# Flowers and Stone

## JAN SIKES

*RiJan Publishing*

*Flowers and Stone* Copyright © 2013 by Jan Sikes

All rights reserved. Printed in the United States of America. No part of this publication may be reproduced, stored in a retrieval system, or transmitted, in any form or by any means electronic, mechanical, photocopying, recording, or otherwise, without the prior written permission of the author except in the case of brief quotations embodied in critical articles and reviews.

Cover Design by Donna Osborn Clark at: creationbydonna.com

Interior Design and Typesetting by: interiorbookdesigns.com

Editing by Timothy G. Green at Inkaissance: inkaissance@gmail.com

ISBN-13: 978-0-9906179-0-7

*This book is dedicated to the endless and undying
impassioned love shared between Rick and Jan Sikes
(aka Luke Stone and Darlina Flowers).*

# Acknowledgments

So many people showed their support and encouragement in the process of writing this book, but first and foremost, I want to thank my amazing sister, Linda Broday for her unwavering support, hard earned knowledge and advice. I thank both of my daughters, Deva Deaton and Crystal Klein for allowing me the time and space to write; my incredible friend, Kay Shields Perot, for pushing me to continue and being excited as each new chapter of the story unfolded. Kelly Wiley was always in my corner cheering me on. I appreciate George Martin, John Beam, Marshall Slayton, Jinelle and Lucky Boyd, Rock and Robin Williams, my writing teachers and so many more for believing in me. I thank Timothy Green for editing the story and Donna Osborn Clark for her creativity in designing the cover and seeing my vision. You are all very special to me.

Most of all, I want to acknowledge the Creator for allowing me to live this life and experience a love that goes far beyond this earthly plane.

# Preface

The gavel hit the block of wood with a resounding force that resonated throughout the courtroom. Luke Stone flinched inwardly, while remaining expressionless outwardly. "Luther Martin Stone, you have been found guilty by a jury of your peers, on one count of robbery of a bank by firearms. The court hereby sentences you to fifty years of confinement in the State Penitentiary. Do you have anything to say?"

Luke looked up at the judge through narrowed eyes. His hands trembled slightly as the cold iron cuffs were placed on them. "No sir."

The thunderous sound of the gavel seemed to suck the very life out of him. It took great effort to force his legs to move, as the bailiff escorted him from the courtroom back to his tiny jail cell. His jaw was clenched tightly and his thoughts whirled like a tornado. What about his family? What about his children, his mom and dad, his brother, his dreams and his life? They had all been ripped from him with the strike of that gavel.

He felt raging anger boiling up inside of him like a volcano about to erupt. There had been so many lies and betrayals. He had never gone inside a bank with a gun and robbed it, so how could he be convicted of a crime he didn't commit? He immediately knew the answer. He had refused to tell the Texas Rangers what they wanted to hear, and let his arrogance take over. Now he was destined to be locked away, like a wild animal in a cage, for a very long time.

The vision of Darlina Flowers floated through the whirlwind of thoughts and for the first time in his life he had no doubt that he had done the right thing in sending her away. The last thing she needed in her young life was to be dragged through a bunch of shit like this. In the next instant, he ached for her and remembered the many hours they'd lain in each other's arms wrapped in a cloak of sweet velvety love...

# Chapter 1

Darlina Flowers adjusted her silver midriff top and black satin shorts while she stood at the counter waiting for her food order. Her gaze wandered around the dimly lit nightclub. Plumes of smoke swirled around the large mirrored ball hanging from the ceiling, as electric yellow, red, blue and green reflected off of it. She contentedly realized how familiar the sights and sounds of the club had become. A vision of her strict religious mother frowning at her flashed through her mind for a brief second. She was extremely disappointed with the lifestyle Darlina had chosen.

The band began a boisterous performance of *Proud Mary*, and she unconsciously moved to the beat of the drum. She observed that places and things forbidden by the church and her mother were what attracted her the most.

Her musings were interrupted by her boss. Marketa had not been in America long enough to lose her thick Czechoslovakian accent. "Darlina, when it's your turn, I want you to try those moves. The customers love it."

"I'll try, but I'm not sure I can." She focused her attention on the stage and how her friend, Sherry, shook her hips and shimmied her boobs at the same time to the rhythm of the music.

Darlina truly enjoyed the time she spent at the nightclub. When Marketa had approached her about working for tips and learning to dance, she never imagined she would have the confidence to be in the spotlight.

"You're up." Marketa affectionately patted her arm. "Show me how it's done."

Darlina climbed the steps to the stage amidst whistles and catcalls. Her insides churned as if hundreds of butterflies fluttered around. She turned to the band leader, a burly man everyone called Buffalo. "Let's do *Suzie Q*."

He took a noisy slurp from his drink. "Okay, little lady."

As the band played, she moved her hips concentrating on the beat of the music. Within seconds, the nerves settled and she became more fluid in her movements.

"Keep it sexy but clean," Marketa taught her.

That wasn't hard for her, since she knew very little about "dirty".

Just as her dance performance was ending, she heard a commotion. Turning, she saw a group of customers being personally escorted by Marketa and seated at the best table in the club. It was totally out of character for this spitfire of a woman make a fuss over anyone. Marketa flitted around with her long elegant ivory cigarette holder in her hand.

Amidst enthusiastic applause, the bright spotlight now off her, Darlina hurried to talk to Sherry.

"Who is that?"

Sherry stared at her in disbelief. "That's Luke Stone and the Rebel Rousers. I can't believe you don't know that."

"How would I know? You forget I don't get out much other than here."

"They are only the hottest band in the whole State of Texas."

"Do you know them?"

"Hell yes, I know 'em. Had a one night stand with the drummer a year or so ago."

With a sudden overwhelming curiosity, Darlina proposed, "Let me wait their table."

Sherry shrugged her shoulders, "Suits me."

Darlina hurried to the table carrying menus. "Evening folks, I'm Darlina and I'll be taking care of you tonight."

Luke Stone, an assuming man over six feet tall with a swagger and crooked grin promptly replied, "Honey, are you sure about that?"

A hot flush rose when she realized what he implied. "Let me rephrase that. I'll be taking your order tonight. What can I get you to drink?"

"Well, seein' as how you don't serve whiskey in here, guess I'll be havin' a cup of coffee," Luke said, leaning back in his chair and lighting a King Edward cigar.

Darlina worked her way around the table taking everyone's drink orders. She could feel Luke's eyes on her and it made her more than a little uncomfortable.

Rushing to the counter to fill the orders, she heard Buffalo's voice boom from the stage. "Folks, we are real honored to have Luke Stone and the Rebel Rousers in here tonight. I wanna dedicate this next song to them." The band played a rousing rendition of *The Fightin' Side of Me*.

Luke yelled from his table, "Hell Yeah!"

Darlina stood where she couldn't be seen and watched this group. It appeared that Luke Stone was the man in charge and everyone around him either seemed to respect and love him or fear him. She couldn't tell which, and maybe it was a little of both.

The attractive dark-haired lady to the left of him must be his wife, she concluded. Many of the customers approached his table and he seemed to know them all personally.

Sherry joined her. "Whatcha' lookin' at, sweetie?"

She quickly looked away. "Just watchin' the show."

"Let me give you a little advice. Luke Stone is bad news and besides that, he's way too old for you."

"I have no intention of getting any closer to him than to take his order and serve his food."

She knew in her heart the words that came out of her mouth weren't true. She was fascinated by him. It's just curiosity, she told herself. She also figured he'd never give her the time of day.

Marketa continued to hover around Luke's table while Darlina served drinks to the group. "Luke, this is Darlina, my up and coming new dancing star and I'm anxious for you to see her perform."

Luke flashed his crooked grin. "Marketa, everyone knows you've got the best dancin' girls in Abilene. I'll look forward to it."

Darlina felt herself blush at the compliment. "Is everyone ready to order?"

She avoided eye contact with Luke while he placed his order. She didn't know why this man unnerved her so, but it seemed as if he could see straight through her. She retreated back to the counter to wait for their food to be prepared.

Marketa sought her out. "Honey, I want you to take another turn up on the stage so Luke can see you dance."

Darlina felt instant panic and replied somewhat breathlessly, "Oh Marketa, I feel really nervous all of a sudden."

Marketa threw back her bleached blonde head and laughed. "Luke Stone has that effect on women. Don't worry, he'll love you."

"I think that's what I'm afraid of," Darlina muttered

As she climbed the steps to the stage, Luke's distinctive voice rang out. "Alright! Now we're gonna get some entertainment."

Darlina addressed Buffalo, "Play *Mustang Sally*."

The music started and she tried to forget about a certain pair of eyes out in the audience. After a few seconds into the song, she relaxed and danced, remembering every move Marketa had taught her.

She finished to whoops and hollers from all over the club.

Marketa rushed up to meet her as she came off the stage. "That was perfect! I knew you could do it!"

Passing through the crowd, everyone showered Darlina with compliments for the performance. Blushing and smiling she reached the counter to pick up Luke Stone's order, suddenly no longer shy about approaching him.

She knew she'd performed well and it gave her confidence. Smiling directly at Luke, she placed the food in front of him.

He put his arm around her waist. "Little lady, you did a hell of a job up there. I really enjoyed watchin' you." He winked as if to emphasize some hidden meaning.

Darlina placed her hand lightly on Luke's shoulder. "Thank you so much. I'm really glad you enjoyed it."

As she started to move away, he asked. "Where are you runnin' off to so fast?"

"Gotta get the rest of these orders out."

"Come back and talk to me."

"Sure, soon as I get a minute," she said over her shoulder as she hurried off, pleased that Luke wanted to talk to her.

She continued bringing the rest of the food to the table and then moved back to the counter after flashing Luke another warm smile.

"What in the hell do you think you're doing?" Sherry did not try to hide her agitation.

"I'm just doin' my job."

"You're flirting with Luke Stone."

Darlina blushed. "No I'm not. I'm bein' friendly 'cause I want a good tip."

"I wasn't born yesterday, honey. I know what I see. I also know Luke. With your blue eyes and long auburn hair, he's gonna be after you like a duck after a June bug."

Darlina brushed her friend's accusation off, but her pulse quickened when she looked toward Luke and his group.

An hour later, she collected the empty dishes. "Can I get ya'll anything else?"

Luke motioned, "Down here, little lady."

She walked to the end of the table where he sat.

"Sugar, I'd like to invite you to go to the motel with me and Mary tonight."

Shaking her head, she replied. "I have no idea what you're asking me, but the answer is no."

"Come on," Luke insisted. "We'll make sure you have a real good time."

Darlina cast a glance at the woman she assumed was Mary only to see her smiling openly at her. "I appreciate the invite, Mr. Stone, but the answer is still no."

"Oh come on now, and don't call me Mr. Stone. I'm Luke and this here is Mary. I promise you we can have one hell of a good time." Luke stood and put his arm around Darlina's waist.

Feeling his large hand on her bare skin made her heart race and she pulled away. "Luke, it's been great meeting you tonight, but I truly don't know what you're talking about and I've gotta go. Ya'll come in and see us again."

Luke let go of her smiling. "Sugar, you can bet on that!"

The rest of the group joined him and they left the club. He looked back when he reached the door, winked at Darlina, and then held the door for Mary as they disappeared into the night.

A confused and shaken Darlina quickly gathered the rest of the dishes from the table, finding a sizable tip.

Sherry was once again waiting for her when she returned with the dishes. "Honey, you're playing with fire if you have anything to do with him."

"He wanted me to go with him and his lady to a motel. I don't know much, but that sure seems wrong. I don't understand why he would ask me that and especially right in front of her."

"You have lots to learn, Darlina. He wanted to have a three-way." Sherry laughed out loud.

"All three of us at the same time?"

"Yes, sweetie, at the same time."

She felt her face flush with embarrassment. "Well, I guess that certainly is different."

"Different is one way to describe Luke Stone."

On her way home that night, Darlina couldn't stop thinking about Luke Stone, his handsome face, the arrogance, his crooked grin and the indecent proposal. She knew she wanted to see him again.

# Chapter 2

The next morning over breakfast, Darlina questioned her older sister, Norma. "Have you ever heard of Luke Stone and the Rebel Rousers?"

Norma took a sip of her coffee. "Hasn't everyone? Why?"

Darlina stirred her Cheerios absentmindedly. "I met them last night at the club and Luke sorta' asked me out."

"How does someone sorta' ask you out?"

"He asked me to go to the motel with him and I told him no. But, I'd really like to hear them play. Everyone says they're a great band."

"I've heard them and they are really good. But, he's way too old for you, Darlina."

"I know, but everybody treated him like a big star. I want to hear their music. Will you and Ray go with me to hear them Saturday night at the Silver Spur?"

"I think Ray has to work, but I'll go with you. You'll need an I.D. to get in though. You won't be 21 for a couple more years."

"Oh, that's right. What should I do?"

"I have an old driver's license I think I can fix up enough to get you in."

Darlina wondered how Norma could do that since they didn't look much alike. Norma had short stylish blonde hair and Darlina was much taller with long auburn hair, but she didn't question her sister.

"I don't tell you often enough how much I appreciate you and Ray letting me live here and all the ways you've helped me. When I came here, I didn't even know how to put on makeup and I'll never forget what you told me about drinking scotch and soda. So far, it's worked every time. I've never gotten sick from drinking. I tell everyone you've taught me almost everything I know."

"Well, little sister, if our mama was here, she would certainly disagree with the things you've learned from me. You know you're welcome to stay here as long as you want or need."

The week flew by and Saturday night came quickly. Darlina changed clothes three times before settling on a pair of tight-fitting white jeans and a lavender ruffled blouse which was one of her favorites. She put on her makeup and combed her hair for half an hour before finally being satisfied with her reflection in the mirror.

She mumbled to herself. "You must be losing your mind. Why are you letting yourself get all worked up? Luke Stone won't even remember you or notice that you're there. You just need to stop worrying about him and go enjoy the music."

Darlina's pulse quickened, when the flashing neon sign of the Silver Spur came into view.

Norma entered the club first, flashing her I.D., and then Darlina followed presenting hers.

The man working the door, looked at the I.D., then at Darlina, back at the I.D., then back at her. "I've seen you before. Aren't you one of Marketa's dancin' girls?"

Darlina squirmed uncomfortably. "Yes, I work for Marketa at the Faded Rose."

The man scratched his chin. "Young lady, I don't really think you're old enough to get in here, but your I.D. says you are so I'm lettin' you in, on one condition."

"What's that?" She twisted the I.D. back and forth in her hand.

"That you'll let me introduce you to the boss man. He's been talkin' about tryin' to recruit some of you girls to work over here. That's how come I recognized you. I've seen you dance at Marketa's."

"Oh you have? Well, I don't have any objections to meeting your boss and by the way, I won't be drinkin' tonight."

"You ladies go right on in and have yourselves a real good time. You're gonna love this band. I'll come around and find you as soon as my relief shows up."

Darlina nodded and they entered the darkened club.

The first thing Darlina heard was Luke Stone's creamy smooth baritone voice singing a Marty Robbins ballad. *"It's a sin, a sin the way I love you. Because I know our love could never be..."*

She was immediately impressed and thought he could give Marty a run for his money.

They stood waiting for their eyes to adjust to the darkness. Looking around, they did not see a vacant table anywhere. They were heading toward the bar when Darlina felt a hand on her arm. She turned to see Mary, the woman she'd met at the Faded Rose with Luke.

"Hey, honey. What brings you in here?"

"My sister and I came to hear the band. This place is packed. We're just gonna go wait at the bar for a table to empty."

"Come sit with me at the band table," Mary invited.

"Are you sure?"

"Sure. Come on! Luke's gonna be thrilled to see you."

Darlina's breath caught in her throat at Mary's casual declaration. She and Norma followed her to the band table.

"Thank you so much." Norma helped Mary re-position chairs around the table. "My name is Norma."

"Nice to meet you, Norma, I'm Mary. It's wonderful that you both came out to hear Luke and the boys. Our table is usually full but none of the other band ladies showed up tonight."

The girls sat down and Darlina turned toward the stage. She found Luke Stone looking directly at her and when they made eye contact, he flashed his crooked grin and winked. She quickly looked away, feeling embarrassed at his boldness, and yet her heart raced.

Norma touched her on the shoulder. "What do you want to drink, sis?"

"Just a Coke."

"Ya'll order whatever you want," Mary said. "I will put your drinks on our tab."

"Oh you don't have to do that," Darlina quickly replied.

"Luke wouldn't have it any other way."

After the waitress had taken their order, Darlina found herself tapping her foot and swaying with the beat of the music. She dared another glance towards the stage and to her surprise Luke's eyes were glued on her. She was thrilled that he recognized her while at the same time felt very uncomfortable to be sitting at his table with his wife, while he openly flirted.

One by one, men approached the table to ask the girls to dance. First Norma, then Mary, hit the dance floor. Darlina found herself sitting alone. This time she looked directly at Luke and gave him a warm smile. He responded with a great big grin and a tip of his black cowboy hat.

A giant of a man, over six foot four, asked Darlina to dance. She accepted and found herself in front of the bandstand. She dared one more glance at Luke to find him no longer smiling but watching her.

She shifted her gaze to her dancing partner, "Do you know this band?"

He let out a loud laugh as he whirled her around the dance floor. "Hell yes, I know 'em. They're all friends of mine. My name is Royce but most folks call me Big Royce."

"Pleased to meet you, Big Royce. I'm Darlina and this is my first time to hear this band."

"Well, sweetheart, you're damn sure in for a treat tonight!"

In spite of his size, Big Royce was light on his feet. When the song ended, he escorted her back to the table. "Thank you, little lady."

"Thank you, Big Royce."

Royce turned to Mary. "Where in the hell have ya'll been keepin' this one?"

Mary laughed. "Royce, you know Luke keeps the best ones hidden."

Just then Darlina heard Luke's voice. "Hey hoss, you ain't over here hittin' on my women, are you?"

Royce turned toward Luke. "Just watchin' out for 'em, Luke".

Luke slapped his friend on the back. "I think I can do the watchin' for now."

Royce nodded and walked away toward the bar.

Luke sat down between Mary and Darlina. After ordering a whiskey and Coke, he turned toward Darlina. "Big surprise seein' you here, sugar."

Darlina suddenly felt very shy at his nearness. "I wanted to hear your band so I twisted my sister's arm and we came out."

Luke looked toward Norma. "And you must be the sister."

Norma took a sip of her drink, "Yes. I'm Norma. I had to keep an eye on my little sister. Thank you so much for the drinks and letting us sit at your table."

Luke looked at Mary for the first time since he sat down. "I hope you put their drinks on my tab."

"Of course I did, Luke."

Just then, the man who had been checking I.D.'s at the door came over to Darlina and motioned for her to come with him.

Luke grabbed the man's arm, "Where the hell are you taking her, Randy?"

He quickly explained, "The boss man wants to talk to her about maybe workin' here some."

Luke took his hand off Randy's arm. "You better not let her outta' your sight."

Randy nodded and then guided a perplexed Darlina through the club to the back office.

Sitting behind a large desk was a middle-age man dressed in a double breasted Ralph Lauren suit, smoking a Montecristo cigar. An open bottle of Johnny Walker Red sat on the desk and two other men relaxed leisurely on either side of the desk. They were drinking and smoking cigars along with the boss.

When Randy came through the door with Darlina, all three men got to their feet.

"Mr. Johnson, this is the little gal I told you about that works for Marketa."

Sonny Johnson came from behind the desk, putting his arm familiarly around Darlina's waist. "Well now, I hear you girls are causing quite a stir over at the Faded Rose. What's your name, sweetheart?"

"Darlina Flowers."

She expertly freed herself from his grip, having become accustomed to groping hands.

"What's the matter, sugar?" Mr. Johnson asked.

"Nothing, sir. Let's keep this strictly about business, if you don't mind."

Mr. Johnson looked at Randy. "Go on back and tend to things out front."

Randy shook his head. "I can't, sir. Luke Stone told me not to let her outta' my sight."

"Oh, so you're one of Luke's women," he sneered at Darlina.

"I'm not anyone's woman, sir. I understand that you may be interested in having some go-go girls here at The Silver Spur?"

Sonny Johnson's eyes roved over Darlina's body undressing her as he went. He sat back down behind the desk. "I'm looking for something to draw more of a crowd on weeknights and I think go-go girls might be just the thing."

"Marketa does get quite a crowd on the nights we dance." She wasn't exactly sure she wanted to work for this man, but kept those thoughts to herself and hoped the expression in her eyes didn't give her away.

"I'll tell you what. Why don't you bring some of your dancin' girlfriends with you for an audition this Tuesday night?"

"I can ask some of the girls over at the club and see if they're interested."

"You just tell 'em Sonny Johnson is interested and they'll be here. We'll have auditions at five o'clock on Tuesday. You come and show me what you can do."

She glanced toward the door hoping this meeting was over and she could get back to listening to the band.

"Take her back to Luke," he instructed Randy.

Darlina extended her hand to Sonny Johnson. "Thank you, sir. It was nice meeting you."

Randy and Darlina had just started down the hallway when Luke Stone appeared out of nowhere. "I'll take it from here, Randy."

"Sure thing, Luke." He walked briskly away.

Darlina confronted Luke. "What is it with you? Do you think I can't take care of myself?"

Luke took a long deliberate draw off his King Edward cigar then draped his arm around Darlina's shoulders, "That's not it at all, sugar. I just know Sonny Johnson and his cronies."

Darlina pushed his arm off her shoulders and faced him squarely. "I don't even know you, Luke Stone, and you sure don't know me and you're all of a sudden acting like I'm your property or something."

Luke grinned and without saying another word, pulled Darlina close to him and French kissed her. A tingling around the base of her spine sent a hot flush through her body. The smell of his cologne mingled with the taste of tobacco on his tongue left her breathless. She melted into the ferocity of the kiss. All of a sudden she remembered he had a wife and resisted the urge to kiss him back.

She pushed him away. "You've got a lot of nerve, kissing me when your wife is sitting out there at the table waiting for you to come back."

Luke laughed out loud. "Wife? What wife?"

"Mary."

"Mary's not my wife."

"Well, she certainly is something and I'm not gonna be involved in anything between you and her."

Once again Luke laughed, as if thoroughly amused. "Little lady, I don't know where you came from, but either you're a damn good actress or you are the most naïve little girl I've ever run into."

"I'm not a little girl. I'm a woman and I may be naïve but I'm not stupid and apparently am not the kind of woman you're looking for."

Luke suddenly became very serious. "How in the hell would you know what kind of woman I'm looking for?"

"Obviously one that will go to bed with you and your wife or girlfriend or whoever she is." Darlina could feel herself starting to shake and tears were very near the surface. She steeled herself against the emotion.

Luke chuckled. "Well at least you figured that much out."

Darlina walked away with no reply. Luke took her arm and turned her back around. "I really want to know more about you, honey, and I promise I'll earn your trust."

Darlina jerked her arm free and continued walking back to the table.

Luke returned to the stage, picked up his red Telecaster and started singing again without looking her way.

Sitting back at Luke's table, Darlina turned over in her mind the things he'd said and done. It seemed as if her head was spinning like a top that had been wound too tight.

Norma leaned over. "You okay?"

Darlina nodded. "Yeah, I'm okay. The owner of this place, Mr. Johnson, wanted to talk to me about getting go-go girls in here on weeknights. There is an audition Tuesday."

"Sounds like fun."

"We'll see," Darlina said, totally avoiding talking about Luke or anything that had transpired.

After a few minutes, Mary touched Darlina's arm. "Let's go somewhere we can talk."

Darlina followed her out the backstage entrance door into a locker room area. Once they were there, Mary turned towards her and started crying.

She immediately reached out and put her hand on the woman's shoulder. "What's wrong, Mary?"

Mary looked down at her hands as she spoke. "Luke told me I had to try to talk you into going with us tonight, or he wasn't going to take me home with him."

"Look, I don't know what you and Luke do and it's none of my business, but I'm just not the girl ya'll are looking for. I don't do things like that."

Mary looked up. "He's gonna be so mad at me. Will you at least tell him I tried?"

"Sure, I'll tell him but I've already told him the same thing I just told you."

Mary smiled through her tears. "Thanks."

"For what?"

"For understanding."

"Well, I can't say as I understand, but like I said, that's between you and Luke."

She hugged Mary and they made their way back to the table, deliberately avoiding Luke's gaze.

The night passed quickly and the band wound down to last call. Luke stepped up to the mic and invited everyone onto the dance floor for some rock 'n roll while they played Pusher Man. Darlina, Mary and Norma hit the dance floor and even though she never looked up, she could feel Luke's eyes on her.

Once the show was over, people stumbled out with many lingering behind to talk to Luke and other members of the band.

Norma told her sister, "I think it's time we headed home."

"Let me say goodbye to Luke first, then we'll go."

Darlina walked to where a group of people were gathered around Luke. She put her hand out to shake his when he took her hand and led her away to a quiet corner.

"Thank you for coming out tonight, sweetheart."

"I truly enjoyed the music. You guys are great. I told Mary I would tell you she talked to me like you asked, so don't be mad at her."

Luke's grin widened, "Well, I'm glad you liked the music and hope I didn't scare you off."

"I don't scare easily."

"So what do you do when you're not dancin' and waitin' tables at Marketa's?"

"I have a day job at the ABCO boiler factory, and that's pretty much about it."

Norma called her name. "I've really gotta run, but I had fun tonight."

As she began walking away, Luke called to her. "What the hell is your name anyway, besides Darlina?"

"Darlina Flowers." She called over her shoulder, following her sister out.

Luke stood watching her until she was out of sight then returned to the crowd waiting for him.

Inside the car was dead quiet on the way home and Norma didn't pry. Once she was in the solitude of her room, she let the events of the night unfold one by one in her head. She thought about Luke's tongue in her mouth, and how much it turned her on. What was she going to do about it? She fell asleep thinking about his strange behavior and about her own feelings that betrayed her at every turn.

# Chapter 3

Luke Stone couldn't remember the last time he'd bought a piece of jewelry for a lady, although lots of ladies had bought jewelry for him. He wondered how in the hell this sweet young girl with sparkling blue eyes had gotten under his skin so quickly. He imagined what it would feel like to run his fingers through her long auburn hair and speculated that it must smell like sweet blooming flowers.

As he stood at the counter in one of the finest jewelry stores in Abilene, he asked the clerk, "What would you suggest for a very sweet young lady that I just met?"

The clerk immediately brought out a tray of necklaces. "These are all very nice, Mr. Stone."

He looked them over and spotted a small gold heart on a very delicate chain with a tiny diamond set in the middle of the heart. "This one oughta' do."

The clerk placed it in a black velvet box and Luke paid for it. He blinked when he walked outside into the bright sunshine. He wasn't accustomed to being out of bed at ten a.m., much less cleaned up and purchasing jewelry. Again, he questioned himself as he drove to the ABCO Boiler Factory.

Darlina sat at her desk typing a contract on an IBM Selectric typewriter this particular Monday morning, her back turned to the door.

The bell rang, announcing someone's arrival. She half turned. "May I..." She paused in mid-question, shocked to see Luke standing there with the trademark crooked grin on his face. "...Help you?" she finished.

"That is exactly what I've been asking myself," Luke replied.

"What are you doing here?"

"I came to see if you were for real or a figment of my imagination."

"For real?"

Luke's smile widened, "Yes, for real. You see, I thought maybe I'd just made you up so had to come and see."

Darlina didn't reply and Luke quickly continued, "I brought you a little something."

She stood and walked to the open window that separated her and Luke. "Okay, what did you bring me and more importantly, why? After all, you barely know me."

She wondered what kind of strings might be attached to any gift from Luke Stone.

Luke fished the small box out of his pocket and handed it to her. Their hands briefly touched and an electrical current passed between them. She looked up at Luke, then down at the box.

"Open it," Luke encouraged.

Darlina gasped as she opened the box to find the delicate gold heart necklace. "Oh Wow! This is beautiful. I'm not sure what to say."

"Well, you could say thank you, and you could say that you'll have dinner with me, just me, and you could say that you'll give me a chance to redeem myself."

"Okay," she said hesitatingly. "I guess so."

"Okay to all of it?"

Words spilled out of her mouth before she stopped to think. "Okay to all of it on one condition."

"What condition?"

"On the condition that you won't ever ask me to sleep with you and Mary again." Her voice trembled slightly and she could feel the blood racing to her face.

Luke chuckled, "You've got a deal, little lady. Now put the necklace around your pretty neck and get back to work. I'll see you at the Silver Spur tomorrow for the audition and then we'll go somewhere, just you and me. I promise you I won't do anything that you don't wanna do."

She looked directly into his eyes. "That's something I think you'll have to prove."

He leaned through the window, kissed her on the cheek, then waved as he opened the door and stepped outside.

She sank into her chair, hands slightly shaking as she fastened the tiny clasp on the necklace around her neck.

Norma came into her office from the back of the plant and immediately spotted the necklace. "Where did that come from, little sis?"

"Luke Stone was just here and brought it to me. He also asked me out and said he would be at the audition tomorrow."

"Are you sure about all this?"

"I don't think I've ever been more sure about anything in my life."

"Just be careful. He's a lot older than you and I don't want to see you get hurt."

"I won't," Darlina assured, as she turned back to typing the contract.

After her sister had left her office, Darlina reached up to touch the beautiful necklace feeling her heart beat just a little faster.

She could hardly wait for her lunch break. Leann was another sister, four years older than herself, that she had lunch with almost every day. Leann had married a man who worked at the boiler factory just two weeks after Norma fixed them up on a blind date.

Leann, like Darlina, had not been allowed to date while living in their very sheltered home, and Darlina worried a little about the quick marriage. She knew Leann wanted out of Hobbs, New Mexico, a suffocating dusty town on the Texas – New Mexico border, and marriage was her ticket.

Leann and Wayne lived in a tiny apartment and Darlina often wished they had a spare bedroom so she could live with them, but since they were a newlywed couple she figured they didn't need her underfoot. Nevertheless, the sisters remained very close. She would never forget how Leann had been the one to comfort and reassure her after she'd unwillingly lost her virginity. She held no secrets from her sister, just as it had been in all their growing-up years.

When Darlina came through the door with a big smile on her face, Leann asked, "What's up with you, little sister? You look like a kid on Christmas morning."

Darlina laughed, pointedly fingering the necklace hanging around her neck. "Look what I got today!"

"Wow! Where did that come from?"

"Remember me telling you about meeting Luke Stone at the club the other night?"

Leann nodded.

"Well, he came by work this morning, brought me this necklace and asked me out."

Leann's smile faded, "Are you sure you want to do that? I've heard some pretty wild things about him and his band."

Darlina laughed, "Yes, I'm very sure. He promised me he wouldn't do anything I don't want to do and for some crazy reason, I believe him."

Leann admired the necklace, "This sure is pretty. It's even got a diamond on it."

Darlina laughed excitedly. "Yes, I know. My very first diamond!"

Leann laughed with her sister and then warned, "Just don't make it the first time gettin' your heart broke."

"No chance! I think my life is finally beginning." Darlina smiled. "Hey, I've gotta' go shopping for a new outfit to wear to the audition tomorrow when I get off work. Wanna go with me?"

"I'd love to, but Wayne'll be home and I better stay here and cook us some supper."

Darlina sensed a little regret in her sister's voice. "Is everything goin' alright for ya'll?"

"I guess so." Leann chewed her bottom lip. "I'm not real sure how it's supposed to go."

Darlina reassured, "It's an adjustment. You'll be just fine."

The two sisters sat across the table from each other in the tiny apartment, chatting and eating their ham and cheese sandwiches, until it was time for Darlina to go back to work.

She had a hard time staying focused on her work the rest of the afternoon. Her thoughts returned over and over again to Luke Stone's boldness. She wondered why, when he had his pick of most any woman in Abilene, he was showing interest in her, a little holy-roller girl from the New Mexico desert?

Five o'clock couldn't come soon enough to suit her. She knew she had to find the right costume for the audition and didn't have time to make one, as she most often did.

She also knew she was more excited about seeing Luke Stone than the audition itself.

Darlina shopped with Sherry and another dancer, Dee Dee, at a small out-of-the-way boutique in South Abilene. Listening to their conversation about the audition, she realized there were several girls trying out, and not just girls from the Faded Rose. She couldn't help but wonder how on earth she could compete with these more experienced dancers.

Sherry held up a bright red sequined top. "Hey, Darlina, what do you think about this one?"

"That would look great with your dark hair. Try it on."

Dee Dee found a black leather mini-skirt with a short cropped matching jacket and settled on it. Both girls prompted Darlina to pick something. She looked through rack after rack without finding what she had in mind.

Sherry began to grow impatient. "Come on Darlina, pick something. Me and Dee Dee are going to the Silver Spur for a while. Wanna go?"

"No, ya'll go ahead. I'm just gonna keep lookin'."

Once Sherry and Dee Dee were gone, Darlina went back to the sale rack she'd already quickly looked over. All she could think about was how she wanted to look for Luke. She hadn't told Sherry anything about Luke or the necklace or the date. It wasn't something she wanted to talk about with the any of the other girls, at least not yet.

Finally, she spotted exactly what she was looking for. A blue and white midriff top with matching hip-hugger bell-bottom pants and a pair of white short-shorts had an alluring look. She liked her reflection in the mirror when she tried them on.

The long flowing sleeves, the low scooped neck and the fitted shorts, all reflected the image she had in mind. She wanted Luke to see her as a woman and not a little girl.

# Chapter 4

Four o'clock in the afternoon found Luke Stone sitting alone at a table in the darkened Silver Spur club thinking and drinking. He knew how the night life that Darlina seemed determined to be a part of, could chew her up and spit her out. He had an inexplicable urge to protect her.

On the other hand, he thought about the honky-tonk man he'd become over the many years of playing music in the clubs. He hardly remembered the hard-working honest man he used to be.

He knew in his heart, she deserved much more than he could give her. Yet, he was drawn to her. He couldn't deny it. She simply needed his protection, he told himself. It had been a very long time since anyone needed him for any reason other than to keep the party going or pay the bills.

His thoughts were interrupted by the sound of giggling girls. He looked up to see several dancers from the various clubs around town entering the club. They immediately spotted him and headed to his table.

Louise Monroe, a tall shapely blonde dancer whose husband was a good friend of Luke's, pulled out a chair. "Hi, Luke. Mind if we sit with you?"

"Of course not, sugar. Where's Johnny?"

"Oh, you know Johnny. He's around somewhere; said he might stop by to see me dance after while."

Two other bleached blondes, Karen and Tonya, both showing lots of cleavage, accompanied Louise. The rough life they lived made it hard to tell their ages, but Luke estimated them to be in their late 20s to early 30s. He had seen them in the clubs around town.

Karen spoke first. "Hi, Luke, didn't expect to see you here tonight."

Luke stood and pulled chairs out for them. "I wouldn't miss it for the world, darlin'. You girls look mighty good and I think you're gonna knock ol' Sonny's socks off."

Tonya held her cigarette for him to light. "You can bet your ass we are."

He lit her cigarette then sat down re-lighting his King Edward cigar. "Ya'll know how this works. You just gotta get up there and shake your cute little sexy asses and you'll have him creamin' his pants."

Karen put her hand on Luke's leg. "And what about you, Luke? Will we have you creamin' your pants too?"

Luke laughed and took a long draw off his cigar. "Sugar, you know I love all of you girls."

Dee Dee and Sherry arrived and joined the others at Luke's table. Dee Dee plopped herself down on his lap and wrapped her arms around his neck. "Oh, Luke! I didn't know you'd be here. Why don't you go home with me tonight? It's sure been a long time."

Luke put his arm around the girl's waist. "Dee Dee, that's a mighty generous offer, but I've got plans for tonight."

"Shit! Just my luck. Well, then some other time real soon, ok?"

Luke patted Dee Dee's ass, "You betcha', sugar."

It was at that precise moment, Darlina entered the darkened club. She stood for a minute adjusting her eyes to the smoky dimness, looking for Luke. She spotted him at the table with all the girls, Dee Dee sitting on his lap, his hand on her bottom.

A wave of nausea washed over her. It was as if she was instantly transported back to high school where she'd been such a misfit with her long dress and hair pulled back in a bun. Her instinct told her to run far away and never look back.

As she turned to make her escape, she heard Sherry's voice. "Darlina! Hey, over here!"

Luke immediately stood, sliding Dee Dee off his lap, and walked toward Darlina. "Hey, sugar! I was beginning to think maybe you'd changed your mind and wasn't coming."

Her voice trembled. "Right this moment, I wish I'd done just that."

Luke draped his arm over her shoulders. "You look sexy as hell tonight. I'm gonna have a hard time livin' up to my end of the bargain."

Darlina pulled away. "Luke, you don't have to live up to anything at all. Looks to me like you've got your hands full."

"What do you mean, darlin'?"

"Looks like you've got plenty of girls to keep you busy. I'll just do my audition then get the hell out of here."

"Whoa. Slow down, little girl. You're not jealous, are you?"

"I'm not a little girl and no, I'm not jealous. I just know when I'm outta' my league."

Luke threw his head back laughing, "Sugar, I guess that's one thing I've never known. I've always been like a bull in a china closet."

"Well, looks to me like you've got plenty of company in that closet with you, so I don't see as you need me for anything."

Suddenly serious, Luke spoke softly, "Those girls don't mean nothin' to me. You've got something they all wish they had and I mean that."

"As usual, I don't have a clue what you mean."

He guided her to the table. "Let's save all this talk for later. Right now, you've got an audition to do."

Darlina couldn't help noticing the puzzled look on Sherry's face as she sat down beside Luke. "Looks like you found the right outfit, honey," Sherry said.

Darlina forced a smile, "Yeah, I found it on a sale rack after ya'll left."

Dee Dee touched Darlina's arm. "Honey, I'm sorry. I had no idea you were Luke's plan for the night."

Luke interrupted by announcing, "Okay, ladies. I'm buying a round for everyone. Order up."

Darlina quickly responded, "I'll have a scotch and soda."

Luke looked at her in surprise. "Hell, I didn't know you drank."

Darlina muttered under her breath, "Now's a damn good time to start."

The girls soon had their drinks and the table buzzed with laughter and chit-chat.

Darlina sat quietly, lost in her thoughts. Why had she come here thinking she could fit in? Why did she think she could compete for a chance with Luke and even more puzzling, why did she care?

Obviously he had no shortage of women waiting on the sidelines. She felt out of place, as she watched the older women interacting, all smoking cigarettes and reeking with confidence and cheap perfume.

Maybe she should try to start smoking. It might make her appear older and more experienced.

A voice boomed from the stage. "Alright. Ladies, if you're here to audition, please come up and give me your names. You're going to be chosen randomly to dance and everyone is going to dance to the same song."

Darlina followed the other women to the stage and signed in. On the way back to the table, Dee Dee looped her arm through Darlina's and smiled openly at her. She hesitantly smiled back.

Luke watched with some amusement. He could tell Darlina seemed uncomfortable around the older women and thought to himself, if only she knew that her innocence was what turned him on. He wondered how long it would take her to become jaded but couldn't picture it. He tried to think of some way he could make her feel more at ease and have more confidence.

He openly admired her as she approached the table. He stood and held her chair. "Don't worry, honey, you're gonna do just fine. You've got one fine lookin' ass on you and I've seen you shake it." He winked at her as she sat down.

Darlina reached for her drink, feeling a little more at ease. "Thanks, Luke."

The other women soon returned and everyone waited anxiously for their names to be called.

"Okay. First up we have Sherry Greenleaf," the voice announced from the stage. "You're all gonna dance to *Honky Tonk Women* by The Rolling Stones and once you're done, I need you to have a seat over here at the table to my left."

Sherry climbed the steps to the stage and the music boomed out. Darlina watched her, listening carefully to the song, as it was new to her. She looked toward the table to the right of the stage where Mr. Johnson and three other men sat. She presumed the other men were judges.

Luke possessively put his arm around Darlina's shoulders as they watched. She started to pull away, but instead relaxed and enjoyed the sense of comfort it gave her.

Darlina's was the third name to be called. As she pushed her chair back, Luke leaned over, kissed her on the cheek and said, "Don't be nervous. Get up there and shake your sweet little ass!"

Once on stage, Darlina closed her eyes, took a deep breath and began moving to the music. A few seconds into it, she relaxed and danced the way Marketa had taught her, giving it her all. She no longer had any awareness of Luke Stone or Sonny Johnson and the other judges, or any of the other women. She got lost in Mick Jagger's music.

As she left the stage, she saw Luke standing at his table, clapping and yelling. She blushed with embarrassment and then thankfully realized the darkness hid her face.

It seemed like a very long time before all of the women had taken their turn and the judges were ready to announce their decisions.

Mr. Johnson got on stage and took the mic. "Ladies, I want to thank you all for auditioning for me today. I can tell you this decision was very hard, because you're all very good. Here are the ladies I've chosen to dance at the Silver Spur starting next Wednesday night. Louise Monroe, Pat Connors, Darlina Flowers, Karen Stacy and Charlotte Locklin. I need to see each of you ladies in my office. Thank ya'll for coming."

When he left the stage, the women all started milling about. Darlina was congratulated by the others and responded as if she were in shock. She couldn't believe she had been chosen.

Luke walked up to her, put his arm around her waist and pulled her in tight to him. "I knew you could do it, princess. You didn't have a damn thing to be nervous about."

Darlina smiled up at him. "Thanks for the vote of confidence."

"Hurry and get signed up so we can get out of here. I've got plans for us!"

She hurried to the office, filled out the paperwork Mr. Johnson wanted and listened to his speech. "I know you're under age and you'll not be allowed to drink in my club. However, when you're not on stage dancing, I want you mingling with the customers. When they offer to buy you a drink, order a Sloe Gin Fizz and the bartender will make it without alcohol. We charge the customer full price and we all make money. Be here at six o'clock next Wednesday. Any questions?"

Darlina shook her head no and hurried out to find Luke waiting outside the door.

"I'd like to change into pants before we go if you don't mind, Luke."

"Honey, you can change into anything you want to as long as you don't change your mind about gettin' outta here with me."

She laughed, quickly ran to her car to get the bell-bottom pants, and within five minutes she was ready to go.

Luke took her hand and escorted her out. Darlina couldn't help noticing the envious looks she received from some of the women as she left with him. She liked the way it made her feel.

Luke's car, a Starmist Blue 1957 Ford T-bird, had been polished and shone like a new penny. He opened the door for her, then before closing it, leaned down and kissed her long and deep. Once in on the driver's side, he leaned over and kissed her again.

She pulled away. "I think you need to slow down a little."

He put the keys in the ignition and started the car. "Whatever you say."

Darlina asked Luke as he drove, "So how is it that you know all those women?"

He looked at her in disbelief. "Well honey, you do know I play music for a livin'. That requires that I spend a lot of time in these ol' honky-tonks and as the song says, they are honky-tonk women so that's how I know 'em."

She fell silent.

Luke glanced at her, again thinking no one could be that naive. She seemed to be totally unaware of the cold hard facts of life. "Okay. My turn," he said.

"Your turn for what?"

"My turn to ask a question. What in the hell is a sweet young thing like you doing shakin' your ass and workin' in the clubs?"

"I guess you could say I'm trying to do it all. I love the music scene so because I'm not twenty-one yet I started hanging around the Faded Rose. Marketa approached me about workin' for tips and teachin' me to dance. And here I am from Hobbs, New Mexico to the honky-tonks in less than a year."

Luke sounded wistful, "It's been a helluva long time since I experienced anything new in life. I can't remember what that feels like."

They pulled into the parking lot of the Saddle and Sirloin and Luke opened Darlina's door, helping her out of the car.

Inside the restaurant, the hostess seated them in a quiet corner at Luke's request. "Sugar, order anything you'd like. I'm not hungry so I'm just gonna order a drink."

"Then what are we doing here? This costs a lotta' money."

"I wanna buy you to a steak dinner. You go ahead and eat. I'm just not hungry."

Darlina accepted a menu from the waitress even though she wasn't sure she wanted to eat if Luke didn't. The waitress, like everyone, seemed to know Luke. She wore a low cut denim top and short skirt and flirted non-stop with him. This time Darlina didn't experience the nagging insecurity. She felt proud to be the one sitting across from him.

Darlina settled on a small sirloin steak, baked potato and tossed green salad. Once the sizzling food arrived, she realized how long it had been since she'd eaten like this. "Are you sure you don't want to eat?"

Luke smiled at her over his Coke. "No, princess. You eat up. I'm just enjoying watching you."

"Where are we going from here?"

"I've got a motel room at the Century Lodge, and don't you go to worryin'. I promised I wouldn't do anything you didn't want to and I keep my word."

"For some crazy reason, I believe you."

A short time later, they pulled up to the Century in Luke's T-Bird. Inside the room, Darlina looked around with curiosity. A dark paneled king size bed dominated the room.

A bottle of Jim Beam sat on the night stand beside the bed, along with a bucket of ice and a six pack of Coke. She didn't see any other personal items in the room.

"Make yourself at home," Luke said as he busied himself making a drink and tuning the dial on the motel radio to a local country station. He sat down on the side of the bed, took his black Tony Lamas off, and then propped pillows comfortably behind his head stretching out. He patted the bed beside him. "Come here."

She sat down stiffly on the side of the bed. "I'm not sleeping with you tonight, Luke Stone."

"I know. You've made that real clear, darlin'. Just come up here beside me and let's talk. Do you want a drink?"

"I've never drank whiskey before, so I don't know if I want one or not."

"I'll fix you one and if you don't want it, I promise it won't go to waste."

Darlina removed her white go-go boots and scooted across the bed beside Luke. He handed her a motel cup with ice, Coke and whiskey in it. She took a sip. "Not bad."

Luke laughed, and lit a new cigar. "Jim Beam, that's my whiskey. King Edward, that's my cigar. Now what would you like to talk about, sugar?"

"You."

Luke took a long drink from his cup. "And what do you want to know about me?"

"Anything you're willing to tell me. How long have you been playing music? Have you ever been married? What is the biggest gig you've ever played? Do you have a bus? What's with the feathers that hang off your guitar?"

"Whoa! That's a lot of questions. I'll start with the first one. I've been playin' music since I was fourteen years old. My uncle gave me an ol' F-Hole guitar. It had rusty strings on it that were a half an inch off the neck and my fingers would bleed from trying to play, but I kept after it. I wanted to play real bad. I'd go to church with my Mom and every Sunday after service, this lady she knew, would teach me a new chord. I'd go home and practice it for a week, then if I went back the next Sunday, she'd show me another one. That was the only time I didn't mind goin' to church. Playin' music was all I ever really wanted to do."

Darlina broke in, "I always thought I wanted to play piano. Every summer my sister and I would go to the Stamps School of Music in Hobbs. I tried to learn to read music, but can't say as I ever did."

"Me neither, but I learned to play by ear and I wrote. I wanted to write my own songs and still do. I've had a few little records and a couple of 'em have done pretty good. Had a record go to number one in Denmark and some others did good out on the West Coast, but somehow the deals always go sour. Guess that's just the music business. I answered one of your questions, now let me ask you one."

Darlina nodded, sipping on her drink.

"What do you hope to gain by dancing at the Silver Spur?"

"I don't know. Maybe just more experience. It's not like I want a lifetime career dancing. It's just something I enjoy doin' right now."

"Can I give you some advice?"

"Sure."

"You're stepping off into a world that I don't think you know anything about. The Silver Spur is a lot different than the Faded Rose. There are assholes out there that will tell you anything to get in your pants and women that will stab you in the back because their ol' man looked at you. Believe me, I know. I've lived in that world for a long time now."

Darlina turned toward Luke, surprised by the serious look on his face. "I think I can take care of myself. I may be young, but I trust my instincts."

"Just remember what I told you."

"Okay. So, have you ever been married?"

"Twice. I'm married now, on paper, but I haven't lived with her in a few years. I've got kids that I take care of and she doesn't have to work, but I can't live there. We just don't get along and that's no good for the kids or us."

"Why don't you get a divorce?"

"Never had a reason to. Things work like they are and I get to see the kids whenever I want. The kids are what matter to me."

"Your first wife?"

"Hell, we were just kids. I was seventeen and she was fifteen. She was a preacher's daughter." He chuckled and took a draw off his cigar. "We were both horny kids that thought you had to get married to have sex. So we did and it lasted about 3 years. She wanted a divorce and I didn't object. What about you? You ever have an ol' man?"

Darlina laughed out loud. "That's a good one. When I lived at home, I wasn't allowed to date. Since I've been in Abilene, I've had a few but nothing serious. Mostly I'm just tryin' to figure out what I want to do."

"Me too," Luke said somewhat sadly. "Guess I'll eventually figure it out or else I'll just get old."

Suddenly, he stopped talking, sat up on the side of the bed and turned the volume of the radio up. "Listen!"

They both listened as Sammi Smith's voice crooned a Kris Kristofferson song. *"I don't care what's right or wrong. I won't try to understand. Let the devil take tomorrow 'cause tonight I need a friend. Yesterday is dead and gone and tomorrow's out of sight. I don't want to be alone so help me make it through the night..."*

Luke turned to Darlina, "That's one helluva a song. Don't think you know it, but you're helping me make it through this night." He put his arms around her and pulled her close with her head resting on his chest. He kissed the top of her head and caressed her hair.

The hours flew by as they lay side by side on the bed talking. She loved the way this rugged forceful man could be so gentle.

She propped herself up on one elbow and looked straight into Luke's eyes, "Luke, I think I want you to make love to me."

Luke kissed her, caressed her skin and replied somewhat breathless, "Nope. I promised I wouldn't and I'm not breaking my word."

"But I changed my mind. I want to."

"Then there will be plenty of time, but not tonight."

Sometime around three a.m., Darlina drifted off to sleep wrapped in Luke's arms. He watched her and thought to himself how lucky he was that this sweet young girl had come into his life. Now, he just had to figure out what to do with her. Most of all, he didn't want her to get hurt. How on earth could he make sure of that?

The sun soon came streaming through the window and Luke moved to wake her. As she sat up on the bed and yawned, he leaned over and kissed her on the neck.

She turned to face him. "Thank you, Luke."

"For what?"

"For keeping your word and not disappointing me."

He laughed, "Sugar, it ain't over yet and I'm pretty damned good at disappointing people, so don't get too far ahead of yourself."

They were both quiet as Luke drove Darlina to her car. She suddenly turned toward Luke. "You never did answer my question about the feathers that hang off of your guitar."

Luke grinned. "It's some of that ol' greasy Indian medicine. They keep the bad spirits away."

They were back at Darlina's car in minutes and he turned off the engine. "I want to see you again and soon."

Darlina leaned over and kissed him. "Me too, but right now, I've got to get to work."

As she drove home, her thoughts were crystal clear. She had never experienced anyone like this man and her pulse quickened as she remembered the kisses and closeness they'd shared. Was she falling in love so quickly? The response her heart gave left little doubt.

# Chapter 5

It seemed to Darlina that everything had changed for her overnight. The sun shone a little brighter and the birds sang a little louder, matching the song in her heart. She didn't think anything could wipe the smile off her face.

She sat across the table from Leann, sipping a glass of iced tea and halfheartedly eating a grilled cheese sandwich. "Leann, I can't stop thinking about Luke and last night. He was such a gentleman and he kept his word. I think I'm fallin' in love with him."

Leann wrinkled her forehead speaking slowly. "Sister, I know you might think you're falling in love, but look at the huge differences between you. He's married, has kids and is so much older. He's a man of the world and you're still young and very inexperienced. Do you really think you could have a life with him?"

Darlina seriously replied, "Yes, I do. I really do. It's just like in the Kathleen Woodwiss romance books that we read where two people meet and fall instantly in love."

"But that's only in books. I'm not sure it happens in real life."

"It does happen because it's happening to me and I think Luke feels the same. Look at you. You married Wayne after the third date. Do you truly love him, or did you just want to get away from home?"

"I don't know if I love Wayne or not, but I had to get away from Hobbs. I knew I couldn't stand another day or night with the guilt the church and mama put on me."

"Then you have to understand. I wanted to get away from home too, but now I want more. I want to love and be loved."

"Well, I can't tell you what to do, but don't be in such a big rush. We weren't raised to know anything about the world and I'm afraid you might be getting in over your head."

"I guess you're right, but I don't want to miss my chance at happiness. I just know there has to be love out there for me and I truly believe it's with Luke."

"I hope so, but I'm also scared for you. It's just a feeling."

"I think I'm going to be insanely happy just like in the fairy tales and I'm not afraid at all."

The two girls sat in silence, each lost in their own thoughts until Darlina had to go back to work. It surprised her that having been up most of the night, she wasn't tired. Her heart was soaring.

She sat behind her typewriter concentrating on her work when the phone rang. "Thank you for calling ABCO Boilers. How may I help you?"

"Hi, sugar," Luke's voice boomed. "I just had to call and check on you. How are ya' doing?"

"Hi, Luke! I'm doing good, but sure glad I don't have to work tonight."

"I just wanted you to know I'm thinking about you and to tell you again how much I enjoyed being with you last night."

"Me too, and thank you for keeping your word."

"You sure didn't make it easy, sweetheart."

"I didn't intend to," she bantered playfully. "Where are you playing tonight?"

"We're playin' at the Boots and Saddle in Angelo tonight and tomorrow, then back in Abilene by the weekend."

"When will I see you again?"

"Real soon, sugar, and that's a promise. You just take care of your sweet little self. Okay?"

"Okay I will. I'm glad you called."

"I'll let you get back to work. Talk to you soon."

She hung up the phone and returned to her typewriter, smiling.

The next few days were a blur. Luke called her daily and it was finally decided she would go with him Saturday night to the It'll Do club. She tingled with excitement and couldn't wait for Saturday night.

She went to work early on Friday at the Faded Rose, and approached Marketa, "I've got a favor to ask."

"Ask anything you'd like, sweetie."

"I need to be off tomorrow night so I can go with Luke to the club where they're playing," she quickly said.

Marketa reached out and hugged Darlina. "Honey, I'm not paying you to work here. You can do whatever you want, but thanks for telling me. Luke, Huh? I had a feeling he took quite a liking to you the night they were in here and I've never seen him not get a woman he went after."

Darlina blushed slightly, "I don't know about that."

Marketa softened. "Oh to be young and in love...but, take it from an old woman like me, people like Luke Stone are good at getting what they want and then leaving once they get tired of the chase or find something new to go after."

"Don't worry. It's gonna be different for me and Luke."

Sherry arrived in a tizzy, interrupting the conversation, "What the hell, Darlina...you don't listen to anything I say, do you?"

"I don't know what you're talkin' about, Sherry."

"Don't play dumb with me! Didn't I stand right here and warn you about Luke Stone?"

"Well, yes you did, but I happen to think you're wrong about him."

"Oh really? Let's see what you have to say about that when you're cryin' the blues because he's dumped you."

Darlina bristled, "There's no need to be mean, Sherry. He's not like you think."

"Which one of us has known him longer? I'll tell you. Me. And I've never known of him to stay with any woman for long."

"You're just upset because of Dee Dee."

"Dee Dee has nothing to do with it. I'm upset with you because you're gonna get your heart broke and don't say I didn't try to tell you."

"Well, I think you're wrong, but thanks for being concerned."

The two girls finished their night's work, with an uncomfortable distance between them.

Darlina simply could not accept what everyone said about Luke. She saw something in him they didn't. They would eventually understand that they were wrong.

This time would be different. She just knew it.

## Chapter 6

Glowing like Cinderella at the ball, Darlina walked into the It'll Do Club on Luke's arm. She felt comfortable at his side, as if it were the most natural place in the world for her to be.

He guided her to the band table where two women were seated. "Rita, Julie, this is Darlina. I want ya'll to take good care of her tonight."

Darlina acknowledged the women with smiles as she sat down. Luke walked to the stage and tuned his guitar.

Rita leaned toward Darlina, "Honey, we're so glad to finally see Luke with a decent woman. It's nice to meet you."

She blushed unable to think of a reply. "Who are you here with?"

Rita replied, "My husband is the lead guitar player, Jerry."

Julie lit a cigarette as she said, "I'm with the bass player, Red. How long have you known Luke?"

"Not very long. We met at the Faded Rose."

Rita patted her arm. "Well, Luke's a hard one to tame. Don't let him scare you off."

Darlina smiled warmly, "Oh I have no intention of letting that happen. It's really nice to meet you two."

Both women ordered Rum and Coke. Darlina ordered a Coke and settled back to watch.

Before long Luke was back at her side. "I usually let the band kick off the show with a song or two before I go up. I like to make 'em want it." He grinned and winked.

One by one, the other band members joined them at the table. Luke introduced Darlina and they each politely said hello, but remained aloof.

The club started to fill with people. Most came to Luke's table to visit. Darlina received some curious looks and everyone she was introduced to, responded in much the same way the band members had. She began to realize they were used to seeing Luke with lots of different women. She wondered if she could possibly become someone special to him, or just another notch in his belt. She didn't know, but was willing to take the chance to find out.

He often put his arm possessively around her, pulling her a little closer to him. Each time he did, her heart skipped a beat. It seemed as if she stood on the edge of a cliff. There was danger yet enticing fascination and appeal.

Around 9:15, the band members took to the stage, starting the night off with a rousing version of *Dixie* to which Luke and many others in the club stood and took off their hats. After a few songs, he joined them, picked up his guitar and moved to the mic.

Darlina quickly got lost in the music, her eyes glued on Luke. Occasionally one of the other women would lean over and say something to her, but she wasn't interested in conversation. She watched every move that Luke made.

He wore a custom made suit with music notes down each pant leg, matching bolero jacket, shiny black cowboy boots and black cowboy hat. She had never seen anyone so handsome, not even in pictures of movie stars.

As the night rolled on, she became aware of the people in the club. This was a much rougher crowd than she was used to being around and made a mental note that she never wanted to work here. Suddenly, someone jostled the table almost spilling the drinks. She looked up to see a very drunk man.

He put his hand on her shoulder slurring his words, "Wouldja' like to dance?"

Darlina removed his hand from her shoulder and shook her head no.

He persisted, "Awww come on. Dance with me," touching her again.

She again shook her head and loudly said, "No, Thank you."

In a split second, the drunken man was hurtled across the dance floor with Luke following, kicking him with the sharp tip of his boot. "The lady said she didn't want to dance, hoss."

A startled Darlina jumped to her feet, feeling a bit sorry for the man but at the same time not wanting Luke to get hurt.

The man tried to get up but Luke held him down with his foot.

"Shit man, let me up. I didn't mean no harm," he slurred.

Luke lifted his boot off him and the man attempted to get to his feet. Luke gave him a shove toward the club bouncer who escorted him out the door.

Luke returned to Darlina. "You okay, sugar?"

She nodded her head as her voice trembled, "How about you? Are you Okay?"

"Of course. I don't think any other sonofabitch will bother you now."

"It's okay, Luke. I'm fine, really," she said.

He kissed her on the cheek and headed back to the stage to rejoin the band. They had not stopped playing nor missed a beat.

She sat stunned at what had just happened.

Rita reached over, patting Darlina's arm. "Don't worry, sweetie, these things happen."

Before she knew it, the night was over. Luke helped the band pack up the equipment then paid them from a stack of twenty dollar bills. He came back to Darlina, "Are you ready to get out of here?"

She nodded her head, standing.

She didn't ask where they were going. It didn't matter as long as she was with him.

As he drove the seventy-eight miles to Brownwood, he talked. "There's somethin' you need to understand. When we're out in the clubs, if someone asks you to dance and you want to, go ahead and dance with 'em. But, if someone makes a pass at you or says anything out of line, I expect you to speak up and tell them to leave you alone."

She searched his face in the darkness wondering where all this was leading. "Luke, I did tell the man I didn't want to dance."

"I know. I saw you. That's why I came off the band stand and took care of it. You did the right thing."

"I'm not sure where you're headed with this."

"Remember Mary?"

"Of course."

"Well, it took me a long time to figure it out, but she liked for me to fight over her. She'd make up shit about someone hittin' on her and expect me to kick his ass. I finally figured it out and told her I wouldn't fight no sonofabitch unless she slapped the shit out of 'em first and that stopped all that."

"Luke, I'm not Mary."

"You sure ain't." He reached across the seat finding Darlina's hand and sliding her across the seat beside him.

They rode in comfortable silence the rest of the way.

Luke's apartment, a modest duplex, sat at the end of Cottage Street. He held her hand as they walked from the car to the door. She expected the nervous jitters to start anytime, but they didn't. It was as if she belonged here.

Once inside, Luke removed his hat, pulled Darlina close and kissed her long and deep. "Now, sugar, let's talk about how you wanted me to make love to you."

Breathless she replied, "Luke, I can't think of anything I want more."

He led her through the kitchen into the bedroom, taking off his jacket as he went. She looked around the small but clean and neat bedroom. She wouldn't allow herself to think about the many women who had been there with Luke. At that moment, she was there and that was all that mattered.

Her heart beat wildly in her chest and she knew beyond any shadow of a doubt this was exactly where she wanted to be.

He appeared to be in no hurry. He casually unbuttoned his shirt, then sat her down on the bed. He slipped her boots off, then his own. Piece by piece, he slowly and methodically removed each bit of clothing, stopping to caress and kiss every inch of skin he uncovered. Her breath came in ragged gasps. She responded by taking off his belt and unbuttoning his pants. As she slid them down she boldly caressed him.

He laid her gently onto the bed, almost as if he were afraid she might break. He lay down beside her and kissed her eyelids, face and then her lips with a sweet tenderness.

"I intend to kiss every inch of your beautiful body," he said hoarsely. "Do you know you're drivin' me crazy?"

When she answered her voice was throaty, "I want you, Luke."

"You've never been with anyone like me."

"No."

"I want you to tell me what you want."

"I want you."

"You've got me. Now tell me what else you want."

How could she say words that she didn't know how to form? "Just make love to me."

"Don't worry. I am, but I'm also gonna teach you how to tell me what you want."

His large hands slid slowly over her body, examining every curve, every soft space as though cherishing the feel of her skin under his fingertips. "Does that feel good?"

Darlina felt her skin sizzle under his touch as a wave of longing overtook her. She felt hot tears stinging her eyelids and shivered with ecstasy. It was just as she had imagined in her wildest dreams. "Yes," she gasped. "It feels wonderful."

He continued caressing, touching and tasting her body. His skilled hands and mouth knew exactly where to go and what to do. Just when she was sure she couldn't go any higher, a new wave of passion washed over her.

Hours passed before Luke, finally spent and satisfied, lay back after lighting a cigar. He pulled her head down onto his chest and held her close. She could hear his heart beating fiercely and smiled realizing how much she had aroused him.

"Luke, I've never felt anything like that before," she whispered softly while kissing his bare chest.

He stroked her hair without replying. Slowly her breathing returned to normal and she gently touched and explored his body.

Luke returned the touches and caresses and after a while, they began to turn more insistent. Almost in shock, she realized he was ready and wanted more, and so did she. They made love until the morning light streamed through the windows.

Exhausted, they drifted off to sleep, wrapped in each other's arms.

# Chapter 7

Darlina slowly opened her eyes, at first not remembering where she was. Then quickly the night all came flooding back. She looked over at Luke, still in a deep sleep, then slowly and quietly, extracted herself from his arms and tiptoed to the bathroom.

Muscles she didn't know she had complained with every movement.

She'd had sex a few times, but it was always quick, usually ending before it started. She looked at her reflection in the mirror unable to wipe the smile off her face. Now she knew what it was like to really make love and glowed with satisfaction.

How she wished she had thought to bring at least a toothbrush. She did what she could to freshen up, putting a ribbon of Colgate on her finger and rubbing it in her mouth. The rumbling from her stomach prompted her to explore the kitchen. Glancing at a clock on the wall she was surprised to find it well past noon.

The lack of food in the kitchen shocked her. Did this man never eat? To be such a large man, he had to eat sometime. She found some saltines and a small container of milk and munched on them until the rumbling stopped.

Back in the bedroom she quietly slipped under the wrinkled sheets beside Luke. He stirred as she came close, instinctively reaching out and wrapping his arms around her.

She touched his face and kissed his closed eyelids softly, then worked her way down to his neck, his chest and then to the part of him that had brought her such pleasure a few short hours ago. As she kissed and caressed him, he began to wake moaning with pleasure.

Soon, she had what she sought. Inside her, he brought wave after wave of intoxicating pleasure.

Darlina didn't care if she never left his arms. She'd read and dreamed about this feeling her whole life and wasn't going to let it go.

Once they showered and dressed, Luke suggested, "Darlin', I better get you something to eat. Let's go down to the Red Wagon café."

"I will admit I'm about as hungry as a horse."

The day began to fade way too soon and before she was ready, they were back in Abilene. "I don't want to leave you, Luke."

He smiled over at her and she slid across the seat to his side. His breath ruffled her hair as he murmured, "You have a job to go to and I'll see you again real soon."

Her throat constricted as the thought flashed through her mind that this was it. This was what everyone had warned her about and now that Luke had gotten her in his bed, she'd never hear from him again.

"Thank you for an incredible night. And I'm not just sayin' that." She intertwined her fingers in his.

"You were amazing, sugar. You sure do learn fast," he chuckled.

"I've always been a fast learner when it's something I enjoy."

He kissed the top of her head and she could only think how she did not want to get out of the car or leave his side.

The next few days passed quickly. She danced at the Silver Spur starting on Wednesday night. She made $40 in tips and had no trouble getting the regulars to order her a Sloe Gin Fizz. Mr. Johnson seemed pleased with her and occasionally gave her a nod or wink.

To her surprise, Luke called every day and she longed to feel his arms around her. Each time she remembered their love making, she ached and longed for him in a way she'd never experienced.

She quickly established rapport with the other girls at the Silver Spur, but particularly liked Louise and felt she could confide in the older woman. She knew Louise's husband was a friend of Luke's and when she met Johnny, she understood why. He was a small wiry man with bright blue eyes and a line of bullshit a mile long.

Louise introduced her to Johnny as Luke's girlfriend. "Sugar, you're scrapin' the bottom of the barrel there. You know Luke's a no good sonofabitch, don't you?"

She started to respond defensively and then realized Johnny was teasing her and playfully answered, "Yep, I sure do."

He laughed, "No really, he's a true friend and a pretty good ol' boy in spite of his reputation."

"I believe that."

"You treat him right and he'll do the same."

She smiled at Johnny, happy to finally meet someone who had a good word to say about Luke.

Darlina found herself exhausted Saturday night at the Faded Rose. Luke and the band were playing in Ft. Sill, Oklahoma and she wished with all her heart she was with him, but he'd told her none of the wives or girlfriends were going as it was a fast trip up and back.

Working all three of her jobs through the week had left her feeling wrung out.

She heard a familiar voice and looked up to see her brother-in-law, Ray.

"Hi, Ray. What are you doing here? Where's Norma?"

"She's home. I just got back off a run with that ol' truck and thought I'd stop in and see my favorite sister-in-law. You look beat."

"I am. Working the Silver Spur, here and the boiler factory is maybe a little much."

"Well, let ol' Ray help you out, little sis. Take this little white pill with some coffee and it'll perk you up in no time."

"Are you sure?"

"Yeah, I'm sure. How do you think I've driven those ol' trucks for so long? It won't hurt you and I promise you'll feel better."

She accepted the pill he handed her and swallowed it. Within an hour, she began to feel the hair tingling on top of her head, her breath came faster and she felt wide awake. She stopped at Ray's table.

"Wow! You were right, Ray. I feel amazing. Thanks!"

"Here, stick these in your purse for later when you need more. Just remember you need to stop and sleep sometime too."

She laughed, "Thanks! I'm gonna head up and dance now. Stick around."

It seemed as though her feet weren't touching the floor when she took the steps to the stage. She had no idea such a tiny pill could make you feel so good. She couldn't wait to tell Luke about it.

Sleep did not come for Darlina until late Sunday night. Luke came to see her on Sunday afternoon and could immediately tell something was different. When she confided in him she'd taken the pill Ray gave her, he laughed. "Darlin', how do you think I make all the miles up and down the roads?"

"I never thought about it. I guess that's one reason you don't get hungry very often either. I haven't wanted a bite to eat."

"Well, I'm gonna go get you a hamburger and you're gonna eat it, then I'm taking you sweet little ass to the motel and wear you out so you'll sleep tonight."

She threw back her head laughing. "I thought you'd never get around to that part!"

"There's something I need to ask you that's been on my mind."

"What's that, Luke"

"Are you on the pill or doing anything to keep from getting pregnant?"

Darlina smiled mischievously. "Why, baby? Don't you want any more kids?"

"I'm being serious, sugar. I sure as hell don't need any more kids."

"Don't worry. I'm on the pill. I'm not gonna get pregnant."

Luke breathed a sigh of relief, "Well then let's get goin' and get you something to eat. Then I'm gonna make you tell me how you want me to take care of your hot little ass."

"You won't have to make me tell you. I will happily tell you every detail," she said pulling his face down to hers and kissing him.

Darlina thought about his concern and felt grateful to Norma for getting her started on the pill. As much as she'd like to have Luke's baby, she knew now wasn't the time.

When they returned back to Norma's house, they sat in the car talking for a long time. "I want you to move in with me, honey. I don't like this business of just seein' you now and then."

"I don't like it either, Luke, but what would I do about all my jobs?"

"Sugar, if you're livin' with me, you don't need a job. I'll take care of you. Just think about it."

"I don't have to think about it, Luke. I love you and I'd happily quit any job to be with you."

"Talk it over with your sister. I don't want you to leave her in a bind. Maybe in a few weeks, we can make it happen."

She boldly kissed Luke, not hesitating to thrust her tongue in his mouth. She wanted this man in every way possible and had no fear of showing it.

"Whoa! Slow down, darlin'. You're gonna get me all riled up again."

Smiling, she said, "I intend to get you all riled up every chance I get, Luke Stone."

"Sweetheart, you do it good. You head on in and talk to your sister and I'll call you tomorrow." He kissed her long and slow, running his hands lovingly over her body. Every touch and every caress left her breathless.

She finally tore herself from his arms and went inside with her mind full of new plans and dreams. Life was truly beginning for her and her heart nearly burst with love for this man. She knew without a doubt she would follow him to the ends of the earth if he asked.

# Chapter 8

Three weeks had passed since Darlina sat in the car with Luke outside her sister's home and Thanksgiving was around the corner. She missed the big family gatherings they'd had every year since she could remember. Tables laden with food along with the sounds of chatter and laughter as they played dominoes or board games were imprinted in her memory.

When she thought about how sad her mother must be with no one coming home this year, she considered calling her. She picked up the phone only to put it back down. The last thing she wanted was to make her mother cry or to listen to another lecture from her. On the other hand, she longed to tell her about Luke and the love she had found. She sighed; it would just have to wait. Perhaps writing her a letter would be best.

Her talk with Norma had gone well and she put in her resignation notice at the boiler factory as well as the Silver Spur. She treasured the talk she had with Marketa about her plans. It pleased her that Marketa assured her a job anytime she wanted and wished her and Luke the best.

Sunday dawned a cool but sunshiny day. As soon as Darlina opened her eyes, she remembered this was finally the day Luke was coming to get her and her belongings and take her to live with him. She bounded out of bed as excited as a kid on Christmas morning.

Norma had planned a family dinner, inviting Leann and Wayne and of course Luke and Darlina. She loved that her family accepted Luke. It was important they understood how much he meant to her.

From the time she was a little girl, she'd believed she would find true love. Her knight in shining armor would sweep her off her feet and make her heart sing. Yes, she was a believer in love and dreams and wishes. This was the way life was meant to be.

She happily joined Norma in the kitchen to help prepare the meal. She laughed and joked with her and Ray. Nothing could take away this moment of joy. When Leann and Wayne arrived, she gave her sister a big hug and kissed her on the cheek.

Leann seemed a little melancholy and Darlina brought her into the living room. "Sister, you know that just because I'm going to live with Luke, I'm not abandoning you. I'll still be your sister."

"I know, but you won't come see me every day at lunch and I'll miss our talks. I'm gonna miss you." Tears came into her eyes and she quickly looked away.

Darlina hugged her again. "You're not losing me. You're gaining another person that will care about you. Luke is a good man."

"I know and I'm happy for you...really, I am. I'll just miss you."

"I'll miss you too but we'll talk often."

They were interrupted by a knock on the door. Darlina couldn't get to the door fast enough. She opened it and flew into Luke's arms. "I'm so glad you're here. I've been ready for you all day."

"Me too, sugar." He looked at Leann, smiled warmly and held out his hand. "I'm Luke Stone. You must be Leann. Darlina's told me lots about you."

Leann dismissed the handshake and gave him a quick hug. "She's told me lots about you too. I'm glad to finally meet you."

The rest of the family joined them and soon they were seated at the table eating, talking and laughing. Darlina looked around the room soaking up the love from every corner, convinced that she would never have anything but good and wonderful things for the rest of her life.

Once dinner was over and dishes cleared away, she went to her room to collect her things. Luke went with her and took advantage of being alone by putting his hands under her sweater, caressing her warm skin and kissing her waiting lips. "Let's go home, darlin'."

She moaned with pleasure. "I've never been more ready."

They said their goodbyes to her family, and she happily hurried off to begin her new fascinating life with the man she had fallen so deeply and completely in love with.

The minute they were in the shiny blue T-Bird, Luke pulled her over close to him and put his arm around her shoulders.

She looked up at him and smiled, then kissed him boldly, thrusting her tongue in his mouth. "Luke, I'm going to take such good care of you."

"Baby, I can't think of anything I'll enjoy more."

The miles between Abilene and Brownwood seemed to fly by and in no time they were parked in the driveway at Luke's apartment. Once inside, he set her suitcases down and she melted in his arms.

She turned her face upward to his expectantly. He placed a large strong hand at the nape of her neck, nibbling softly on her ear. Pursing his lips, he gently moved to that sweet soft spot on her neck where her pulse quickened. Soon their breaths mingled as he teased and taunted with his mouth. Finally, his tongue slipped between her slightly parted lips and she pressed herself into him as the intensity of the kiss rose.

Breathlessly, she whispered, "Take me to our bed, Luke. Make love to me."

He picked her up, carried her into the bedroom and laid her on the inviting black and gold iron frame bed. She didn't know if it was possible for someone to die of happiness, but if it was, she would surely die right here and now.

Hours later, as she put her belongings away in the empty dresser drawers Luke had provided, Darlina paid more attention to the details of the apartment. When she had been there before, she didn't notice the Akai reel-to-reel tape recorder sitting by the bed or the Colt 45 long barrel pistol that hung from the iron bedstead in a custom tooled black leather holster. Beside it hung a large Bowie knife also housed in a black leather sheath. On the wall above the bed was an authentic Civil War sword complete with CSA engraved on the handle protected by a silver metal holder. She did clearly remember the Martin guitar that sat beside the bed and it was still there.

A large charcoal drawing of Robert E. Lee hung on the opposite wall. As she browsed through the bookshelves, she couldn't help but notice a large assortment of books on the Civil War.

Luke explained. "I've always been a big Civil War buff. Robert E. Lee was the finest general that ever lived. I have a great affinity to

Sam Bass too. I'll tell you all about it sometime, but right now I just want to get you settled in."

"I want to hear all about it. I've always been an avid reader and it makes me happy to see that you have so many books."

A Dearborn heater sat in one corner of the room and the best she could tell, this was the only heat source in the entire apartment except for the stove in the kitchen.

She slowly took in the surroundings that were now her new home.

Luke pointed out the recorder, "Lots of times in my sleep, I dream songs so I sit up on the side of the bed, grab the ol' guitar and turn on the recorder. When I listen back the next day, I usually have no memory of what I recorded, but that way I don't lose the song."

She was fascinated by this kind of creativity. "Well baby, don't stop doing that just because I'm here. It won't bother me at all."

"There's something else I need to show you." He walked to a small intercom box attached to the wall. "This intercom is hooked up between mine and Red's apartments, so if you ever need anything, just hit this button and you can talk to him. His apartment is the other side of this duplex."

"I can't imagine that I would ever need to do that, but at least I know what it's for."

"Red is as close as a brother to me and because I love you, he'll look out for you."

"That's sweet. I'll enjoy getting to know him."

"Tomorrow I'll take you to Piggly Wiggly so you can buy a few groceries. The kitchen's pretty bare."

"If it's the same as when I was last here, it's very bare."

"I don't eat many meals here, but you need to eat and keep your strength up 'cause I'm gonna wear that beautiful body of yours out."

She loved the playful banter, "You can try, mister, but I'm tougher than I look."

"You look like a fairy princess to me. All this talk is makin' me want you in a bad way."

She flew into his arms, kissing and caressing him and in no time, found herself back on their bed in the throes of passion.

True to his word, the next day, he took her shopping and she stocked the kitchen with food staples. With Luke's permission, she began to make the apartment more inviting. She moved an overstuffed chair into a corner placing a lamp and vase of dried flowers on an oak end table beside it.

Luke had told her she could do anything she wanted as long as she didn't move the recorder, the guitar or anything in his office.

What he called the office was the actual living room in the apartment and was strictly off limits to everyone. Luke had bits and pieces of paper scattered across a large office desk. Three guitars and an amplifier sat against one wall along with two big filing cabinets.

He explained that all of the bits and pieces of paper were song ideas he was working on and as long as nothing got moved, he knew where everything was. He called it his eccentric filing system.

Darlina loved settling into daily life with Luke. She loved every facet of being his woman. To her it was as natural as breathing.

She'd been living with Luke for a week when he told her they were playing at the Lakewood Club in Brownwood Saturday night and his brother would be there to play keyboards. She excitedly anticipated meeting a member of his family.

They arrived at the Lakewood Club early to find some of the other band members already setting up equipment and instruments and testing the sound. Luke escorted her to the table where they would all sit and told her to order anything she wanted. She watched while they began a routine that was quickly becoming familiar to her.

Suddenly the door flew open. "Where are those damned ol' Rebel Rousers?" a voice boomed.

"Right here, you sonofabitch," Luke replied. The two men took strides towards each other then embraced. Luke brought the man to the table where she was sitting. "Bobby, I want you to meet my new lady, Darlina. Darlina, this is my brother, Bobby."

Bobby reached out and lifted Darlina off her chair. "So this is the newest cunt?"

"Now Bobby, don't start any shit. You're already drunk, aren't you? I've told you over and over not to show up to play for me drunk. Put Darlina down, you crazy sonofabitch."

Bobby dropped Darlina, who luckily landed in her chair, and turned to face his brother, "Don't you be tellin' me what to do, you white eyed bastard."

"Come on, Bobby. Let's not do this tonight."

"Do what, you coward?"

Luke grabbed Bobby by the arm. "Come on man, let me take you home. I don't need this shit. Besides that, you owe Darlina an apology."

"I don't apologize to no damned broad and you ain't takin' me nowhere, you big overbearing white eyed sonofabitch."

Enraged, Luke drew back his fist and hit Bobby square in the mouth, knocking him backwards into some tables and chairs. Bobby got to his feet and lunged toward his brother. They tangled with each other, throwing punches and obscenities.

Darlina quickly scooted off into a corner like a frightened rabbit, her heart in her throat and stomach churning. She didn't want either man to get hurt.

The owner of the club and the other band members came running. Red tried to grab Bobby and hold him while the club owner and Jerry grabbed Luke.

"You two knock it off or get the hell out of my club," the owner irately shouted.

Luke, wiping blood from his mouth, apologized. "I'm sorry, Gene. Bobby showed up drunk and you know how he gets."

Bobby yelled, "Yeah, you know damned well how he gets. Let go of me and I'll teach this sonofabitch not to mess with me." He persistently struggled to get loose from the men who held him.

"Dammit, Bobby. Would you shut up and go home and sleep it off?" Luke implored.

"Hell no! I wanna finish this shit with you."

Luke looked pleadingly at Red and Jerry. "Can you two take him home and put him to bed?"

The two men dragged Bobby out of the club as he continued to struggle to get lose from their grip.

Luke came to Darlina, "Baby, I'm really sorry you had to meet my brother when he was drinkin'. He can be one mean sonofabitch, but when he's sober, he's totally different. He'll apologize to you for insulting you. I'll make sure of that."

With trembling hands, she began to wipe the blood off Luke's face with a napkin. "Let's go to the house and get you cleaned up."

Luke yelled at the rest of the band, "I'll be back. Ya'll go ahead and finish settin' up. You can take down the keyboard and put it back in the trailer."

They returned to their apartment where Darlina helped Luke get cleaned up and changed into clean clothes, then headed back to the Lakewood Club.

In the car Luke apologized again, "Honey, I truly am sorry."

"It's not your fault, Luke. I just hate that you had to fight your brother."

"That's not unusual when he's drinkin'. He gets a big brother complex or something I've never understood. I'm used to him, but you don't deserve that kind of shit."

"Is he older than you?"

"No, I'm four years older than him. We've gone through this fightin' shit for years. I even let him whip me once thinkin' that would put an end to it, but it didn't and I wound up layin' his head open with a coke bottle that night."

"I don't know what to say, Luke. I'm sorry for you and for him."

"That's why I love you, sweetheart. You manage to see the good in everyone." He reached across the seat and intertwined his hand in hers.

The days turned into nights and nights turned into days as it all started to become a routine for Darlina. She loved going with Luke every night to play music and slowly but surely, the band members were warming up to her somewhat. Maybe, she thought, they were beginning to accept that she was in Luke's life to stay. She knew beyond a shadow of a doubt, she wasn't going anywhere.

# Chapter 9

Luke excitedly woke Darlina up at ten o'clock in the morning, a few days after the Lakewood Club incident. "I just had the most brilliant idea! I can't believe it took me this long to think of it."

She sleepily rubbed her eyes. "Okay, baby. What is it?"

"I wanna start havin' go-go dancers as a part of the Rebel Rouser's shows and honey, you're gonna be my star dancer."

"That's a really great idea. I don't know of any other band that has dancers, especially not country bands. I'd love to do it, but you're gonna need more than me."

"I know and I've already thought of that. I'll either get Louise, Sherry or Dee Dee, depending on who's free on the nights we need 'em."

"I love it, Luke. I think it'll make your band even more popular than you are now, if that's possible."

"We're playing the Westwood Club in Abilene this coming Saturday night and that'd be the perfect place to try it out. A bunch of snooty rich doctors and lawyers are always at that club. I'd be willin' to bet some go-go girls would liven the place up."

Fully awake now and excited about the new idea, she immediately began to think about her costumes. "I think I'll get all my costumes out today and see if I can spruce them up a little with sequins or beads."

"Honey, let me help make you a costume. I'm pretty damn good with my hands and I can picture you in a leather costume with long beaded fringe hanging down from the top."

"Oooohhh I love that idea. Let's go get some leather and whatever else we need and get started."

Luke laughed at her enthusiasm. "Slow down a little, sweetheart. We're butt naked in bed and I haven't had any lovin' or coffee or anything yet."

Laughing with him she said, "Let's start with the lovin' and figure it out from there."

Several hours later found them at the kitchen table with a large piece of supple deerskin leather and a pattern spread out. She loved that they worked together easily and in no time at all, it was taking shape. They were interrupted by a knock on the kitchen door.

Luke opened the door. "Come on in, hoss."

Bobby walked through the door straight to Darlina. "I came to apologize to you, little lady. I'm sorry I insulted you the other night." Turning to Luke he said, "Brother, I owe you one too. Sorry I showed my ass. I don't know what makes me do it."

Darlina stood and gave Bobby a warm hug. "Apology accepted, Bobby, and it's nice to finally meet you."

Luke slapped his brother on the back. "Shit man, it's no big deal. You know I don't hold grudges. I shoulda' whipped your ass, though."

Bobby jokingly replied, "You only wish you could, you big overbearing bastard."

Darlina made a fresh pot of coffee and Bobby sat at the table looking on while they worked.

"What are ya'll makin'?"

Luke explained, "I've got this crazy idea. I'm gonna add go-go dancers to the Rebel Rousers show. Darlina used to work for Marketa and at the Silver Spur and she's a damn good dancer. She's gonna be my main girl, then I'll get Louise, Sherry or Dee Dee to fill in so I can have two girls at each show."

Bobby looked at his brother in amazement. "That's one hell of an idea! No other country band I know of has dancers. I wanna be there when they debut."

"Well, that'll be this Saturday at the Westwood. Why don't you come and play with us? Sober that is."

"You got it! I'll be there and the Westwood is the best place I can think of to start."

"That's what I thought too. Those ol' doctors and lawyers will loosen right up when the girls get up there shakin' their cute little asses."

Bobby tipped his chair back and slapped his knee. "It's a great idea."

Darlina served up steaming cups of Folgers coffee then she and Luke returned to work on the costume. Bobby sat visiting and watching the progress. She thought to herself that Luke was right. When he wasn't drinking, Bobby could be pleasant to be around and had a very unique sense of humor.

She could see some similarities between the brothers, but Luke was the dominant one and that, she surmised, was Bobby's problem when he got drunk. Maybe she could do something to help.

After an hour or so, Bobby left and Luke told Darlina he needed to go meet with the band and bounce this new idea off them. He kissed her before he went out the door.

Once he was gone, she looked at the costume they were working on and tackled it feverishly. She couldn't contain her excitement about dancing again and this time for Luke! She remembered the two little white pills that Ray had given her, still in her purse. Maybe if she took one, she could get more done because she wouldn't have to waste time sleeping.

By the time Luke returned, she had the top sewn together and it was ready for the fringe to be added.

"What did the band think?" She asked.

"They loved the idea. We're gonna do it. Damn baby, you sure got a lot done while I was gone."

"I had a little help," she said holding out the other white pill to him.

He chuckled, "Nah, sugar, you keep it. I've got plenty. Looking at you working away with that leather is turning me on big time. Come in here and take care of your man."

"With pleasure," she said getting up from the table.

Back in the bedroom, she fit easily in his arms and the sheets were soon damp and wrinkled, her breath mingled with his.

At four that afternoon, listening to the water running in the shower, Darlina looked at the Confederate gray pants with a lighter gray stripe, black satin shirt with large collar and gray jacket with black piping around the lapel and down the front that Luke had laid on the bed. She went to the closet, found his black Tony Lama boots, and proceeded to bring them to a lustrous shine. She felt useful and hoped he would be pleased.

He emerged from the shower rubbing his wet hair with a towel. He stopped when he saw his boots. "Sweetheart, you didn't have to shine my boots for me."

"I know I didn't, but I wanted to. Like 'em?"

"Like 'em? I love 'em. From now on, you're my official boot shine girl."

She smiled, pleased with herself. "I love you, Luke."

"And I love you right back, sugar. Your turn in the shower but I ain't shinin' your boots for you while you're in there."

She laughed, "I would never expect you to, my dear."

The weather was turning colder and the 1964 Lincoln Towncar that served as a band car had no heater. She brought a blanket to keep warm and loved huddling under it with Luke. Tonight they were going to Junction to play at the SPJST hall. Red, whose name was Tommy Johnson, always drove the car, pulling the band trailer with rebel flags painted on each side. He stood right at 6' tall, had an unruly shock of red hair, wore thick coke bottle glasses and was practically skin and bones.

Red was Luke's right-hand-man and he depended on him to keep things running smooth. The way Red looked up to Luke and tried so hard to please, reminded her of a faithful dog and his master.

Jerry and Rita normally drove their own car to the gigs unless Rita wasn't going, then Jerry would ride in the Lincoln with the rest of the band. Jerry stood 6' tall and Rita was 5'5" and a little on the heavy side. She had a warm smile and Darlina was quickly growing fond of her.

The drummer, Charles, whom everyone called Preacher, was 6'2" and thin, but not as skinny as Red. He had straight dark hair that he kept cut just above his ears. He usually rode in the Lincoln.

On this particular night, Preacher had a girl with him who Darlina had never met. Her first impression of her was that she was a little rough, and didn't particularly like her.

Even though she'd been introduced to her, she couldn't remember her name. She guessed she should pay more attention.

They sat in the backseat, making out, not caring who watched or heard. The heavy breathing, rustling and moans were very distracting to Darlina and left her feeling uncomfortable.

Luke wrapped his arms around her under the blanket. "A penny for your thoughts."

"They aren't worth a penny right now," she said laughing. "Honestly, I'm mostly thinkin' about the new show and gettin' to be a part of it. I can't wait to get my costume finished and try it on for you."

Red piped up. "Luke, I really think you've come up with a good idea about the go-go girls. I think the crowds are gonna love 'em."

"Me too, hoss. We'll find out Saturday night."

As they traveled down the highway, Darlina reflected on how good it felt to be accepted in this group. She loved being some small part of the music. She knew she could never tell Luke about how she'd always fantasized about being a singer. She was afraid, if she did, he'd find a way to get her up on the stage to sing. So, she contentedly rode at his side and vowed to keep that secret to herself.

She had beamed with pride when Rita told her how happy she was that she and Luke were together and how she could tell that she was good for Luke. The encouragement was nice because it reflected what she felt as well.

The SPJST hall was packed to overflowing by the time the night was under way. She continued to be amazed at the numbers of people that came to hear Luke and his band play wherever they went. They were, without a doubt, the hottest band in Texas.

Driving down the two-lane Texas Hill Country road at two o'clock in the morning, pulling a band trailer, could be a little nerve wrecking. There were deer everywhere on the sides of and in the road.

Luke told Red, "Next one of them sons of bitches you see, graze 'em with the fender and let's take back some of this deer meat."

Darlina felt her insides tighten at that thought, but remained silent.

She could see a deer on the road just ahead and watched in fright as Red drove a little faster and headed straight for it.

"Shit! Missed that one. I'll get the next one," he said.

"There! Get that one," Luke commanded.

Red turned the steering wheel sharp to the right and hit the deer with the right fender, knocking it off the road. He brought the car and band trailer to a screeching halt and he, Luke and Preacher all jumped out at the same time.

She watched in horror as Luke drew his pocket knife and expertly sliced the deer's throat. Once it stopped kicking, they picked it up by the legs and threw it into the trunk of the car.

"And that's how we get meat to feed the families," Luke told her.

"Okay," she mumbled, unable to think of any other reply.

"I've killed lots more deer out of season and without a gun than any other way." Luke carefully cleaned his pocket knife before folding it and placing it back in his pocket.

Red laughed. "Shit man, there've been times we had more deer meat than we knew what to do with. Damned good eatin'. Remember those goats we got that time?"

Luke chuckled. "Yep, sure do. My kids loved that goat meat and we all ate on it for days."

She sat in silence not knowing what to say. She'd never tasted deer or goat meat and certainly had never seen them killed. It made her a little queasy to remember the deer flopping at the side of the road and to know it lay in the trunk of the car bleeding out.

"You okay, sweetheart?"

"Sure," she replied with a false jovialness.

What else could she say? She wouldn't let Luke know that what they'd just done grossed her out. She had to pretend it didn't bother her at all when in truth it did, very much.

By the time they reached Brownwood, they had two deer in the trunk of the car.

All in all, it had been a rather disturbing night. Between Preacher having sex with the girl in the backseat and the deer slayings, she had an uneasy feeling, but remained determined to keep a good front and not let Luke see that any of it troubled her.

She was finally accepted, and damned if she was going to do or say anything to threaten that. She almost wished she hadn't taken the little white pill so she could go to sleep and forget about everything but she knew it would be many hours before she would sleep again.

Once they reached the apartment, Luke, Red and Preacher all changed clothes and unhooked the band trailer. Then they grabbed a full bottle of Jim Beam and left to take care of the deer in the trunk of the car.

Darlina assumed the girl Preacher was with had gone home because she didn't see her again.

She looked around their apartment, her gaze landing on the unfinished leather costume. She was determined to have most of it done by the time Luke returned.

She glanced at the clock as the final stitches were being sewn. The only thing left to do was make the fringe and add beads. She was leaving that task for Luke, as she wasn't quite sure how to tackle it. At five a.m. she wondered what was taking the men so long.

She went to the dresser drawer where her things were, got out the rest of her costumes and laid them on the bed. Next, she got a box of beads, sequins and other decorations that Luke owned. He'd explained how he used them to decorate their band costumes from time to time. She expertly sewed new decorations on the costumes and then stood back appraising her work. Not bad, she thought.

This was everything she'd ever wanted. Life with Luke fulfilled all of her dreams. By being included in the band shows, she was getting to live out yet another dream. It felt incredibly wonderful to finally be totally accepted and cared for.

# Chapter 10

At six o'clock in the morning, as the sun was coming up over the horizon, Darlina heard the door fly open. Luke, Red and Preacher tromped in, dumping a large trash bag on the kitchen counter.

"Darlina!" Luke called out.

She came into the kitchen from the bedroom. "Yes, Luke."

"Make us a pot of coffee and get this meat all packaged up and put in the freezer." He grabbed her, roughly.

She could smell the whiskey on his breath and he seemed a little wobbly. In fact, to her, they all appeared to be drunk. "Luke, you're getting blood on me," she objected, pulling away.

He grabbed her arm harder and gave her a bruising kiss. "I'll put blood or anything else I want on you, sweetheart. Remember, you're my ol' lady now."

She didn't understand why he was treating her so rough. "Yes, I remember, but you're hurting me," she said choking back tears that threatened to fall.

"Well then, by God, get us some damn coffee made and get started on this meat."

"Okay Luke, but you don't have to talk to me like that."

He stomped off to the bathroom and she was left in the kitchen with Red and Preacher. She turned her back to them to hide the emotion in her face.

Red spoke softly, "Sugar, tell Luke me and Preach went on to bed and we'll see him later."

"I will."

Once the coffee was brewing, she turned to the daunting task at hand. The smell of fresh blood assaulted her nostrils when she opened the trash bag and she started to gag. She had to pull herself together and do what Luke asked. She didn't know what to think about his behavior. Maybe it was just to show off in front of Red and Preacher or maybe he'd drank too much whiskey. She didn't know but was determined she would not accept that kind of treatment from him.

When he came back from the bathroom, he headed to the coffee pot. "Where did Red and Preacher go?"

"They said to tell you they were goin' on to bed."

"Pussy sons of bitches," he growled.

"Luke, are you okay?"

"What the hell business is it of yours?" He snapped as he stomped off into the bedroom, spilling coffee as he went. Soon she heard him strumming on his guitar.

She wasn't sure how she did it other than pure will, but she managed to package the meat and put it away in the freezer.

Snores coming from the bedroom let her know that Luke was asleep. Maybe he'd wake up in a better mood. The smell of deer blood was strong and pungent in the kitchen. After getting out all of the cleaning products she could find, she scrubbed the counter, sink and floor until the only thing she could smell was bleach. Then she went to the shower to wash the smell off her.

After she was cleaned up and could no longer smell deer blood anywhere, she got under the sheets close to Luke. Instinctively, he reached out and wrapped his arms around her. She sighed softly and hoped that when he awoke, everything would be normal again.

It was late afternoon when Luke opened his eyes. Darlina was awake, snuggled close to him and he began nuzzling her neck.

She pulled away slightly. "Luke, why did you treat me so rough and talk ugly to me when you came in this morning?"

"What are you talking about, baby? I don't even remember gettin' home."

"Well, you did and you weren't very nice. You must've been way drunk."

"I'm sorry, sweetheart. I truly have no memory of any of it. Forgive me?" He asked caressing her face.

She answered his question with a gentle kiss that quickly turned to a hot searing passionate kiss. She felt soothed that he didn't remember the incident and knew in her heart he'd never intentionally be mean to her.

Darlina proudly showed him all of her costumes and the work she'd done on them through the night.

"Wow sugar, those look great. I need to attach the fringe to the leather top and you'll be all set."

"I'm really looking forward to dancing tomorrow night."

"I know you are and you're gonna be my shinin' star up there on the stage shakin' your sweet little ass."

"Who's dancin' with me?"

"Louise. You know, she's one of the best."

"Yes she is and besides that, I really like her. I like Johnny too. He's truly your friend."

"Yep, they don't make many like ol' Johnny. I'm gonna get this fringe cut. How about you cook us up a mess of that fresh deer meat?"

"Okay. How do I fix it?"

"Don't tell me you've never cooked deer meat before."

"Sorry, but no I haven't."

"Dip it in milk, then flour and fry it like chicken fried steak. It's the best meat on earth besides maybe buffalo."

Taking out a package of the meat that had just been put away, she dreaded opening it and smelling the blood again, but didn't want to break the good mood Luke now appeared to be in.

She carefully opened the package and breathed through her mouth to avoid the smell. Within 30 minutes she had it fried and ready to eat.

Luke cleared off the table and sat down with a plate in front of him. He piled it high with the meat. "You really need to eat some of this."

"I don't know if I can, Luke. Remember I took a white cross yesterday?"

"Yeah, I remember, but if you eat, it'll start to bring you down so you can sleep tonight."

Taking a small piece of the meat, she cut it into bite size pieces. Once she had it in her mouth, she was surprised to find it fairly delectable. "This ain't too bad."

"Told ya'. You can trust what I tell you."

She smiled at Luke very happy that the foul mood from earlier had dissipated.

"I'm gonna leave you home tonight, sugar. You need to get rested up and be at your best for tomorrow night."

"But, I love goin' with you."

"And I love havin' you with me, but I think you need more rest than you're gettin'."

"I'll do whatever you say, but I'll miss bein' with you."

"You just be here when I get home and I'll be a happy man."

"I'm not goin' anywhere, Luke. I love you."

Once he'd eaten his fill of the meat, he leaned back in the chair, lit a King Edward cigar and said, "Come here, princess. Come sit on daddy's lap."

She got up from her chair joining him. He gently stroked her hair. "You're the very best thing that's ever happened to me. I don't know what I'd do without you."

"You'll never have to find out," she said, lovingly tracing the lines on his face with her fingertips.

He gently picked her up and carried her to their bed where he slowly and methodically aroused her to the heights of passion that she was becoming accustomed to.

That night, as he was getting dressed for the gig, Darlina asked him, "Do you mind if I give Leann a call tonight?"

"Hell no, I don't mind. Tell her I said hello."

"I will. I won't talk long and run up the phone bill."

"Talk as long as you girls want to. I'll see you when I get home."

She stood on her tiptoes and kissed Luke, thrusting her tongue in his mouth and pressing her body against his.

"Now, don't go gettin' me all stirred up or I'll just not go play at all tonight."

She laughed, "Go on. Just remember what's waitin' for you right here."

"How could I forget?"

Once he was gone, she picked up the phone and dialed Leann's number. As soon as she heard her sister's voice, tears she'd been holding back came in a flood.

"Oh sister, it's so good to hear your voice. I've missed you terribly," she said when Leann picked up the phone.

"What's wrong, Darlina? Why are you crying?"

"Nothing's wrong, I've just missed you, that's all."

"I've missed you too. So, tell me all about your exciting life with Luke."

"I do love being here and going with Luke to all the places they play and everyone accepting me as his woman. It's all I ever dreamed it would be."

"But, something's wrong. I can hear it in your voice."

"Not really. Guess I'm just feelin' a little emotional. It's so close to Christmas and I'm thinkin' about family and mama."

"Yeah, I know. Me too. Wayne's family has totally accepted me and we're a big part of their daily lives, but I miss mama and daddy too."

"Do you think I should call them?"

"I don't know. I talked to mom a couple of weeks ago and she was cold and distant, but at least I'm married to Wayne and you're not married to Luke. You know that goes totally against her beliefs."

"I wish she could just accept us as we are."

"Maybe in time, but it's too soon. Her and daddy are putting the house up for sale and moving somewhere in Northern New Mexico."

"I wrote her a letter when I moved in with Luke and all I got back was a package with some new towels in it and a note saying she didn't approve of what I'd done, but there was a gift."

Leann laughed. "That's our mama. Always proper even when she don't wanna be."

"Well, I think I'll call and wish her a Merry Christmas sometime in the next few weeks. Luke's gonna start havin' me go-go dance as a part of the Rebel Rousers shows. We've been makin' a new leather costume with long fringe and beads on it and tomorrow night is the first night."

"That's exciting. Where are ya'll gonna be?"

"Some place called the Westwood Club. Luke says it's an upper class club with rich snooty doctors and lawyers."

"Well, me and Wayne could never get in a place like that, but next time ya'll play in Abilene, let me know and we'll come out and see you. Don't guess you've talked to Norma."

"No, I really should call her. I'd love for you and Wayne to come out and see us and maybe Norma and Ray too. You have no idea how much I've missed you."

"Yes I do, 'cause I've missed you as much. Norma might come out with us, but her and Ray are split up."

"On no! What happened?"

"Apparently Ray decided he needed a younger woman and Norma found out he was having an affair. It's been pretty rough on her."

"I'll call her soon. Guess I better get off here. Tell Wayne I said hi and Norma too."

"And tell Luke hi for me. I'm serious about lettin' us know when you play in Abilene again."

"I will. I love you, sister."

"Love you too. Glad you called."

Once she hung up the phone, she sat thinking about her family and especially Leann. She was filled with a longing to see all of them. She wished their mother would stop being so hard on them for trying to live their own lives.

Her thoughts turned to Norma and felt sad that Ray had cheated on her. She knew she had to see her sisters soon. She'd talk to Luke about it when he got home.

She felt very alone and wished she was at the club sitting in her place listening to Luke and the band. She hoped he was sincere in just wanting her to rest and get ready for tomorrow's show and there wasn't any other reason he wanted her to stay home tonight.

No, she told herself. She would not let doubts start to creep in. Luke loved her and she loved him and he would never do anything to betray her.

She decided to do as he suggested. She took a long hot bath, washed her hair then settled down on their bed to wait for him. She sat cross legged looking around the room.

She spotted some photo albums on a shelf. Curiosity won out and she got the books down, bringing them back to the bed with her.

The first album she opened contained family pictures. She saw an older man and woman in many of the pictures and thought that must be Luke's mom and dad. There were lots of pictures of babies and older children with Luke holding one or the other of them.

She thumbed through the pages thinking about Luke's children and wondered when she would get to meet them. She made a mental note to ask. There were several pictures of a dark haired lady holding the babies and she knew this must be his wife. She looked at the pictures very carefully taking in every detail. Even though in many of the pictures, the woman was smiling, there always seemed to be a hint of hardness about her face.

It made her sad to see the family split apart and was very glad she wasn't the cause of it. She also felt sorrow because her own family was also split apart in their own way. Why couldn't everyone just live and let live and love each other?

The next book she opened contained promotional pictures of Luke and the band. A picture of Luke and the band standing on a train track, all wearing holsters and pistols or carrying rifles as if they were about to rob a train, caught her interest. Another intriguing picture was of Luke in a confederate soldier's uniform with the pistol and sword that hung over his bed strapped around his waist.

There were lots of pictures of Luke with singing stars like Bob Wills, Bobby Bare, Red Foley, Loretta Lynn, Little Jimmie Dickens, Ernest Tubb and many others covering more than a decade.

She began to understand how long Luke had been in the music business. She wondered what went wrong and why he never made it big. He was good enough, that was for sure.

She'd always believed there was more to Luke Stone than most people seemed to think and now she had evidence from all these pictures. Apparently, he had many sides and wore many different hats.

She thumbed through the rest of the pictures then placed the albums back on the shelf. Even though she didn't think she was tired, she drifted off into a deep sleep.

# Chapter 11

Luke slipped quietly into bed at two o'clock in the morning, trying not to waken Darlina. She stirred and then snuggled close to him.

"You okay, sweetheart?" he asked.

She mumbled sleepily, "Yes. How did it go tonight?"

"The same...every club, every night, every crowd, it's always the same."

She heard tiredness in his voice that went deeper than just being tired from the night. "Baby, did something happen tonight?"

"Mary was at the club."

"Okay. Wanna talk about it?"

"Nothin' much to talk about. She wanted to come back here with me and I told her she needed to go home to her husband and kids."

"I didn't know she was married."

"I knew she was married when I started goin' with her. I went to her house, called her husband outside and told him I was gonna go with her and if he had anything to say, say it to my face, man to man."

"What happened?"

"The coward sonofabitch, tucked his tail between his legs, went back into the house and sent Mary out. He'd keep the kids while she went off with me for days at a time."

"That seems a little weird."

Luke sighed, "To you it would. Anyway, I told Mary tonight that we were done and I was with you now. She cried and begged, but then she left the club with some other poor bastard."

Darlina held him as tight as she could. "Make love to me Luke."

"Now that you mention it, I believe I will."

Darlina opened her eyes the next day sometime around noon. She felt a new surge of excitement. Today was the day she would first dance on stage with Luke and the band! She could hardly wait to be in the car and on the way to Abilene. She felt confident that she would be able to make Luke proud.

Bobby dropped by around four o'clock, looking as though he'd been spit polished and shined. "Mind if I ride along with you to the show?"

"Hell no. At least I know you'll get there sober."

"Then I'll be back in an hour or so. What outfits are we wearing?"

"The contract says the band has to wear tuxedos, but not a word about what the band leader has to wear. So, I'm wearin' my faded blue overalls."

Bobby laughed, "My brother; always the rebel. I'll see you in an hour."

"Don't be late or we'll leave your ass here."

"I'll be here."

Once he left, Darlina questioned Luke, "Can you get away with not wearing a tuxedo?"

"Hell yeah. They want us. We draw a crowd and crowds spend money. They may bitch and complain, but I'm fulfilling my contract. Besides that, they're gonna be watchin' you and Louise."

She laughed, unable to disguise her excitement. "We're gonna give 'em a show too!"

He fondly patted her bottom, "You betcha'!"

By five p.m. they were in the car headed to the Westwood. Everyone looked really nice in their tuxedos. Everyone except Luke. He stood true to his word and was wearing blue overalls. She hoped there wouldn't be any trouble for him tonight.

When they arrived at the club the band immediately started unloading and setting up the equipment.

The manager of the club, a short balding man named Sam, approached Luke as time drew near for the band to start playing. "Mr. Stone, you're going to change into your show clothes, aren't you?"

Luke chuckled. "I'm wearin' my show clothes, stud."

"But the contract said the band would wear tuxedos."

"And they are. It didn't say a word about what the band leader would wear."

"It was assumed you'd be dressed the same as your band members."

"Then I guess you better re-write your contracts, hoss, because there wasn't a damn thing in there specifying what the band leader had to wear."

"Oh dear. Mr. Holloway isn't going to like this."

"Well you just tell Mr. Holloway to come see me if he has any problem with me or my clothes."

Darlina listened to the conversation and felt sorry for the man. Luke seemed to be hell bent on going against the grain no matter the cost. She couldn't say that she understood that part of him or why he liked making other people uncomfortable. Maybe it was his way of always being in control.

The night started slowly with the crowd responding just as Luke predicted. They sat in their formal evening wear and sparkling diamonds while stiffly interacting with each other.

Luke stepped on stage, picked up his guitar and spoke into the mic. "I don't know what you folks are here to do tonight, but the Rebel Rousers are here to have a good time and provide you with some entertainment. So get yourselves a fresh drink and let's have some fun."

The band began playing a rousing rendition of *Ring of Fire* and Luke let out a big rebel yell.

Darlina watched with Louise and felt the excitement of the show starting to build in her. She leaned toward her and said, "This is gonna be fun!"

Louise smiled, "It sure is."

Luke had told both girls that he was going to bring them up right after the first break. He explained it would give the crowd a little time to get a few drinks down and then the girls would come up and really get 'em going. Darlina could hardly wait for the first break.

From the stage, Luke announced, "Ladies and gentleman we're gonna take a pause for the cause and when we come back we've got a very special surprise for all of you; so don't anyone go away."

He joined them at the table. "You girls ready?"

Both Darlina and Louise nodded.

"When the band goes back on, they'll do one song. Then, I'll go up and announce you girls."

Darlina squeezed his hand. "I'm ready!"

Once back on stage the band played *Silver Wings* while Red sang.

They were finishing the last stanza when Luke walked onto the stage. As soon as the last chord faded he announced, "Now, Ladies and Gentlemen, here's the part of the show you've all been waiting for. Thank you for stickin' around and havin' a good time with us. I want you to put your hands together and welcome to the stage, Darlina and Louise, the Rebel Rouser go-go girls!"

The band began playing *Poke Salad Annie* as Darlina and Louise took their places on opposite ends of the stage. The crowd came alive as some of the men began to stand. They were whooping and hollering while the girls danced.

Darlina looked over at Luke. He was grinning from ear to ear. He mouthed the words, "Told you so."

The girls gave a dynamic performance, going right into a second and then third song. They finished their part of the show to boisterous applause from all over the club.

Breathless, Darlina left the stage with Louise and they were both immediately surrounded by people. Everyone congratulated them and offered to buy drinks while inviting them to their tables. Both girls graciously accepted the praise, but went back to their own table.

Luke quickly joined them there; giving Louise a hug and then Darlina a big kiss. "You girls were fantastic and look at the response you got! I knew this would work."

Many of the patrons began to approach Luke offering to buy the band rounds of drinks and asking him to join them at their tables.

Darlina watched as Luke interacted with the crowd. There was no question; he was very good at what he did. She had never felt more proud to be the lady at his side than right now.

The girls took one more turn on the stage before the night was over. By the time the show was finished, the crowd had loosened up. Some of the men had shed their coats and ties. Some of the women had taken off their shoes and were dancing wildly on the dance floor. Luke's idea was a tremendous success.

Everyone's mood in the car was elated as they drove back to Brownwood. They passed around a bottle of Jim Beam and everyone took shots except Darlina. She could drink it mixed with Coke, but shivered when she thought of drinking it straight.

Bobby laughed and joked, "Man, did you see that fat rich bitch shed her fur and shoes and start shakin' it out on the dance floor?"

Red replied, "Which one, Bobby? I saw several."

"We helped those people relax and live a little tonight." Luke winked at Darlina and pulled her a little closer. "And our dancin' ladies helped us pull it off. You were great, baby."

Bobby reached over the seat, patting Darlina on the head. "You were outstanding tonight, sweetheart. My ass of a brother finally picked a winner."

Darlina soaked up the praise but Bobby's words made her beam. She had a warm glow all over and loved that everyone was beginning to accept her as a permanent fixture in Luke's life. "Well, that's the most fun I've ever had dancin' and can't wait to do it again!"

She smiled up at Luke who immediately leaned down and kissed her passionately.

"Okay you two, get a motel room!" Bobby joked.

"We don't have to. We're almost home." Luke took a swig off the bottle Bobby passed to him.

Once they were home, they quickly said their goodbyes and rushed into the apartment. As soon as they were inside the door, they feverishly shed their clothes. It seemed to Darlina that their passion continued to soar to new heights and she wondered how that was even possible.

They were on the bed, touching, caressing and kissing when Luke stopped and got up. "Don't go anywhere, darlin'. I'll be right back."

Darlina wondered where he was going and why he stopped in the middle of their love making. But, she didn't have to wonder long.

Luke came back from the kitchen with a fresh clove of garlic in his hand. "This is an old Mexican folklore. The Curanderas say that if a man rubs garlic on his penis and then makes love to a woman; it is believed that no other man will be able to satisfy her for the rest of her life, except him."

He began to rub the garlic on himself and Darlina watched in fascination. "It might surprise you that I know what a Curandera is. Growing up in New Mexico and most of my friends being Mexican, I do know. She's like a witch."

"Yeah, or kinda' like the Indian medicine man. They use potions and ceremonies to heal their people or to cast spells."

"I like the kind of magic we make together, honey. I want you Luke."

Darlina thought that Luke had never made more complete love to her than he did that night. She doubted the ceremony would ever be put to the test because she wanted only Luke forever.

She'd found her true place of belonging. This man, who was a rebel in the truest sense of the word, had captured her heart completely.

She understood that he lived life on his own terms and rarely apologized to anyone for it. She also knew that he enjoyed making people sit up and take notice. Boy did they ever!

# Chapter 12

With Christmas not far away, Darlina had family on her mind. The weather had turned cold, along with a drizzling rain. The Dearborn heater in the corner of the bedroom put off a warm glow, as she and Luke got out of bed to start their day at the crack of noon.

She remembered what she had told Leann on the phone and mentioned it to Luke. "Next time we play in Abilene, is it alright if I invite Leann, Wayne and Norma out to see us?"

Luke pulled on his boots as he sat on the side of the bed. "Of course it's okay. How about we go shopping today and you pick up some gifts for them? I need to buy some things for my kids."

"That reminds me of somethin' else I've been meanin' to ask you," she said somewhat nervously. "When am I gonna get to meet your kids?"

"I don't know," he said reaching for her hand and pulling her down on his lap. "Their mother is pretty set against them meeting any woman I'm with. It's confusing to little kids. They still think we will work things out and I'll be back in the house with them."

"And what do you want?"

"I want to be with the kids every day but there is no way in hell I can live with their mother. We're poison to each other."

"Well, I'd love to meet them, but I understand and when you're ready, I'll be ready."

"Let's go see what we can find for them and for your family. I want to buy my mom and dad something too. You can help me. I never was very good at the whole shoppin' thing."

"I don't know about that," she said, as she fastened the heart necklace Luke had given her. "You did pretty well with this, but I'd love helping you shop and I'll look for some gifts for my family too. I really wish my mama wouldn't be so mad at me. I miss her, but there is no point in me sending them anything."

"Don't worry, sugar. She'll come around. I've disappointed my mama more times than I can count, but she always comes around."

"I'd like to meet your folks."

"Maybe someday. Let's go shopping."

Since the weather had turned bad, they shopped in Brownwood, driving to the local J.C. Penney and Woolworth stores.

Darlina helped Luke pick out trains, cars and toy guns for his boys. She relished the experience of shopping for his daughter. She found so many things that she knew any little girl would like and finally decided on a pink transistor radio and a princess dress-up kit. She found a purse for Leann, a bracelet for Norma and a wallet for Wayne.

Once they were back home, she gathered wrapping paper, bows, ribbons, tape and scissors and began wrapping everything they had bought.

"Sweetheart, I've gotta go take some money to my wife and see my kids for a little while." Luke put his jacket on. "I'll be back by dark."

"Okay, baby. Enjoy your kids." She stood on her tiptoes to kiss Luke warmly and he responded by pulling her body close to his and placing both hands on her bottom.

Once he was gone, Darlina hummed Christmas carols to herself as she wrapped each gift. She took great pains to make them all beautiful packages. She even tried to picture the children's excitement as they would unwrap them.

True to his word, Luke was back by dark and came in the door holding something behind his back.

"What are you hiding?" Darlina asked.

"Just a little somethin' I picked up for you. It's not wrapped or anything though."

Darlina jumped to her feet. "Oh Luke! You didn't have to get me anything."

"Yes I did." He handed her a sack from Wilson's Western Wear store.

She opened it and gasped, "I love it."

Inside the sack was a supple deer skin leather purse, with a long beaded fringe that hung down from the flap. It was the most beautiful purse she had ever seen.

She threw her arms around his neck and kissed him. "Thank you, Luke. It's perfect and I love it."

"You're perfect and you deserve something pretty. You haven't asked for a thing since you've been here and I'm pretty much an idiot when it comes to buying gifts, but this just looked like you."

"I love it and I love you. Thank you, honey!"

"Rita and Jerry invited us over to their place tonight for supper and I told 'em we'd be there. I don't remember often enough to feed you and you're gettin' mighty skinny."

Darlina laughed. "Well, that part is true. You sure don't spend much time thinkin' about anything to eat, but I'm doin' alright. I manage to rummage up enough to keep me goin' and hang in with you."

"That you do, and do it well." Luke gave her bottom a resounding slap. "Now go get ready and let's go visitin'."

Darlina enjoyed the warmth and acceptance that Rita always showed towards her. She appreciated the woman's friendship.

Luke and Jerry discussed a big show that was coming up soon at Laughlin Air Force Base. They talked about the go-go dancers and how the Air Base would be the perfect place to bring the girls.

Rita interjected, "Are you guys gonna take us girls over into Boy's Town?"

"What's Boy's Town?" Darlina questioned.

Luke chuckled, "You bet your sweet asses we are and we're gonna have ourselves one helluva time."

"Is Bobby going? Hell, last time he damned near got us all thrown in the Mexican jail," Jerry said, while opening himself a beer and mixing a Jim Beam and Coke for Luke.

"Nope, Bobby's staying home this time. He's too big of a risk."

"What's Boy's Town?" Darlina repeated her question.

"It's hard to describe," said Rita. "It's something you'll have to see for yourself, but it's across the border in Mexico."

"Well, I'm sure it'll be fun," Darlina said. "When I was a kid we went to Juarez pretty often, so I'm familiar with Old Mexico."

"This'll make Juarez look like Mayberry," Luke declared.

"Oh stop tryin' to scare me. I'll look forward to it, and especially gettin' to dance at the Air Base."

Rita popped bread into the oven. "I've been meaning to tell you how proud I am of you. I'd never have the courage to get up on the stage and dance."

"I don't think its courage, Rita; just a lot of want to."

The night passed quickly and Darlina's excitement about the show at the Air Base grew as she listened to their conversation. She knew this was important to Luke and that made it equally important to her.

On the way home, Darlina asked Luke, "When is this big show?"

"It's the 16th and I think me and you'll go in our own car, separate from the band and make it a little vacation trip. How does that sound?"

"That sounds wonderful."

A few short days later, it was time to go to Del Rio for the show at the Air Base. Luke had asked Sherry to come along and dance with Darlina and she was happy that her friend would be joining her.

Luke and Darlina left Brownwood on the 15th, in Luke's T-Bird. He drove south into the Texas Hill Country. He'd told Darlina they would stop in Sonora for the night. She was thrilled to be going alone with Luke and not in the band car.

She sat close to him and they talked. Luke pointed out landmarks as they traveled. Occasionally, she would mix him a Jim Beam and Coke from the portable bar that always accompanied him.

He told Darlina a story as they passed through Brady, Texas. "I played here with Willie Nelson in 1965, at the Country Club. He didn't have a road band at the time and me and the Rebel Rousers backed him. About twenty people showed up that night. No one had heard of Willie back then. At the end of the night the promoter said he'd have to mail us our pay and I never got a dime. Don't figure Willie did either."

"Was that the only show you played with him?"

"No, we played several shows with him and his first wife, Shirley, that year. Willie's a helluva nice guy and never forgets anyone he meets."

When they passed through Eldorado, Luke talked about living there and working in the oil fields before he was married and had a family.

She loved these glimpses into his past. She wanted to know everything there was to know about Luke Stone.

They were about 10 miles outside of Sonora when the motor started making a knocking noise.

"Shit!" Luke exclaimed. "Looks like we've got trouble."

He pulled the car over to the side of the road. Then he got out and opened the hood. He closed it after a few minutes, got back in and started creeping along down the shoulder. "It'll be a miracle if we make it into Sonora the way this motor is sounding."

Darlina sat quietly as Luke anxiously tried to baby the car enough to get it into town. She breathed a sigh of relief when she saw a sign that read, "Sonora 2 miles".

"I think we're gonna make it. I'll call Red when we get there and have them stop by here tomorrow and pick us up. Damn! This wasn't what I had in mind."

"It'll be okay, baby. We'll still get some time together before they come through tomorrow and maybe we'll be able to find a garage that can fix the car."

"Always the optimist. You're right, though. It'll be just fine."

JJ's Auto Repair had a closed sign on the door when Luke pulled in the parking area. Conveniently, across the street at the Mustang Motel, a vacancy sign blinked off and on. Luke gathered their bags and they walked across the street to the motel.

Once they were checked in, he picked up the phone and made the call to Red. He explained what had happened and they discussed the possibilities. Red assured him he would pick them up the next day.

"Well, darlin', here we are. Some vacation, huh?"

"Luke, this is a just fine vacation, but I'm really hungry. Let's go find something to eat."

"Dammit, I always forget about that. I'm sorry I'm starvin' you."

She laughed. "I'm not starvin', but I am hungry."

They walked two blocks down the street to Rosie's Cafe and ate a warm dinner. To Darlina's surprise, Luke ate with her. She thought to herself that he must not have taken any pills.

"Do you ever think maybe you drink a little too much, Luke?"

His blue eyes twinkled and he chuckled. "Darlin', I ask myself that all the time, and every once in a while I quit cold turkey, just to make sure I still can. So far, I still can."

"I will say that I've only seen you drunk once since I met you. Most of the time I can't even tell you're drinkin'."

"I don't like to lose control and usually know when to stop. I've watched my brother let alcohol control him for years and I'm determined not to let that happen to me."

Darlina rubbed his leg under the table. "Hey, cowboy, wanna go to the motel with me?"

"Now you're talkin' my language. Let's go."

They walked back to the motel hand in hand. They both seemed oblivious to the cold biting Texas wind blowing out of the North.

Darlina awoke the next morning to find Luke dressed and ready to go. She quickly threw the covers back. "Why didn't you wake me? I'll get ready as quick as I can."

Luke gently pushed her back towards the bed. "You crawl back under those covers and stay here, princess. I'm just gonna walk across the street and talk to the mechanic. I'll be back in a little bit to take you to breakfast."

He leaned over her, kissing her waiting lips warmly. She reached up and wrapped her arms around his neck. "Sure you don't want a morning delight before you go?"

He chuckled. "Honey, I always want a morning delight, but I better go see about the car. You just rest and I'll be back before you know it."

She snuggled back under the covers as she heard the door click shut. The next sound she heard was the door opening. She sat up while sleepily rubbing her eyes. One glance at the clock told her two hours had passed.

Luke entered the room, throwing the keys onto the desk.

"What did you find out about the car?" she asked.

"The mechanic said it was a rod and luckily it hadn't gone through the block yet so he thinks he can fix it, but I'll need to talk to Red first. He's a damned good mechanic himself. How about you get your sexy little ass out of bed and get dressed so we can go eat?"

"Okay. I didn't mean to sleep so long."

"That's exactly what you needed to do."

"I'll take a quick shower and be dressed in no time."

When Darlina emerged from the bathroom, Luke was sitting at the desk hunched over a writing tablet. She walked up behind him, putting her arms around him and leaning over his shoulder.

He immediately turned over the tablet he was writing on.

"Whatcha' workin' on?"

"Nothin'. You ready to go?"

"Yep. I'm ready."

Luke went into the bathroom and Darlina put on her coat. However, curiosity got the best of her and making sure Luke couldn't see her, she quickly turned over the tablet. What she saw puzzled her. It looked like a floor plan layout and a map. She wondered what it could be but turned it back over as soon she heard the toilet flush.

"Let's go, beautiful."

Hand in hand, they walked back to Rosie's Café where they ate a hearty breakfast and downed several cups of coffee.

"We'd better be gettin' back to the motel. Red'll be here in a couple of hours to pick us up."

"Oh Luke, I'm starting to get real excited about dancin' at the Air Base and it'll be fun having Sherry with me. Then there's Boy's Town. You've got my curiosity aroused about that."

"Let's get back to the motel and I'll get something else aroused before Red gets here."

Darlina replied seductively, "I like that plan."

Three hours later, the two of them sat in their places in the Lincoln under the blanket, riding down the road to Del Rio. For a moment, the drawing Luke was sketching flashed in her mind and she quickly dismissed it.

Red looked over at Luke. "Did you get the banking business tended to in Sonora?"

Luke nodded. "Got it done. We'll talk about it later."

This left more room for Darlina to ponder. What did any of that mean? Oh well, it was none of her business. She was happy to be going down the road with them; excitedly looking forward to performing with the band at the Air Base. She felt almost giddy with anticipation of the show and going across the border into Old Mexico with Luke. Somehow she just knew this was going to be a night to remember.

# Chapter 13

The officer's club at Laughlin Air Force Base was larger than any night club Darlina had ever been in. It was more like an auditorium than a club. The band members were given dressing rooms and she shared Luke's. Eyes glowing with excitement, she dressed in the new fringed leather costume she and Luke had made.

Luke held her at arm's length admiring her, and then he twirled her around. She laughed as she dipped backwards on his arm. "This is going to be so much fun," she proclaimed.

"We've always drawn big crowds down here and looks like tonight it's packed out. I know you girls will be a big hit with the soldiers."

"When do you want us to come out?"

"I think we should do like we did at the Westwood and bring ya'll up right after first break."

"We'll be ready."

Luke kissed her and left to go check out the stage. He'd let Darlina pick out his costume. She thought he looked dashing in the black bell-bottom pants with Mexican Conchos down each leg, a satin insert at the flare, along with a matching black bolero jacket and black satin shirt. Of course, she'd polished his black boots with the silver tips until they shined like patent leather. It was a task she took pride in.

No sooner than he'd gone, there was a knock on the door. Darlina opened it to find Sherry. "I was hoping you'd come hang out with me while we wait to go on. How have you been doing?"

"I've been doin' pretty good. Sure looks like you and Luke are happy."

"We are. Now do you want to take back the words you said to me at the Faded Rose?"

"Not just yet, but I'll happily take them back when I know he's for real."

Both girls heard the music start and knew the show had started. They could smell cigarette smoke drifting through the building from the crowd.

Darlina chatted about things she and Luke had been doing and showed Sherry the leather fringed purse he'd bought her. "So, it looks like you're with Preacher tonight. I thought you were done with him."

"Oh well. It's convenient for the night but I'm not crazy about him or anything."

"Out of all the band members, he's the one that I just can't warm up to. He always appears to be a little sneaky or underhanded."

Sherry laughed. "Guess you've got him pegged. Hey, got anything in here to drink?"

"You know Luke. Wherever he is, there's something to drink. Want a Jim Beam and Coke?"

"I do. I need some courage to go out and face this big crowd."

"Oh honey, you'll do just fine. It'll be just like old times when we danced at the Faded Rose." Darlina handed her a drink in a Dixie cup.

"Thanks. By the way, you look absolutely stunning tonight in that leather costume. It makes mine look shabby."

"Oh, don't say that. You look wonderful and red has always been your color. We just have to dance like Marketa taught us."

Before long, Luke was back to get the girls. He escorted them to the area behind the stage where they would wait for their cue to go on. Darlina's heart began to beat fast and her breath came in short gasps. She reached out for the drink in Sherry's hand and took a big swig, as she made a conscious effort to calm the nerves. She wanted tonight to be perfect.

Luke squeezed her hand reassuringly. "Okay baby, I've gotta go back so you girls just hang tight and we'll get you up soon."

The girls could hear the audience and it sounded as if the place was full. Darlina peeked out and was not surprised to find a standing room only crowd.

Sherry moved close beside her. "Look at all those men in uniforms!"

Darlina nodded. "I see them. There must be 500 or more and now I'm really nervous all of a sudden."

The girls shared the rest of the drink and soon Luke was announcing them to the audience. "Ladies and gentlemen, the Rebel Rousers have a real treat for you tonight. All the way from Abilene, Texas; we bring to you the Rebel Rouser Go-Go Girls!"

As they burst onto the stage they were met with cheers, whistles, and hollers from all over the building.

The band played *Mustang Sally* and the noise from the crowd rose to a crescendo. The excitement was like electricity in the air and the girls danced exactly as Marketa had taught them, bringing round after round of applause and cheers from the soldiers.

Darlina glanced at Luke and saw him beaming. He winked and blew her a kiss.

The four hour show ended and Luke and Darlina were back in the dressing room changing into their street clothes. They were interrupted by a knock on the door. Luke opened it to find a uniformed officer standing there.

"Luke, that was the best show you've ever brought us. I can assure you that you'll be booked back here again soon. The soldiers need entertainment and that's what you gave 'em tonight. I just wanted to let you know how pleased we are."

"Thank you, Commander. We enjoy coming out and entertaining ya'll. I'll be in touch about another booking."

The man handed Luke a large amount of cash and left after shaking his hand.

"Did you hear that, baby? You girls make us more of a success wherever we take you."

Darlina wrapped her arms around Luke's neck. "That makes me very happy. I love being a part of the show."

"Okay, sweetheart. Let's get finished up here and get everyone rounded up. We're goin' to Old Mexico!"

At the border crossing, the clock said two a.m., as the group hurried into Mexico. A December chill hung in the air and everyone was in good spirits.

Once across the border, they headed south toward Boy's Town, with Luke in the lead. "Ya'll wait here. I'm gonna get us a bottle of Anise."

He darted into a liquor store and came out carrying a bottle. He removed the cap and threw it away. Taking a big swig, he let out a rebel yell. "We're gonna party tonight!"

He handed the bottle to Darlina. "Ever had Anise, baby?"

"No. What does it taste like?"

"Tastes a lot like licorice. Have a swig."

She turned the bottle up and then shivered, as the hot liquid burned down the back of her throat. "That's actually pretty good," she said as she passed the bottle on to Rita.

As they continued on their way down the streets of Villa Acuna, Darlina's senses were bombarded with the sights and sounds. There were brothels with Mexican women blatantly advertising their wares on the street. Mariachi music came from inside the cantinas and a bustle of activity kept her looking in different directions. She noticed lots of American soldiers on the street.

Red tugged on Luke's jacket sleeve. "Hey, hoss, I'm gonna go find me a Mexican whore."

"Go ahead. Just make sure you meet us back at the bridge by sun up."

Preacher joined in, "Wait for me Red. I wanna go with you."

Sherry looked at Darlina and rolled her eyes. "Mind if I hang with you and Luke?"

Luke answered, "Hell no, we don't mind. Let Preacher go get crabs off some meskin whore. I swear that boy's got no sense."

Luke, Darlina, Sherry, Rita and Jerry continued down the street. By the time they covered a city block, they were approached by street vendors offering to sell them pills, marijuana, cocaine, LSD, or any variety of drug paraphernalia. Luke examined the contents of one box presented to him. He picked out some pink pills and broke one in half handing it to Darlina. "Here, take this, sweetheart. You'll like it."

"What's it called?" she asked.

"Pink heart. You'll feel like you're walking about six inches off the ground in a little bit."

She swallowed it with a drink of Anise as Luke purchased several different types of pills from the vendor. He offered Sherry, Rita and

Jerry some and they all continued on their way. He stopped several times to make purchases and began stuffing large amounts of pills inside his boots.

As Luke predicted, within a short period of time, Darlina began to feel euphoric and lighthearted. Even though she wore a jacket, she shivered from the cool night air, so Luke took off his soft fringed leather jacket and wrapped it around her shoulders.

The group stopped at many of the Cantinas they passed by. The noise and loud music filtered out into the street, openly inviting them in. By the time they made it to Mamasita's Restaurant, everyone was a little drunk and high.

In the front window, an animal carcass turned slowly on a spit, over an open flame.

"Let's go in and get some cabrito," Luke suggested.

Darlina didn't have the slightest idea what cabrito was, but she was up for anything Luke suggested at this point.

"Wait," said Rita. "I want someone to take a picture of all of us."

She stopped a soldier who was walking down the sidewalk. "Sir, would you mind taking our picture?"

"No, ma'am."

They all huddled together as he clicked the picture. "Let me get one more just for good measure."

Luke climbed into a garbage can sitting outside the restaurant and everyone made silly faces as the soldier clicked another picture.

He handed the camera back to Rita.

"Thank you so much," she said.

"No problem. Ya'll have a good time."

"I want a copy of those pictures when you get them developed," Darlina said.

"Okay. I'll get doubles."

They entered the warm glow of the restaurant and were seated at a big table.

"I hate to sound stupid, but what's cabrito?" Darlina asked.

Luke chuckled as he gave his answer. "Darlin', that's barbecued goat."

"Oh. I don't feel hungry."

"Of course you don't, but I want you to try it. It's one of the many reasons I love Mexico."

Surprisingly, the meat tasted delicious and Darlina decided maybe deer and goat meat weren't so bad after all.

They spent a good two hours in the restaurant eating, drinking and talking. Finally, Luke announced. "We'd better head back toward the bridge. The sun will be up in a few minutes."

"Wow! Time sure did fly by," commented Rita.

"Time does tend to fly when you're havin' fun." Luke put his arm possessively around Darlina's shoulders.

"Sure hope we don't have to hunt Red and Preach," Jerry said.

"Hell, I'll leave their sorry asses here, if they don't show up," Luke threatened.

Luke paid the bill and they all walked back out onto the street as the sun was starting to peek over the horizon. Somehow, it didn't seem right to Darlina that it was turning daylight already. She and Luke held hands as they walked back through Boy's Town toward the International Bridge. She still felt euphoric and wished for some alone time with Luke.

He put his arm around her waist. "I know what you're thinkin', baby."

"How do you know?"

"I can read your mind."

"Oh yeah? Then what am I thinkin'?"

"You're wishin' we were somewhere alone."

"How did you know?"

"I can feel your heat and I'm wantin' the same thing."

"Well, my dear, we'll just have to wait, huh? But, you better get ready 'cause when we get back home, you're gonna get all my lovin'."

Luke stopped, pulled her close and kissed her gently, planting his hands firmly on her bottom and giving a squeeze. She moaned softly and returned his kiss, as she moved her hands over his broad back and down to his bottom.

When the bridge came into sight, they saw Red and Preacher standing and waiting. They walked back across the bridge to the car and were soon on the road, with Red driving. She nestled her head comfortably on Luke's arm as he tucked the blanket snugly around them.

Her heart beat strongly with love for her rebel and nothing could ever change that. Contentedly she sighed as she listened to the whine of the wheels on the asphalt and XERF from Ciudad Villa Acuna, Mexico; playing on the radio.

# Chapter 14

Demons haunted Luke Stone and had for what seemed to him, a very long time. Though he struggled to rid himself of them, they consistently persisted and threatened to swallow him and everyone around him.

He glanced at Darlina, who was humming as she washed the dishes. How could he hope to have a happy loving life with her when he was saddled with so much baggage from the past? There were many things he could not tell her and so much he wished he could undo and take back. The troubling feeling that it was too late gnawed at his gut. He sensed danger all around them and feared he would be unable to protect her from it.

It was around noon when an insistent knock came on the back door of their apartment.

Luke opened the door to find his long time friends, Big Royce, Indian Joe and Butch standing there. He glanced over his shoulder at Darlina as she busied herself in the kitchen. "Sugar, we're going next door to Red's for a little bit."

"Okay."

He saw her wrinkle her forehead and couldn't help but notice an unspoken question in her eyes. He'd always been good at reading people, and he had quickly learned to read her every thought. He left before she could voice her question or worry; winking at her as he went out the door.

Inside Red's apartment Luke addressed the three. "I have what you came for."

"That's good, Luke. Me and the boys were startin' to think you'd forgotten us," Royce said.

"I've been busy," growled Luke.

"Now Luke, don't go gettin' all bent out of shape. We just need what we agreed on from you," Butch cajoled.

"And you'll damn well get it. I don't want you comin' to my apartment ever again. I'll either see you in the clubs or you come over here to Red's."

"No problem, man. We were just gettin' anxious."

Red spoke up trying to ease the tension in the air, "You boys wanna a drink?"

"Hell yeah, we want a drink! Thought you'd never ask," Royce laughed, as he nervously ran his fingers through his hair.

"I'll be right back." Luke walked slowly and deliberately out to the Lincoln, looking over his shoulder and glancing to each side, unable to shake the feeling that someone was watching. He ignored it, blaming it on nerves, but he had a strong premonition that something was about to break bad. He shuffled through some papers in the glove box. Then, with his tablet in hand, he walked back to Red's apartment.

"Here," he said pitching the tablet in Butch's direction.

Butch frowned with concentration as he looked it over and then passed it to Royce. Indian Joe seemed unconcerned, intent on finishing off his beer and paying no attention to the others.

Royce carefully tore the page out of the tablet, folded it and stuffed it in his pocket. "As usual, you'll be hearing from us in a few days and we'll have your money."

"Like I said, just don't come to my apartment. Either call me and I'll meet you somewhere, or come out to the clubs."

Luke took the Beam and Coke Red handed him and sat down at the table. The other men pulled out chairs and joined him.

"Luke, I don't like the way you're actin'," Royce stated.

"Well then you can kiss my ass, you fat sonofabitch."

"Now, don't start gettin' all mad. What the hell's wrong with you anyway?"

"I want out."

"We had an agreement."

"I know we did and now I want out. I'm done with this shit. I've got a bad feelin'."

"Oh hell! It's just because of that new, sweet young thing you've got waitin' for you next door. You'll get over it," Royce said laughing.

"You leave her out of all this!" Luke pushed his chair back and clenched his fists.

"Hell man, you're gettin' all tore up over nothin'. We've got all this handled and nothin' is gonna go wrong."

"Damn sure better not. I'll go to Oklahoma and take care of that one for you and then I'm done. You'll have to find some other way to get what you need."

Red spoke trying to soothe the situation, "Luke, I'll go with you to Oklahoma and we'll talk about all this on the way."

"No, I want you here to look after Darlina while I'm gone. I'll take Johnny with me."

"I don't give a shit who goes or doesn't go," Royce interrupted. "I just want the job done."

"Get off my back, man. I'll get the job done. Haven't I always?"

"Yes you have and you've been paid well, so let's just keep our shit together and don't mess up somethin' that's workin' good," Butch said.

"I'm tellin' all of you sons of bitches right here and right now that I want out," Luke emphatically stated. "After Oklahoma, you can find some other way to get what you need."

"Aw, Luke. Now don't be that way. Just think it over and you'll see that this arrangement works real good," Royce said softening.

"I ain't sayin' it hasn't worked. I'm just sayin' I'm through. You assholes can do whatever you think you have to, but this is fair warning that I'm done."

"Okay, okay," Butch appeased. "We trust you, Luke and know that you ain't no kind of a rat. Don't ever give us a reason to think otherwise."

"You chickenshit sonofabitch. I ought to kick your ass right here and now. I've never given you any reason not to trust me and I ain't givin' you one now."

"I know. That's what I just said, you big overbearing piece of shit."

Luke halfway rose out of his chair. Red placed a hand on his shoulder intervening. "Why don't you guys leave and let me and Luke talk?"

The three stood. Royce offered his hand to Luke and he shook it staring him dead in the eye. They left the apartment with the paper they had come for.

"Red, I've got a bad feelin' that I can't shake. You know how I am, hoss. I have to go with my feelings."

"I know, Luke. We'll just do the Oklahoma job and I'll get out with you. You know I'll do whatever you want me to."

Luke looked at his faithful friend. "Red, we've been through a helluva lot together. Big Royce was right when he said all this was because of Darlina. I love her, Red Hoss, and I want a life with her. I'm afraid it's too late."

"Maybe not. If we can slide out of this without any problem, then you can get a new start."

Luke sighed and put his head in his hands. "I swear to you I won't let anything hurt her. I'll protect her with my life."

"I will too, stud. She's good for you and a sweet sincere girl. It'd be hard not to like her."

"Promise me that if anything happens to me, you'll look out for her."

"I promise."

"You know those crazy fevers I get from time to time?"

"Yeah, it's been a while now."

"When it comes again, she's gonna need your help. She'll be scared."

"Don't worry, I'll do everything I can to help."

Luke stood slapping his friend on the back. "See you later. We gotta go pick up my T-Bird tomorrow. I wanna leave early in the morning."

"No problem. I'll be ready when you are."

Luke hesitated at the door, "Thank you Red...for everything."

"You're welcome, man."

He walked slowly back to his apartment. He suddenly felt as if the weight of the world rested on his shoulders. Had he brought Darlina into something that might destroy her? He sighed as his breath fogged in the cold December air. He squared his shoulders with determination and slipped back into the warm sweetness that he had come to love and expect in their home.

# Chapter 15

Luke and Red had left early that morning to go pick up the repaired T-Bird and Darlina couldn't wait for them to get back so they could go to Abilene.

Once Luke was back, she rushed around the apartment getting ready. Unable to contain her excitement, she dropped two of the gifts as she tried to get them gathered up and into the car.

"Baby, slow down a little. Your sisters will be there and they are just as anxious to see you as you are to see them," Luke chuckled. "I love seeing you this excited about Christmas. That's what it's all about."

"I know, Luke. It really seems like forever since I've seen them."

She'd called Leann and told them they were playing at the Four Aces Club that night and invited them all to come out. She couldn't wait to see both of her sisters.

"I feel like I've been depriving you from your family," Luke told her.

"Oh no, baby, you haven't deprived me of anything; but I can't wait to see my sisters again!"

He laughed and gave her bottom a playful slap as they headed out the door. "I love seeing you smiling and happy."

She looked up at Luke as they walked to the car, "I'm always happy when I'm with you Luke. It's the only place on earth I want to be."

"I'm glad you decided to send your mom and dad something for Christmas."

"I had to. I just wish we could see them so they could meet you and understand how happy you make me. I'll give them a call in a day or two."

"If you want, you can go with me out to Lake Brownwood tomorrow to see my mom and dad."

"Are you serious?"

"Yes, I'm serious. I think it's time you met them."

"What about your wife though? Won't they think badly of me, for being with you, when you're still married?"

Luke laughed. "My mom and dad are so used to me and my brother doin' shit they don't approve of, they don't pay much attention anymore."

"Well, I can't wait to meet them, but only if you're sure it's okay."

"It's okay or I wouldn't mention it. Let's get movin'. Time for us to hit the road."

Darlina watched the door anxiously once they arrived at The Four Aces Club. She could hardly wait to see her sisters. Norma was the first to arrive. As soon as Darlina saw her walk through the door, she jumped up and ran to greet her.

"Oh Norma, I've missed you terribly," she said hugging her sister.

Norma returned her hug. "I've missed you too. You look like you've lost weight. Aren't you eating?"

Darlina laughed. "I eat now and then. I was so sorry to hear about you and Ray."

"Oh well, things happen, I guess. I'm better off without him."

"I know it isn't easy and I feel bad that I haven't called, but I've thought about you a lot."

"You're busy with your new life. You don't have time to worry about me. I'm doing just fine."

"Come say hi to Luke. He's glad ya'll came out to see us tonight."

The two sisters walked arm in arm to the band table and Luke left the bandstand to join them.

"Hi, Norma. It's good to see you."

Norma gave him a quick hug. "It's good to see you too, but even better to see my little sister. Looks like you need to make her start eatin' now and then or she's gonna dry up and blow away."

Luke chuckled. "Yeah, I have a hard time remembering to feed her, but she's gettin' better about tellin' me when she's hungry. Sorry to hear about you and Ray."

"That's water under the bridge. I'm gettin' along just fine."

Keeping her eye on the door, Darlina saw Leann and Wayne the minute they walked in and ran to greet them.

As she hugged them both she expressed, "I've missed you so much Leann. Hi, Wayne. I'm really glad ya'll came."

"You have no idea how much I've missed you. I miss you most around lunch time every day," Leann said, as she looped her arm through her sister's.

"I know and I really should call more. I'll do better."

The trio walked to the band table where Luke was still visiting with Norma. He turned to greet them, extending his hand to Wayne and hugging Leann. "So good to see ya'll."

Norma hugged Leann and greeted Wayne. It was almost like a mini-family reunion.

The three sisters chatted non-stop while Luke and Wayne visited. Darlina gave each of them their Christmas present and they in turn had brought her gifts as well. Her eyes sparkled with joy as they settled in at the table.

"Are you going to dance tonight?" Leann asked.

"No. Luke said this club doesn't pay him enough to add dancers to the show. However, I did dance at Laughlin Air Force Base in Del Rio and there was a standing room only crowd."

"Ooooh, dancin' for the soldiers. Bet that was fun."

"It was. Then we went across the border to Villa Acuna. I thought I'd seen Mexico going to Juarez as much as we did when we were kids, but I'd never seen anything like Boy's Town."

"I've heard about it, but have never seen it. Don't figure I will."

"I'm so very happy to see ya'll. It seems like it's been closer to a year instead of just a couple of months. How are mama and daddy?"

"They're about the same. They've moved and I need to give you their new phone number."

"I'm gonna call and wish them a Merry Christmas. I mailed a gift, but haven't heard a word back from them."

"Well, mama is acting like we've both died and daddy's having a hard time with her."

Leann fished around in her purse for a pen and paper. She wrote the number down and handed it to Darlina.

"I'll call them soon. Just wish things could be different with them," Darlina said wistfully.

The band headed to the stage and started the show off with their standard rendition of *Dixie*.

Darlina couldn't have been happier. She'd enjoyed introducing her sisters and brother-in-law to Red, Jerry and Rita. Rita responded to them in her warm friendly fashion.

Proudly, Darlina watched Luke and the band deliver another great performance and loved that her sisters seemed to enjoy being there.

However, Leann had her own problems to deal with. Wayne ordered drink after drink and before long he was so drunk that he couldn't walk. Leann was angry and embarrassed.

Promptly at 1 a.m., Luke made the last call announcement and as had become their routine, ended the show with a rock 'n roll song, inviting everyone to the dance floor.

Too soon Darlina was saying tearful goodbyes to her sisters. She hugged each of them tightly, as if it were the last time she'd ever see them.

Leann said, "I loved seeing you Darlina, but it don't look like I can bring Wayne out like this. I'm ashamed of how drunk he is. Guess I'll have to drive us home."

Darlina hugged her sister again. "I'm sorry Leann. Try not to be too mad at him. He was just trying to have a good time."

"Too late. I'm already mad, but I'm glad I got to see you."

Darlina felt tears rush to her eyes and she wished she could make everything alright for her and for Norma too.

Luke came to her side and embraced her. His presence helped soothe her and he promised they would see her sisters again very soon.

The next day dawned cold and rainy. Luke and Darlina left their apartment at two o'clock in the afternoon, headed for Luke's parents' home at Lake Brownwood.

"I have to say I'm a little nervous about meetin' your folks." Darlina gave herself one more inspection in the car's rearview mirror.

"Aw, don't worry, sweetheart. My folks will treat you real nice and if they don't they'll have to answer to me."

"I just don't ever want to be the cause of any problems."

"Just one more reason I love you. You always care about other people."

"I can't help it. It's the way I am."

"I love that you can't help it. Don't worry. You'll see. It'll be just fine."

They arrived at a modest house sitting close to the banks of Brownwood Lake. There were flower beds bordered with rocks and Christmas lights twinkling around the windows. As they approached the door, Darlina could hear dogs barking.

"Those damned little Pekingese. I'm the one that got her started with the little shits and mom just loves them to death."

Luke knocked lightly on the door, then opened it and led Darlina inside. He was greeted by three small dogs jumping up on him and whimpering. He leaned down and patted each of them on the head. "Dad, mom, where are you?"

"We're in the kitchen, son," a voice replied.

They walked through the living room into the kitchen where Mr. and Mrs. Stone sat at a round oak table. Mr. Stone stood when he saw Darlina. "Who is this young lady?"

"Dad, mom, this is Darlina."

Mr. Stone extended his hand and Darlina shook it. Mrs. Stone coldly eyed her but politely said, "Nice to meet you. Can I get you both something to eat or some coffee?"

"I'd love a piece of your good ol' chocolate pie, if you've got any made and a cup of coffee." Luke gave his mom a warm hug.

Darlina spoke shyly, "That sounds real good Mrs. Stone. I'll have the same."

Mrs. Stone busied herself making coffee and taking the pie out of the refrigerator.

"Here, have a seat," Mr. Stone said, pulling a chair out for Darlina.

"Thank you, Mr. Stone."

"And don't call me Mr. Stone. My name is Albert but most folks call me Al."

"Okay, Al. Thank you so much."

Luke pulled out a chair and sat down. "We brought ya'll some Christmas presents. I put them under the tree when we came in."

"Son, you didn't have to get us anything. Heck, at our age there ain't much of anything we need," Mrs. Stone said, while avoiding looking at Darlina.

"Well, we got you something anyway. How is everything going?"

"Oh son, you know, about the same. I'm gettin' a few little carpenter jobs here and there and we're scrapin' by. Fishin's been pretty good though. I'll send a mess of bass home with you," Al said, as he lit a cigarette.

"That sounds real good, dad. You know I do love fish."

Mrs. Stone returned to the table with the pie and some saucers. "Have you seen your family, son?"

"Yes mom, I see 'em two or three times a week. I go take 'em money and check in on 'em real often. The kids are growin'."

"Me and daddy go by every once in a while to see them, but Joyce won't ever invite us into the house." She accepted the lit cigarette Al handed to her.

"Mom, let's not talk about all that right now. We just wanted to visit and I wanted to introduce you both to Darlina." Luke puffed on his King Edward.

"Okay, son. I just worry about those little kids; that's all."

"I know. I do too, but I make sure they have what they need."

Darlina sat quietly, feeling very out of place at this family table. It was obvious to her that Mrs. Stone did not approve of her being there with Luke and she also understood why. After all, he was still married and had small children that he was responsible for.

Trying to make polite conversation, Mrs. Stone asked. "Where are you from, Darlina?"

"I grew up in Hobbs, New Mexico, ma'am."

"Where did you meet my son?"

Luke interrupted, "Mom, please don't give Darlina the fifth degree. I met her at a club in Abilene and she's the best thing that's happened to me in a very long time."

"Son, I didn't mean any harm. Just askin'."

Mr. Stone made an attempt to lighten up the conversation. "When are you gonna go huntin' with me, Luke?"

"Soon, dad. I pretty much work all the time, but I'll make some time before long."

The conversation remained strained and after an hour, Luke stood and pushed his chair in. "We better be gettin' back to town. Gotta play in Angelo tonight."

Darlina stood as well. "Thank you for the pie and coffee, Mrs. Stone."

"You're welcome," she said. "Son, don't wait so long to get back out to see us."

"I'll try, mom." He hugged her and shook his father's hand.

"It's sure good to see you, son," he said. "And it was nice to meet you, Darlina."

"You too, Al."

Once they were back in the car, Darlina breathed a sigh of relief. "Well, that didn't go too bad, I guess, but your mom sure didn't approve of me bein' with you."

"She's old fashioned, but she knew better than to say anything out of line. Dad seemed to take a liking to you."

"He was very sweet, and I'm glad I got to meet him. You know, until I heard your mom say it, I didn't even know your wife's name."

"Didn't figure it was anything you wanted to know."

"Well, I was a little curious. It's kinda' nice to know."

Luke gazed intently at Darlina. "Honey, I'd give anything if I'd met you ten years ago."

"Luke, I'd only have been nine years old. I was still in elementary school."

He laughed. "Just my damned luck."

She slid across the seat next to him and he draped his right arm over her slender shoulders. As she rested her head on his arm, she wished that somehow they could have met before Luke got tangled up in a bad marriage. But, the truth is, that it was too late. She wondered how he'd ever get out of it and whether or not she would ever get to be Mrs. Luke Stone.

Without any doubt, she knew that was what she wanted more than anything in the world. She could make him happy and there was no question in her mind how happy he could make her because he already did; beyond her wildest dreams.

# Chapter 16

Darlina called her mom and dad the next day after the visit with Luke's parents. As she picked up the phone and dialed the number, she felt very apprehensive. Luke sat at his desk in the office within earshot, but she knew he was purposefully giving her some privacy.

"Daddy? This is Darlina. How are you?"

Her father's voice sounded sad on the other end. "Darlina. I'm fine. How are you?"

"I'm fine, daddy. Leann told me you and mama moved. Where did you move to?"

"We're up in Northern New Mexico. I had a chance at a job up here and it seemed like a good opportunity for us to get out of Hobbs."

"Did you sell the house?"

"Not yet. We're waitin' to see what happens. You want to talk to your mama?"

"I sure do, daddy and I want to wish you a Merry Christmas and I miss you."

"Merry Christmas to you too, little girl. Here's your mama."

"Hello." Darlina heard a strained tired voice.

"Mama. It's Darlina. How are you?"

"Oh, I'm as alright as I can be, considering I've lost both of my daughters at the same time."

"Mama, you haven't lost us. We just had to have lives of our own. I sure wish you and daddy could meet Luke. He really makes me happy."

"Darlina, you know you weren't raised to take up with a married man. I have no desire to meet him and I'm ashamed of you for the way you're living."

Tears came into Darlina's eyes and she choked them back. "Mama, please don't be that way. I love him."

"You don't even know what love is. I wish you well, but I'd rather you not even call as long as you are living with him. It just upsets me more."

"I don't mean to upset you. I just wanted to wish you and daddy a Merry Christmas."

"Well, it won't be very merry, but we'll have a Christmas."

"Mama, I love you. I don't want to hurt you, but I need to be happy and Luke makes me happy."

"Okay, Darlina. I've got to go. You take care of yourself."

She whispered into the phone, "I will, mama, and you too. I love you."

Her mother had already hung up on the other end before she got the last I love you out. She sat with the phone in her hands, silent tears running down both cheeks.

Luke came to her side, gently took the phone from her hands and hung it up. Gathering her up in his arms, he held her and rocked back and forth. "Don't cry, sweetheart. Everything's gonna be alright."

She nodded her head as her throat was too choked up to force any words out.

The two of them sat this way for a long while. Luke caressed her and held her tight. She could tell it tore him up to see her hurt.

After a while she lifted her head and wiped her tears away. "Thank you, Luke. You do know I love you, don't you?"

"Of course I do, darlin'. Don't worry, she'll come around."

"I hope you're right, but I've got my doubts. Anyway, I did what I could. At least I tried."

Luke leaned down and kissed her mouth gently, then held her close. She breathed in the scent of his cologne mixed with the familiar smell of King Edward cigars and relaxed in his arms.

It was a cold but clear Christmas Eve night in Abilene, Texas. Luke and the Rebel Rousers were playing a private party for Shamrock Oil Company in the conference center of the Starlight Inn Motel. Darlina felt and looked very festive. She was dressed in a red satin blouse and tight white bell bottom pants. She sat proudly beside Luke, as he introduced her to the many people who greeted him.

She thought he seemed somewhat jittery and knew he'd taken some pills before they left the house. She hoped he hadn't overdone it. He seemed to be drinking heavier than usual as well. He'd offered her one of the pink hearts he'd bought in Mexico and she'd taken a half. It was just enough to get the euphoric feeling she enjoyed.

Maybe his mood was simply because of the holidays and not getting to be with his kids. She didn't know but silently vowed to stay close and keep a watchful eye on him. Funny, that tonight she felt like his protector.

She was thrilled to look up and see Norma walking toward her. "Norma! What are you doing here?"

"Hi, Darlina. This is Greg and he works for Shamrock. When he asked me to come out with him, I jumped at the opportunity, especially when he told me Luke was playing the party. You look fantastic, little sister."

"And you do as well. It's so nice to meet you Greg. Ya'll sit here with me."

Luke returned to the table after checking out some last minute details on stage. "Norma, this is a nice surprise."

"Luke, this is Greg. He works for Shamrock."

Luke extended his hand. "Nice to meet you. You work for one of the nicest guys I know. Ted Riley's a good friend of mine."

"Nice to meet you Luke, and you too, Darlina. I've heard ya'll play a bunch of times and danced lots of miles to your music."

"Well, we're gonna make sure everyone has a chance to dance a few more miles tonight." He leaned into Darlina, kissing her on the cheek. "It's time to get this show started. Glad you have some company for tonight."

She smiled at Luke, "Me too, sweetheart. Go knock 'em out."

The music, euphoric feeling, party atmosphere and having her sister there with her, were totally uplifting to Darlina. She smiled and laughed more than she had in a very long time.

Suddenly, there was a tap on her shoulder. A nicely dressed young man stood behind her. "Would you like to dance?"

She smiled, but shook her head, "No, thank you. Maybe later."

He walked away but she noticed him staring at her across the room. She hoped there wouldn't be any trouble.

The band took a break and Luke joined her. "What did that man ask you?"

"Just to dance and I said no. He was real polite."

"Yeah," he growled, "And I've been watching him stare at you."

"Luke, it's okay. He's not causing any problems."

"We'll see about that." He downed the glass of Jim Beam and Coke and got up to go to the restroom.

Darlina thought no more about the incident. She enjoyed visiting with her sister and was pleased that she and Greg were keeping the dance floor hot. Darlina thought it was good for Norma to be out having fun and suddenly wished Leann was with them as well.

When Luke returned, she noticed an increased darkening in his mood. "Are you alright, baby?"

Luke smiled, what looked like a forced smile to her. "Hell yeah, I'm alright. You look absolutely delicious tonight. I can't wait to get you back home."

Darlina flirted back. "Hope you're up to it, cowboy."

He leaned down and kissed her lightly on the forehead. "I think I can handle it."

Red interrupted them, motioning for Luke to come with him. Darlina wondered what was going on, but was sure it was just band business.

Luke didn't come back to the table, but instead went straight back to the stage with the band. Darlina didn't have another chance to talk to him and felt a twinge of worry. Something was just not right.

The band played until midnight and Luke announced the last song of the evening. "Alright ya'll. Grab your partner and let's get out on the dance floor for a little belt buckle shinin'."

As they began to play the Platters Song, *Twilight Time*, Darlina felt a tap on her shoulder again. She looked up to find the same young man standing there. "You said later. It won't get any later than this. Will you dance with me?"

She glanced at Luke before answering as politely as she could, "I'm very flattered that you asked me, but I really don't think I want to dance. Thank you anyway."

His face grew red and before he walked away he said, "You're just like all the other bitches. Lead a man on and then don't follow through."

"I really think you'd better walk away."

"Oh yeah? Think your big ol' boyfriend might hurt me?"

"I don't think it. I know it. Please leave."

"I'll leave, but I promise you when I get through with him, your boyfriend won't be fit for anything else tonight."

Darlina arose from her chair. "That's enough. Leave!"

She looked directly at Luke to see his face change into a grimace. She smiled reassuringly at him and mouthed the words, "It's alright."

He nodded his head, but the expression didn't change. As soon as the song was finished, she saw him immediately leave the stage and walk over to the man. Her stomach tightened with fear.

Red followed Luke and the two of them stood talking to the man. She wished she could hear what they were saying.

Norma put her hand on Darlina's shoulder and asked, "Everything alright?"

"I don't know. Will you and Greg stay for just a little while longer?"

"Sure we will," Greg said. "Need me to go see about Luke?"

"No, I'm sure he'll be fine. It's the other man I'm not so sure about."

"We'll stay with you until Luke comes back," Norma reassured.

Thirty minutes passed before Luke returned. His suit had blood splatters on it and his expression was even more ominous.

"Luke, are you alright?" Darlina asked.

"Sure. I'm alright. You ready to get out of here?"

It seemed unusual to her that he didn't stay to help gather all the equipment, get paid and pay the rest of the band, but she didn't question him.

"I'm ready if you are."

Luke, Darlina, Norma and Greg had just made it out the front door when the ambulance siren blared to a stop in front of the building.

Norma gave Darlina a questioning look, but they all kept walking pretending they didn't see it. She gave her sister a hug and she and Greg got into their car.

"Sugar, do you feel like driving?" Luke asked.

"Sure. I don't mind."

They got into the blue T-Bird and Darlina adjusted the seat and mirrors. Luke sat with his head back on the seat, eyes closed.

She reached over, taking his hand in hers and squeezing it.

He opened his eyes, "I'm so tired of all this shit. It's always the same. It's always gonna be the same. I'm just tired."

She quietly put the car in reverse and they backed out with the flashing lights of the ambulance reflecting off the mirrors.

She turned on the radio and reached over to caress Luke's face. "Luke, what happened back there?"

He sat up opening his eyes. "Red heard the little bastard bragging in the bathroom that he was gonna get you to leave with him tonight. That's when Red came and got me."

"Okay, but there was an ambulance and that's serious."

Luke growled. "He got what he had comin' to him. I gave him every opportunity to back down and he wouldn't, so I carved his face up a little. He'll live."

"Oh dear, I feel so bad, like I caused it or something."

"No, sweetheart," he said tiredly, "You didn't cause anything. He was an arrogant little bastard who wanted a go at me. He only used you to make that happen."

"Well, I'm still sorry Luke. I don't ever want to be the cause of any trouble."

He laid his head back on the seat; closed his eyes again and Darlina drove the rest of the way home, with the radio making the only sound in the car. Every once in a while she would glance over at Luke. She felt an overwhelming urge to protect him. There was always bound to be trouble and he certainly wasn't the kind of man who would ever back down or walk away from it. She loved that about him, while at the same time hating it. She wondered if she could ever really make a difference in his life. She only knew she had to try.

# Chapter 17

By the time they arrived back in Brownwood, it was 1:30 in the morning. Darlina had grown concerned that Luke had not opened his eyes since they'd left Abilene. She parked the car and turned the motor off.

"Luke. Baby, we're home."

He didn't answer. She shook him and spoke louder. "Luke honey, we're home."

He finally stirred and with her help, got out of the car and into the house. He fell onto the bed and she took off his boots and undressed him. She made a mental note to work on the blood spatters on his suit before it went to the cleaners.

Once she had him under the covers, she went into the kitchen and poured herself a glass of milk. She sat at the table with an uneasy feeling that something was definitely wrong. Things had not been right with Luke all evening and now he was passed out. It just didn't add up. She'd seen him swallow several of the pills they'd brought back from Mexico and normally they would be keeping him awake for hours. Maybe it was all the alcohol he'd mixed with them.

When she returned to the bedroom, she found Luke tossing and turning restlessly. Occasionally, a groan escaped from his lips. She felt his forehead and it was warm but not hot enough to cause alarm.

She got out of her clothes and under the covers with him. Wrapping her arms around him as much as she could, she spoke soothingly to him as if he were a child. He would settle down for a few minutes and then would start thrashing around again.

After a couple of hours, she slipped out of bed and got dressed. Something was very wrong. She remembered what Luke had told her about the intercom and his instructions to call Red if she ever needed help.

She walked to the intercom box on the wall and pressed the button. Red didn't answer, so she pressed it again.

Finally, she heard Red's sleepy voice, "What's up?"

"Red, it's Darlina. Something's terribly wrong with Luke. Can you please come over?"

"Sure, sweetheart, I'll be right there."

She unlocked the door and within five minutes, Red was there. His shock of red hair was tousled and she knew she had awakened him, but he didn't seem to mind.

He took one look at Luke and told Darlina, "Honey, it's the fever. It's been a while since he's had one. You did the right thing to call me."

"What do we need to do?"

"Mostly just wait it out and try to keep him comfortable. I wanna warn you though; he might say some things that are disturbing. He can explain it all to you when he wakes up."

"What do you mean when he wakes up? How long will that be?"

"Maybe a couple of days if we're lucky. One of us'll need to stay with him at all times."

With a trembling voice, Darlina replied, "A couple of days? Shouldn't we get him to a doctor?"

"Oh no, Luke sure wouldn't want that. I've been through this with him before. He'll be alright. We're just in for a few hard days and nights until this passes."

"Okay. What can I do?"

"Get a cool washcloth for his forehead. It'll help the fever some. If you're up to staying with him a few hours, I'll go back to bed and then I'll come and relieve you so you can get some rest."

"I'm fine to stay up with him. I'm not the least bit sleepy."

Red placed his hand on her shoulder. "I promise you he'll be alright. We just have to wait it out."

She looked up at him with tears in her eyes. "Red, you know I'd do anything for Luke. I just can't let him die."

"He's not going to die, sugar. This happens every so often and he always comes back out of it. He'll talk out of his head and that's what

I mean about him saying things that are disturbing. All we can do is try to keep him comfortable."

"Okay, I'll do whatever I can. Thank you Red."

"I'll be back in a few hours, but if you get scared or he gets worse, just buzz me."

She nodded in agreement as he turned to go. Looking back at Luke, she wondered how she could make him more comfortable. She pulled a chair up beside the bed and sat holding his hand and wiping his brow with a cool cloth.

He tossed and turned violently at times and Darlina became afraid he'd throw himself off the bed. She held onto him until he would settle down again and she'd breathe a short-lived sigh of relief.

She alternated between sitting beside the bed and getting into the bed with him; doing everything she could think of.

"No! No!" Luke screamed out, grabbing his left leg with both hands. "Please not the leg!" He followed with a guttural scream of pain.

What could be going on in his mind to make him cry out so? She had no answers, only endless hours of listening to it and watching him writhe in pain and suffering. The agony in his voice sent chills up and down Darlina's spine.

She sat in the chair beside the bed, put her head in her hands and cried. For a while he settled down to the low moan and she took advantage of the opportunity to dash into the kitchen and brew a pot of coffee. She was going to need all the stamina she could gather.

Six hours had passed when she heard a soft knock on the door. She quickly ran to let Red in and felt relieved to have him there.

"He's not any better, Red."

"That's okay. I'm here to take over for a while. You try to get some rest."

"I can't leave him."

"I know. Just get a blanket and curl up in that chair over there and see if you can get a little sleep."

"I'll try. There's some coffee in the kitchen."

"That sounds good. I'll help myself."

Darlina curled up in the big chair with a blanket wrapped tightly around her. She knew she couldn't drown out the sounds coming from the bed, but she could relax a little knowing that Red was there. Before she knew it, she dozed off.

She awoke to a blood curdling scream. She jumped to her feet and in two bounds, was beside the bed. Red stood at the bedside holding on to Luke with all his might.

"What's happening, Red? I don't understand at all."

"He's re-living a Civil War battle and it's the same every time. He gets his leg cut off on the battlefield with no anesthesia. He'll have to explain it to you more, but it's like a past life he's lived."

"I've never heard of past lives. Do you think it's true?"

Red chuckled. "Honey, I have no idea. All I know is Luke lives it over and over again. That's one reason you see all the Civil War stuff around the apartment. He's read every book he can get his hands on. Hell, maybe he did live back then. Who am I to say?" Luke settled back down to a low moan and Red sat back in the chair.

"I suppose you're right. I'm gonna go take a shower and see if I can feel alive again. Is that alright with you?"

"Sure. When you get out, maybe you could rustle us up something to eat."

She leaned over the bed, kissed Luke's forehead and smoothed back his hair. "I sure will. We've got some eggs and biscuits I can fix."

"Sounds good. I'll stay right here. Go do what you need to."

While the warm water ran over her head, she thought about what Red had said. Could it be possible that people have lived before and remember it? She'd never heard that theory talked about in church. She decided that if she'd lived before, she hoped it was with Luke.

A short time later, feeling somewhat refreshed, she had a heaping plate of hot biscuits and eggs cooked. She and Red sat beside the bed and ate. Luke had settled down some for the moment, with only an occasional groan escaping his parched lips.

"Let's see if we can get a sip of water down him," Red suggested.

Red lifted his head, while Darlina held a cup up to his lips. The water trickled down his chin, with very little going into his mouth. He licked his lips as if he wanted more. They tried again, with a little more going in this time.

This encouraged Darlina and she wished there was some way she could change the damp and wrinkled bed sheets. She tried to smooth them down the best she could with him in the bed.

A little after noon, Red went back to his apartment for a while and Darlina picked a book off the shelf to read while she kept watch. The book she chose was titled *A Pictorial History of The Civil War*.

As she turned the pages, she saw picture after picture of soldiers lying on the battlefield, bleeding and dying. She wondered again if what Luke was experiencing could be real.

Her eyes were drawn to a detailed photograph of a doctor's bag. Its contents included forceps, several tweezers like instruments, bandages, small bottles of antiseptic, a saw, and other assorted items. She shivered when she looked at the saw. The caption below the picture stated that on the Confederacy side, doctors usually had no access to ether or chloroform, therefore having to perform surgeries with the patient fully awake.

This sounded exactly like what was going on in Luke's head.

She laid the book down after a while and sat looking at Luke. His face was twisted into a permanent grimace and the agony he was experiencing was clearly etched in the lines.

She replaced the cloth on his forehead with a new cool one and he seemed to relax a little.

It occurred to her that this was Christmas Day and Luke's children must be wondering where their Daddy was. She thought about Joyce and how she most likely would assume he was just hung over and didn't feel like coming to see the children. She wondered if Joyce had ever gone through this with Luke.

She wished she could explain to them what was happening, but knew that was impossible. She could only hope he would wake up soon. How could it be, that this larger-than-life, strong vital man was lying here helpless, caught in a nightmare that seemed to have no end?

Red came back a few hours later. "Sugar, I'm gonna go try to find us a hamburger or something. This bein' Christmas Day, don't know what I'll find open, but I won't be gone long."

"Some Christmas, huh?" she said ruefully.

Red placed a comforting hand on her shoulder. "Yeah, some Christmas. I'll be back shortly. Will you be okay?"

"Sure. He seems to be settling down a little."

"Well, it comes and goes. Hang tight and I'll be back."

She tried to smile at Red. She couldn't think of any way she could show how much she appreciated him being there and helping them through this. "Would you mind terribly stopping at a grocery store, if one's open, and pick us up a little fruitcake or something?"

"Not at all. See you in a bit."

Once he was gone, she settled back in the chair beside the bed. Her mind turned to her parents and she could imagine the bleak Christmas they were having. She was suddenly filled with an ache of loneliness. Without Luke there with her, the world seemed to stop turning.

She looked at him tossing and turning, so caught in this nightmare of torment. If only he would wake up, or her for that matter and find that she'd been having a nightmare of her own.

Instead, the hours slowly crawled by, one after another torturous other.

Red returned with a bag of hamburgers and fries and had managed to find a small, dried out fruitcake. "This was the best I could do. Any change?"

"None that I can tell." Tears clouded her eyes. "I feel so helpless."

"I know. Me too, but I swear this is all we can do. Why don't you go in the office and use the phone to call some of your family," Red suggested.

"I'm not sure I trust myself to talk to anyone right now. What about you, don't you have family?"

"Nah. None to speak of. Luke's the closest family I've got."

Darlina could see loneliness reflected in his face. "How long have you known Luke?"

"He picked me up hitchhiking about ten years ago and I've been with him ever since. It worked in my favor that I knew how to play bass guitar. I've learned a lot with Luke and am a much better musician than I was ten years ago."

They were interrupted by another violent scream and more thrashing around on the bed.

This went on through the rest of the day and into the next night. Twenty four hours had passed and Luke seemed to be as far away as he was when it started.

Red and Darlina took turns sitting with him and resting. She knew she'd forever be indebted to Red for staying close and helping.

He'd been sitting with Luke for the past four hours while Darlina dozed. When she awoke, she could see he was getting tired, as he ran his hand through his hair and took off his glasses to rub his eyes. "Why don't you go home and get some sleep? If anything changes, I'll buzz you."

He stood up. "I think I will, sugar, if you're alright. I could use some shut eye."

At five o'clock in the evening on December 26th, Luke opened his eyes.

Darlina was sitting by the bed, with her head resting on Luke's chest when she felt his hand touch her hair. She jerked her head up to meet his gaze.

"Oh Luke!" she exclaimed. "You're back." Tears flooded her eyes and he gently wiped them away.

"How long have I been out?"

"It's been about thirty six hours. I thought you'd left me for good. I was so scared."

"Didn't you call Red?"

"Yes. I couldn't have got through this without his help. He is truly your brother in all ways that count."

"Yes he is. Where is he now?"

"He went home to get some sleep. He'll be back when he wakes up."

Luke gingerly tried to sit up and Darlina put her hand behind his back to help him. "Every muscle I've got hurts," he said.

"Luke, you've got to explain to me what just happened. Red said you were re-living a past life in the Civil War."

"That's true. I don't know how it happens, but it's the same every time. I live the agony of the battlefield and I always get my left leg amputated without any anesthesia. I don't know the whys or the hows; I just know it happens."

"I don't know either Luke, but I do know it's very real to you."

"Sugar, I need to get off this bed. Can you help me into the bathroom?"

"I'd be happy to."

She put her shoulder under his arm and slowly they walked into the bathroom.

Once she was sure Luke could stay on his feet, she returned to the bed, stripping off the damp and tangled sheets.

By the time Red returned, Luke and Darlina were sitting at the kitchen table and he was drinking coffee and eating eggs.

"Hey, hoss. It's damned good to see you up and eating something."

Luke smiled at Red. "It's damned good to be up and eating something. Thank you for helping Darlina, stud. You know I appreciate it."

"Yeah I know, Luke. She never left your side. She's a trooper and you're a lucky man."

Luke turned to Darlina, reaching across the table to intertwine his fingers in hers. "I sure am, hoss. I sure am."

Darlina returned his squeeze and smiled warmly at him. "I don't know, but I kinda' think I'm the lucky one. I'm lucky you came back."

"I'll always come back, sweetheart. Don't ever forget that."

# Chapter 18

Three days had passed since Luke had gone into his unconscious state and now that he was fully recovered, he told Darlina, "Sweetheart, I've gotta go see my kids. I feel like a heel for missin' Christmas Day with them, but it was a little out of my control."

"Yes, I know. I thought about them while you were laying there fighting the fever and hoped they weren't too disappointed."

"Disappointing people seems to be the one thing I'm best at, but I need to go see 'em."

"How about you drop me off at a Laundromat and let me get our clothes washed and dried?"

"Okay. I'll help you gather everything up."

Darlina grabbed a book off the shelf and with the bundles of laundry, she and Luke headed out the door.

"I see you picked a book about my ol' buddy, Sam Bass."

"I wanna know everything there is to know about you, baby, and if Sam Bass is some part of that, I wanna know about him too."

Luke jokingly said, "Just don't find out too much. I don't want you to get scared away."

"Luke, if what just happened with you didn't scare me away, I don't think anything will."

He chuckled. "Guess you're right about that."

As he helped her carry the bundles of laundry into the Laundromat, she assured him, "Don't feel like you've got to hurry back. Go spend time with your kids. I'll be just fine doing the laundry and reading this book."

He kissed her lightly on the cheek. "I love you, sweetheart. You're one in a million. See you in a bit."

The Laundromat was fairly empty and Darlina quickly went to work separating the clothes and putting them in the washers. She then sat down with her book and was soon engrossed in the story.

Luke wasn't having such an easy time. When he arrived at the house, Joyce coldly met him at the door. "Thanks for ignoring the kids on Christmas Day."

"Don't start on me Joyce. I was laid up in bed sick."

She snorted. "Yeah, I bet you were laid up in bed, but I doubt you were sick."

"Think what you will. I didn't come here to argue with you. I just wanna see the kids."

"What if they don't wanna see you?"

Just then Luke's daughter came running and wrapped herself around his leg. "Daddy, daddy. Come see what Santa brought me for Christmas."

He looked at Joyce as he reached down to pick the little girl up. "Does that answer the question?"

She stepped aside and let Luke enter the room. The three little boys quickly came running to him and they each clamored for his attention. He sat down on the couch and put Alexis on his lap.

His oldest son, Joseph, brought the new BB gun Luke had gotten for him. "Dad, let's go outside and shoot my new gun. Mama won't let me. She says I'll get hurt."

"Okay, son. Let me see what everyone else got and we'll put on your coat and go shoot it."

Joyce coldly interrupted, "Luke, do you have any money? I need to go buy groceries and run some errands while you're here with the kids."

He handed Joyce several twenty dollar bills. "Sure. Go ahead. I'll be here 'til you get back."

She put on her coat and went out the door without saying goodbye to any of the children. Luke sighed and turned his attention back to them.

His daughter, Alexis, whom he affectionately called Lexxi, came running with the pink transistor radio that Darlina had picked out for Luke to give to her. "Daddy, listen. I can get the radio stations that play your music. I listen to it every night 'til mama makes me turn it off."

He smiled at the little girl, ruffling her hair. "That's real nice, Lexxi. I'm glad you like it."

The two younger boys, Martin and Nathan, were always pushed back by the older two, but he called them to him and asked them to bring toys they had gotten.

Each eagerly ran off and came back with their toy guns. "Okay, boys. Looks like it's time for us to go outside and shoot some guns. Whadya' say?"

They all clamored excitedly. Lexxi pouted. "What am I gonna do daddy?"

"Oh, honey, you're gonna come with us and help me keep score to see who can shoot the best."

She grinned mischievously, thrilled to get a chance to judge her brothers. "Can I bring my radio?"

"Well, I think you should bring your radio. We just might need some shootin' music."

Luke played outside with the children, praising each of the boys on their shooting abilities and helping Lexxi tune in her favorite radio stations. Finally, they were all shivering from the cold, and had to go back in.

Once inside, he fixed them hot chocolate with tiny marshmallows on top and they sat around the table. He loved his children. He wished with all his heart he didn't have to be away from them, but he knew he'd never live with their mother again. He never loved her or even liked her. She'd gotten pregnant with Joseph and he'd felt obligated to marry her. The fact that she was under age at the time didn't leave him many choices.

Now, as he looked around the table, he soaked up the sparkle in his children's eyes and vowed to always take care of them, no matter what.

Lexxi looked up from her hot chocolate. "Mama's comin'."

She said it in such a matter of fact manner that Luke thought she was already in the door. It amazed him that she seemed to know ahead of time when her mama was on the way. Five minutes later, Joyce walked in.

Joseph bragged to her, "Mama, daddy let us shoot our guns and I shot the very best."

"Really? Luke, you know that BB gun ain't safe, don't you?"

"Oh, lighten up Joyce. Joseph's old enough to have a BB gun and he knows how to handle it. He'll be just fine."

Luke stood up from the table. "Okay, kids. I've gotta get goin' but I'll be back to see you real soon."

Tears filled Lexxi's big brown eyes. "Daddy, I wanna go with you."

"Now, sweetie, you have to stay here with mama and your brothers. I promise I'll be back in a day or so. Ya'll be good for your mama."

He hugged each of the children and started walking toward the door.

"Here, these need to be paid," Joyce said tossing him a stack of bills. "The electric bill is overdue."

Luke sighed, "I'll take care of it." He took the stack of bills and left, turning around to wave goodbye to the children one more time.

He sat in the car a few minutes before starting the engine. He couldn't help thinking of how different life would have been if only Darlina had come along before he'd messed up so badly. He shook his head as if to clear the fog. No need in thinking about what could have been; there was nothing to do but deal with what was.

When he got to the Laundromat to pick up Darlina, all of their laundry was folded in neat piles and she sat engrossed in the book. She didn't look up until Luke touched her arm.

"Ready to go, baby?"

Her eyes lit up and a warm smile curved her pretty lips. "Yep. All ready."

"Did you learn anything about Sam Bass?"

"I learned that he wasn't really an outlaw and that he had a friend much like Red is to you named Seaborn Barnes, and that they raced horses and bet on them. That's about as far as I've gotten. How'd it go with the kids?"

"They were glad to see me and I was very happy to get to spend some time with them. Wasn't sure Joyce was gonna let me in when I got there, but my little girl fixed that."

"Well, the important thing is that you got to see them."

"Let's go get something to eat. I wanna treat you to a steak dinner or anything you want."

"This cold weather's got me wantin' Mexican food. Let's go to Gomez's and get some enchiladas."

They sat with steaming cups of coffee waiting for their order to be served. Luke looked across the table at Darlina and his heart melted. "Honey, we haven't made love since I got sick. I'm pretty sure I'm feelin' well enough now. When we get home, I need to take care of my beautiful lady."

Darlina's face lit up as she replied, "Well, I don't wanna push you or nothin', but I'm more than ready to be in your arms and feel you inside me."

Luke chuckled as he lit his King Edward cigar. "I think it's time I got back to livin' instead of bein' a sickie."

Several hours later, Darlina glowed with contentment. She was most certain Luke was totally well now. Thank goodness that ordeal was over and they could get back to what was normal living for them.

Five days had passed since Christmas Eve and the band was playing their first gig since that night. Darlina felt at home and in her place beside Luke in the Lincoln. Red drove and Preacher, Jerry and Rita sat in the back. The only thing missing was the companion bottle of Jim Beam. Luke hadn't touched it since the fever. They were driving to Big Spring, Texas to do a show at the Stampede.

Luke was back to his old self and there was never a mention of what the three of them had just been through. "Wish I'd been thinkin' straight, we should've had the Rebel Rouser go-go girls tonight. The Stampede is a big ol' joint and the girls would've been a hit."

"That's true," said Jerry from the back seat. "When are we gonna have them again?"

"I don't know yet. We're playing the NCO Club at Dyess in February and I definitely plan to have them there."

"Oh that sounds good," Darlina said excitedly. "Where are we going to be for New Years?"

"A place you're gonna love," Luke said. "We're playing London Hall at London, Texas and that is one of the most unique places you'll ever see in your life."

"London, Texas? I didn't know there was such a place. What's different about it?"

Red spoke up in his slow drawl, "It's one of the oldest dancehalls in the State of Texas and everyone comes from miles around. Grandmas, grandpas, mamas, daddies, little kids, the cedar choppers...everyone comes out of those hills."

"Oh wow! Sounds like fun," said Darlina.

It was a long drive from Brownwood to Big Spring and Luke had gotten the band motel rooms for the night. With the weather turning snowy and icy, he didn't want to risk driving back in the wee hours of the morning and sliding off the road.

Luke talked about Hoyle Nix while they were driving. He owned the Stampede Club and was a good friend of Luke's. "I swear to you, when Hoyle plays, it is impossible to tell if it's him or Bob Wills. If there'd never been a Bob Wills, Hoyle Nix would have been as big as Bob ever was."

The Stampede Club was packed with oilfield workers, cowboys and their ladies making up the majority of the crowd.

Darlina was happy to be watching the band setting up and getting ready to play. She and Rita sat at a table reserved for the Rebel Rousers. She looked around the room, once again amazed at the huge crowds the band drew. She vowed there would be no trouble tonight no matter what she had to do.

The band appeared happy to be back playing again and started another night of music with their standard rendition of *Dixie*. Luke sat at the table with Darlina and Rita for the first three songs, and then took the stage, with his commanding presence.

He wore a buckskin leather fringed jacket, tan faux leather pants that had silver conchos tied with strips of leather down each leg. His brown boots, with their silver tips, shone like a mirror and his tan cowboy hat was trimmed with a beaded hat band.

Darlina thought he sounded better than ever as he belted out song after song. The crowd responded enthusiastically and the dance floor was packed.

She breathed a sigh of contentment. Things were finally back on track and they were closer than ever after Luke's ordeal with the fever. She felt a little older and wiser as well as a whole lot stronger than she did before the days that she'd sat with Luke through his agonizing nightmare.

Everything was going to be alright now. He looked down at her from the stage with a grin as he winked. She returned his gaze with sparkling eyes and mouthed the words, "I love you."

# Chapter 19

The picturesque rambling dance hall sat amidst a grove of giant oak trees. As the band pulled up to the building, Christmas lights twinkled all around the front roof line, giving off a festive glow in the quickly fading Texas Hill Country sunset.

London Hall was like a scene out of a 1920's movie. The way it had been described to Darlina didn't begin to do it justice. The age of the building, the wood floors, the fold out wooden windows, and the preservation of its original structure impressed her.

The only modernization she could see was electric lights and one inside bathroom for ladies. Men had to use an oak tree outside.

There wasn't a way to pull around back and unload the band trailer, so Red had to back it up to the front door and unhitch from the car.

Posters from music acts that had performed there, such as *Easy Adams and the Top Hands, Adolph Hofner, Luke Stone and The Rebel Rousers, Doug Sahm, Augie Meyers* and numerous other artists lined the walls.

As they walked around looking at the posters, Luke explained to her, "Easy Adams is a good friend of mine and he wrote *Bandera Waltz*. He once told me I sang it better than anyone he'd ever heard besides himself. That was a real compliment to me."

As Red had predicted, people ranging from age 90 to tiny babies crowded into the dancehall.

Luke had taken Darlina shopping and she'd purchased a pair of tan bell bottom pants and a matching western style blouse, with cream colored fringe hanging from the yoke and down the sleeves.

Darlina thought the outfit matched the purse Luke had gotten her for Christmas just perfectly.

She hung the purse on the back of her chair and became mesmerized by the scene unfolding before her eyes.

She watched as Luke moved through the gathering crowd. Most everyone seemed to know him. He patted little kids on the heads and shook hands with the old men. He'd told her that he once had rented London Hall for a year and he and the Rebel Rousers had played there on a regular basis. Maybe, she thought, this was how all of these people knew him.

As the crowd grew, it became standing room only on New Year's Eve in London Hall.

The band started the show without Luke, as was the normal routine. Once they were into the second song, someone in the crowd started calling for Luke and soon the chant echoed throughout the building. "Luke Stone. We want Luke Stone."

Luke stood, waved to the crowd and made his way to the stage. The moment he picked up his Martin D35 guitar, the crowd went wild with applause. It was a few seconds before anyone could hear Luke as he sang *Danny Boy*. He didn't pause between songs and went right into *Standing Room Only When I Die* and from there into one of the songs he'd penned titled *Den of Sin*.

People packed the dance floor. Children danced with each other and with older folks. Grandmas danced with grandpas and even sometimes two women cut a rug together. Darlina sat in amazement, taking it all in. If she closed her eyes, she could imagine the way it must've been on the frontier in the old West days.

Her attention was drawn back to the stage as Luke finished singing *Be Nobody's Darling but Mine*. He announced, "Thank you so much. It's my pleasure to be here tonight and help all of you good folks see in 1971. We've got a special treat for you right now. A young man that you all know has been standing in front of this stage since we started, singing along with every song and I want to get him up here and let him sing for you. Make welcome little John Beam!"

There was a large round of applause at the announcement and a young boy climbed the steps to the stage, approaching Luke shyly.

Darlina guessed him to be about ten years old. Luke took the guitar from around his neck and placed it on the boy's shoulders. It swallowed him and Luke had to adjust the guitar strap as small as it would go. Then, he lowered the mic so the child could reach it.

"What are you going to sing for us young man?" Luke asked.

The boy's voice trembled slightly as he replied, "*Sweet Thang.*"

The band started the opening rift and the boy strummed along on Luke's guitar. He bravely began singing into the mic. He knew every word and as the song progressed, he grew more and more confident and sang louder.

Darlina beamed at Luke, catching his glance. Her heart warmed at the act of kindness Luke offered the child.

When the song ended, Luke took his guitar back and put his hand in his pocket. He took out some money and handed it to the boy.

John looked up admiringly at Luke. "Thank you, Mister Stone."

"You did good, son. You earned this money." Then, into the mic he said, "Give this young man a big round of applause."

The crowd applauded, cheered and whistled as the young man ran from the stage. With his money in hand, he joined a group of children his age who were waiting for him. Within a few minutes, they all ran off to buy candy with their newfound wealth.

Luke put his guitar down and left the stage. The band continued playing with Red taking over the mic. He joined Darlina at the table. "Well sugar, what do you think so far?"

"I think this is one of the most amazing places you've taken me and I'm having a ball watching everyone."

"At midnight, I want you to join me on stage for a New Year's kiss."

"I wouldn't miss it. I love you so much, Luke. What you did for that little boy was one of the kindest things I've ever seen."

"I've known him and his family since he was just a little tyke and he always stands directly in front of the stage, mouthing the words to the songs and playing an air guitar. I just figured it was time to let him get up and get his feet wet."

"You made his night. He really did pretty well too."

"He comes from a very poor family. There's a shitload of them Beam kids, but they make it to every dance we play down here. I think that boy's got the music in him."

Luke sat close to Darlina with his arm around her shoulders, while the band finished out the set. There was a steady stream of people who came to shake Luke's hand, slap him on the back, or praise him for his kindness to John.

Darlina graciously acknowledged each person as they conversed with Luke. She noticed that Luke was still not drinking and knew he'd not taken any pills since the night he got the fever. She liked this sense of getting the real Luke, not altered in any way.

As midnight approached, Darlina got ready to go onto the stage for her New Year's kiss.

He picked up the mic and made the announcement. "Okay folks, it's gettin' damn close to midnight. It's time to grab your special someone and let's get ready to count down."

Red handed Luke a stopwatch and Luke began to count as Darlina joined him. "Ten, nine, eight, seven, six, five, four, three, two, one...Happy New Year!"

He pulled Darlina close to him, kissing her passionately to which she responded equally. "I love you, baby", he whispered in her ear.

"I love you too, sweetheart."

He picked up his guitar, removed the strap and handed it to her. "I've made a practice of giving the woman I'm with on New Year's my guitar strap for many years and this one's yours."

She accepted the guitar strap and then made her way off the stage, as the band played *Auld Lang Syne*.

The night came to a magical end. The band was packing up and people still lingered. They visited with each other and with the band. The clock said half past two a.m. before they were finished loading up and headed back to Brownwood.

They'd travelled down the road for about an hour before Darlina reached for her purse to get something out of it. Her heart stood still when she realized she had left her purse at London Hall.

"Oh no," she exclaimed. "Luke, I left my purse hanging on the back of the chair I was sitting in tonight."

"Are you sure?" he asked.

"Yes, I'm sure. Can we go back and get it?"

"No sugar, not now, but I'll call tomorrow and see if anyone turned it in. If they did, it'll be waiting there."

"But Luke, it's the purse you bought for me and I love it." Tears sprang up in her eyes. "I don't wanna lose it."

He put his arms around her and held her, "Don't worry, baby. It's just a purse. I'll get you another one if we don't get it back."

She mentally lectured herself for being so distracted and forgetting it. How could she have let that happen? She hoped and prayed with all her heart that it would be there and they could go back and get it.

Unfortunately, when Luke called the next day, no one had turned in the purse. It was gone. She couldn't hide her disappointment and even Luke's promise to buy her another one didn't take away the huge sense of loss.

Although Luke didn't seem to think it was a big deal, it was hard for her to stop beating herself up over it. She'd screwed up. She would have to pay more attention and be more careful.

After taking Darlina to get her driver's license replaced and a new social security card ordered, Luke stopped at the same western wear store where he'd bought the purse. She picked out another one, but it wasn't the same and she still felt a sense of loss.

"Thank you, Luke. You know I don't deserve another purse though."

"Would you please stop beating yourself up? It was a simple mistake that anyone could make. It's no big deal."

"It is to me. That purse meant the world to me because you bought it for me, just like this necklace that I wear all the time." She reached up and lovingly touched the little gold heart necklace that was nestled around her slender neck. She would always treasure the necklace, because it was the first gift Luke had given her.

"Honey, it was just a purse. Don't worry. There'll be plenty more gifts 'cause I intend to buy you all the pretty things you deserve."

She wiped away a tear that trickled down her cheek. "I love you, Luke."

He leaned down kissing her gently, "I love you too. Now let's forget about all this shit and get happy again. Okay?"

"Okay."

"I'm gonna run you back to the house and go see the kids for a little while. You sure you're alright?"

"I'm sure. Go see your kids and enjoy them."

Once Luke had left, Darlina got the new purse out and began to try to replace what she'd lost. No matter how hard she tried, she couldn't shake the feeling that she'd lost something that could never be replaced.

When Luke returned, he walked in the door with a newly purchased bottle of Jim Beam. From the look on his face, she could tell something was wrong.

"What happened, Luke?"

"That bitch wouldn't let me see the kids. Said she was done lettin' me just drop in whenever I want and from now on I'll have to call and make a damn appointment to see them."

"Oh no!"

"Well, I'm not settling for it. I pay the bills at that house and they're my kids. I'm gonna let her cool off and then I'll go back."

"I'm so sorry, honey. I know you were lookin' forward to seein' them. Any idea why she would do that?"

"I don't know. The bitch is crazy if she thinks I'm gonna stay away from my kids." He unscrewed the lid from the Jim Beam bottle and took a swig.

"Don't let her upset you. I know you'll figure something out."

"She can't keep me from seein' them. That's what I know."

He grabbed a Coke, a glass and a few ice cubes and then disappeared into his office and shut the door.

Darlina felt an instant apprehension. Why would Joyce all of a sudden decide to restrict Luke? She didn't understand that, but she did understand how much it hurt him. She glanced toward the closed door and her heart broke for him.

She busied herself in the kitchen by thawing out and cooking some of the venison from the freezer. She knew the only thing she could do was give Luke some room and hope that he would find peace with the situation.

After an hour, Luke emerged from the office, carrying the nearly full bottle of Jim Beam and his empty glass. Darlina instantly sensed he was in a lighter mood, and felt relief that he'd obviously only had a drink or two out of the bottle.

"Baby, I cooked us some venison. Feel like eating?" Darlina asked pleasantly.

He didn't reply, but walked over to her, put his arms around her and held her tight. "What would I do without you?" he asked.

"You'll never have to find out," she replied, turning into his arms and kissing him. "Why don't you fix me a drink and refill yours. Then, let's eat."

Luke fixed drinks, while Darlina placed delicious smelling food on the table and the two sat close together; eating, drinking and soaking up each other's warmth and love.

Darlina hadn't really known what to do to help Luke with his difficult situation, but she did know how to light up the house with her love. From the look in Luke's eyes, she knew she'd done what he'd needed the most. She felt that she was growing and learning more from each situation they faced together.

Perhaps this was what it felt like to really be a grown woman taking care of the man she loved; just the way she'd always dreamed about.

She reached across the short distance between them, took Luke's hand in hers and squeezed it. He looked deeply into her eyes, gently squeezed her hand in return and quietly they sat knowing conversation wasn't necessary. Their eyes and hearts said everything that was needed.

# Chapter 20

The next morning, Darlina overheard Luke on the phone. She knew he was talking to Joyce and from the side of the conversation she could hear, apparently the sour mood from yesterday had passed and she was telling Luke that he could come to see the kids.

As soon as he hung up the phone, he said, "Darlin', she said I could see the kids, so I'll be gone for a bit. Looks like she got over whatever bullshit she had going on yesterday."

"That's great, baby. Don't forget to stop by the dry cleaners and pick up your suits while you are out."

"Okay," he said, as he kissed the top of her head. "See you after while."

"Enjoy the kids," Darlina called out, as he went out the door.

By the time he returned, it was mid-afternoon. He'd started explaining to Darlina that he had to make a trip to Oklahoma and she couldn't go with him.

"Why can't I go with you, Luke?"

"Sugar, this is a business trip and I need for you to stay here."

Darlina looked away with tears welling up in her eyes and a lump forming in her throat. She didn't understand why Luke wouldn't let her go to Oklahoma with him. With each passing day, the closeness between them grew. They did most everything together and now all of a sudden, he didn't want her to accompany him.

"I'll stay because it's what you want, but I'd rather be with you."

"I know honey, but this is a trip I need to take without you. Johnny's going with me."

"Johnny? Why not Red?"

"Because I need Red to stay here too. I've already got it arranged. After the gig tomorrow night at The Oasis, I'm takin' you to Sherry's apartment. I'll pick you up from there when I get back."

"Really? Why Sherry's?"

"Guess you'll find out sooner or later. Johnny's livin' with Sherry. Him and Louise split."

"Oh no! I didn't know. So, is Sherry dancin' with me tomorrow night?"

"Yep. Then we'll drop you girls off and high-tail it to Oklahoma. We oughta' be back sometime in the afternoon."

"Why do you have to go in the middle of the night? Wouldn't it be better to wait 'til mornin'?"

"I need to be there when everything opens. You gotta trust me on this, sugar."

"I do trust you, Luke."

"Then stop questioning me. This is the way it has to be," he said, with growing agitation in his voice.

"Okay, baby. I'm sorry."

Luke wrapped his arms around her. "Nothin' to be sorry for. Just trust me."

No matter how hard she tried, Darlina couldn't shake the feeling that something wasn't right but there was nothing to be gained by badgering him.

It'd been a while since she'd danced with the Rebel Rousers and she looked forward to it.

With the holidays past, life had returned to normal again for Darlina. The band returned to playing the nightly gigs and she occupied her place beside Luke with more confidence than ever. With each struggle they went through, their bond became stronger.

Their conversation was interrupted by the ringing of the telephone. Luke went to answer it.

"Hello."

Darlina could only hear Luke's part of the conversation, but his voice immediately took on sharpness.

"Dammit, I told you I'd get what you need. I'm leavin' after the gig tomorrow night."

Again, Darlina was haunted with a feeling that something wasn't right. She went into the kitchen and left Luke with privacy to complete his conversation.

She couldn't stop thinking about all of it. The strange way Luke was acting, the fact that he didn't want to leave her at their house alone, and the edge in his voice on the phone. She hoped he wasn't involved in something that could hurt him.

Later that night at the It'll Do Club, Darlina saw the three men who had come to their apartment a few weeks back. She remembered Big Royce from the first night she'd gone out to hear Luke and the Rebel Rousers play. The other two, she only recognized from seeing them briefly at the apartment.

Luke seemed particularly on edge. He'd hardly gotten on the stage at all and sat beside Darlina with his arm protectively around her.

Big Royce approached the table. "Hey, hoss. Mind if we sit here?"

Darlina felt the muscles in Luke's arm tighten. "Suit yourself."

The three men pulled out chairs and sat with Luke and Darlina.

Big Royce appeared to be the spokesperson for the group. "Howdy, young lady."

"Hello," she replied.

"Luke, how come you're not up there entertaining us tonight?" Butch questioned.

"Reckon I ain't feelin' much like entertaining tonight," Luke snapped.

"Shit man. We came out tonight to hear you sing," Big Royce said, slapping Luke on the back.

"Guess you're gonna have to catch me in a better singin' mood," Luke said. "How about we go outside so we can talk?"

Big Royce nodded and the three stood up.

"I'll be right back, sugar."

"Sure, baby." She sensed that Luke's uneasiness had something to do with the three men, even though they appeared to be friends.

She also noticed that as Luke stood up with the three men; Red laid his guitar down on the stage and quietly slipped out the back door. The rest of the band kept playing.

Something was going on, but she thought it best to do as Luke asked, so she sat quietly at the table.

Rita reached across the table, laying a reassuring hand on her arm. "Don't worry, Darlina. They're Luke's friends."

"I sure hope so," she replied with a worried tone in her voice.

Luke and Red came back into the club through the back door a few minutes later. Both went straight to the stage and picked up their instruments.

As soon as the band finished the song they were in the middle of, Luke stepped up to the mic. "I want to send this next song out to some friends of mine here tonight and you know who you are."

He hit the guitar strings hard and began singing, "Take this job and shove it. I ain't workin' here no more..."

He looked over at Darlina and winked at her as if to say everything was alright. She thought he looked dashing in his gray mock Confederate suit, white boots and white hat. He appeared as though he was ready to step out on the battlefield to fight for the cause. Her heart beat steadily with love for her rebel.

She looked around the darkened smoky club and found that the three men were still there, standing at the bar drinking. Big Royce let out a big whoop as Luke sang.

The rest of the night passed without incident and Luke's mood seemed to lighten. Whatever was going on between the men, she was relieved that there was no fighting involved and no torn bloody clothes or busted lips.

Luke had returned to his old routine of emptying a bottle of Jim Beam every couple of days or so. He was back to the way Darlina knew him before the fever. She almost regretted losing the Luke she'd gotten a glimpse of during those weeks when he didn't drink at all. As far as she knew, he'd still not taken any pills and she certainly hadn't. She secretly blamed the pills for the onset of the fever.

Later that night, on the way home from the gig, Darlina casually asked Luke, "Honey, those three men at the club tonight; do they have anything to do with you going to Oklahoma?"

He took a big swig of his Jim Beam and Coke before replying nonchalantly. "Nah. They're just old friends of mine. Don't worry your pretty head about anything."

"I just can't help feeling that something isn't right and I love you so I do worry."

He wrapped his arms around her reassuringly. "Why don't you let me do all the worrying? I've heard it causes wrinkles."

She grinned at him. "Well, I sure don't want wrinkles."

"Then let me take care of things. You just worry about taking care of me."

"I love doing that part."

He leaned down and kissed her gently. She sighed and snuggled closer to him. Whatever the problem was, it was plain to her she would have to let Luke handle it.

Luke awoke early the next day. "Sugar, I've got some errands to run, bills to pay and I'm gonna go see my kids again."

"Alright. Hope she'll let you in this time. Think you oughta' call first?"

"Nah. I think she got the burr out of her ass."

He got dressed, while Darlina made breakfast and coffee. She no longer felt the anxiety from yesterday and fully trusted Luke to handle whatever it was.

"Sweetheart, breakfast is ready," she called from the kitchen.

"Be right there."

She heard a knock on the kitchen door. Goodness, it looked like everyone was up early today. She opened the door and was surprised to find Luke's father, Al, standing there. "Al! Come in. What a nice surprise."

Al entered the kitchen just as Luke came out from the bedroom. "Dad! What are you doin' here? Is everything okay?"

"Yeah, everything's okay. I was just in town and thought I'd drop by and say howdy."

"Glad you did. How about a cup of coffee?" Luke offered.

"I believe I will, but I don't wanna interrupt your breakfast."

"You're not. Want something to eat? Darlina will fix you some eggs and bacon if you're hungry."

"No, I ate before I left the house. I will take a cup of coffee though." He sat down at the kitchen table, lighting a cigarette.

Darlina got a cup from the cabinet, filled it with steaming black coffee and handed it to Al.

"It's not often you drop by, dad. Are you sure everything's alright?"

"I'm sure, son. Like I say, I came to town and was thinkin' about you. I was afraid you wouldn't be awake yet."

Luke chuckled. "It wouldn't be the first time you caught me in bed, would it dad?"

Al fidgeted, glancing toward Darlina. "Now son; I don't think it'd be very nice to bring that up."

"Bring what up?" Darlina questioned.

"Dad stopped by one morning to visit and caught me in bed with two ol' gals. I think it embarrassed him."

"Well, it sure did. Can't understand what one man would need with two women. Hell, one's plenty enough for anybody."

Darlina laughed at Al's uneasiness with the subject. "Well, as long as I'm here with Luke, you won't have to worry about that happenin', Al."

"That's good to know. I've been tryin' to talk mama into having you two come out to the house some Sunday afternoon for fried chicken and maybe a game or two of dominoes."

"Let me guess," Luke said. "She ain't likin' that idea."

"You know your mama son. To her, you're still married to Joyce and she can't tolerate you bein' with another woman. No offense, little lady."

"None taken, Al. I totally understand."

"Well dad, you and I both know it's damned near impossible to change mom's mind when she gets it set on something," he took a sip of coffee. "But I do appreciate you trying."

"I'd just like to see you more often. We see Bobby pert near every day and it looks like him, Cindy, and the kids will be movin' back in with us. I swear that boy can't keep a job."

"I'm sorry to hear that. He can work with me all he wants, but he has to stay sober."

"That seems to be the problem. Anyway, me and mama will help all we can."

"Dad, I hate to run, but I've got to go pay some bills and go see the kids. I went the other day to see 'em and Joyce wouldn't let me in."

"You know I hate to say anything bad about anyone, but she can be pretty hateful sometimes. Last time me and mama went by, she told us the kids were asleep, but we could hear them inside the house. She's got a big chip on her shoulder."

"I guess so, dad. Anyway, you can stay as long as you'd like. Darlina would love to visit with you, wouldn't you, sweetheart?"

"Of course. Stay as long as you'd like Al."

"I appreciate that, but guess I'd better be moseying along too. It's good to see you kids."

"Good to see you too. Give mama my love."

"I will. Goodbye, little lady."

Darlina gave Al a quick hug. "Stop by anytime you want. You're always welcome here."

Luke gave Darlina a hug and kiss. He then followed his father out the door.

As she gathered their dishes and cleaned up the kitchen, she thought about Luke's family and wondered if she'd ever be accepted as a part of it.

She wished there was something she could do to help win over Mrs. Stone. She knew in her heart that, just as with her own mother, as long as Luke was married to Joyce, she'd never be fully accepted.

She was content loving Luke exactly as things were, but dared to dream what it would be like to actually become Mrs. Luke Stone. She allowed her mind to wander as she washed the dishes and pictured herself in a flowing white gown saying wedding vows with Luke standing beside her.

She brought herself back to the present and tucked that daydream away for safe keeping. Maybe someday it could be a reality. For now, she was just Darlina Flowers, the little holy-roller girl from the New Mexico desert, who was in love; truly in love. For now, that was enough as long as Luke was by her side.

# Chapter 21

Later that evening, a heavy fog set in, making it difficult to see the road. Darlina breathed a sigh of relief when she saw the neon sign of the Oasis club up ahead. It blinked on and off, distorted by the thick fog. The Oasis sat at the edge of town and was one of the biggest and newest nightclubs in Abilene.

Luke and Darlina had driven Luke's T-bird since he was leaving for Oklahoma right after the gig. Darlina was quiet, lost in her thoughts while radio station KWKC blasted out one country hit after another.

Luke glanced over at her. "You've been very quiet since we left the house. Wanna tell me what's on your mind?"

"I'm sure you know what's on my mind. This trip you're taking to Oklahoma, in the middle of the night, has me worried."

"Honey, I told you to let me do the worrying for us. It's perfectly safe and I'll be back before you know it."

She sighed. "I hope so. I don't know what I'd do if anything ever happened to you."

"Nothin's gonna happen. It's just a business trip. You need to get your head off that and start gettin' excited about dancin' tonight. Here." Luke reached in his pocket and took out a small bottle. He opened it and handed Darlina one of the pink hearts he'd bought in Mexico. He then popped two black capsules in his mouth and swallowed them down with a swig of Coke.

Darlina accepted the pill and broke it in half. "I guess I need somethin' to get me feelin' good. What did you just take?"

"They're called Black Mollies and they'll keep me good and awake for the trip."

"I don't intend to lay my head down and sleep until you're back."

"Sugar, please don't worry. I promise this is nothing to be concerned about. Now lighten up and let's go give these people a show." He put the bottle back in his pocket and lit a King Edward cigar.

"You're right, baby. I truly am excited about dancin' tonight."

"That's more like it." He reached across the seat for Darlina's hand and she scooted closer to him.

Maybe everything would be okay. Perhaps the pill would make her feel good again and quit worrying. She lay her head on his shoulder and when he'd come to a stop in the parking lot of The Oasis, he leaned down and kissed her soft full lips.

"Now put a smile on that pretty face and let's go entertain some folks."

"Okay. Let's go give 'em a show," she said as she gave herself one last look in the rearview mirror.

Inside the sprawling nightclub, an early Thursday night crowd had already gathered. Couples danced to the juke box, cowboys played pool and the atmosphere was charged with energy. Within minutes, Darlina let her worries fade away and started to relax.

The rest of the band was already there setting up the equipment. Luke showed Darlina where she would be changing clothes and then went to help finish setting up. She sat her bag on a small table in the dressing room and hurried back to join the others.

She'd just sat down at the table reserved for the band when Sherry and Johnny come in. They immediately went to the dance floor. As they danced, Sherry jumped up and wrapped her legs around Johnny's waist. Watching them, it occurred to Darlina that Luke had never danced with her. He was always on the bandstand. For a moment, she wished he would come down and dance one dance with her. That was the downside of being a musician's lady. They were always making the music for everyone else to enjoy.

The song came to an end and Sherry and Johnny made their way to the table, where she sat. Darlina stood and hugged Sherry, then Johnny. "Hey you two...looked like you were enjoying yourselves out there."

Sherry laughed; throwing her arms around Johnny's neck. "I can't speak for Johnny, but I sure was."

Johnny gave Sherry a resounding slap on the bottom. "I see you're still hanging with that sorry assed ol' musician," he said to Darlina teasingly.

"Yep, sure am," she replied laughing.

Johnny pulled out a chair for Sherry. "Why don't you sit here with Darlina? I'm gonna go aggravate Luke and the band."

Sherry sat down and Johnny walked up to the bandstand.

Darlina turned to Sherry and looked her straight in the eye. "Well, miss high and mighty, who couldn't tell me enough bad things about Luke. Looks like you need to practice what you preach."

"I don't know what you're talkin' about," she said, with a grin and twinkle in her eye.

"When did you start going with Johnny?"

"A few weeks ago. I'd always see him around the clubs and then one night he asked if he could take me home. I told him I didn't date married men and that's when he told me that he and Louise had split."

"Well, I do have to say you look happy."

"I am, Darlina. I think I could really fall in love with Johnny."

"Then I'm happy for you. It's about time you settled on one man."

The girls' conversation was interrupted by the men returning to the table, along with the rest of the band members.

Luke hugged Sherry. "Hi, sugar. Are you ready to dance tonight?"

Enthusiastically, she replied, "Damn right I am."

"Then you girls need to go get changed and ready. It's almost time to start and I wanna bring you up in the first set."

Darlina jumped to her feet excitedly. "Honey, will you order me a Coke and whatever Sherry wants, while we go get dressed?"

Luke grabbed her around the waist and playfully held her. "I don't know if I wanna let you out of my sight long enough to go change clothes. You are beautiful tonight, baby."

She laughed carelessly, looking up into Luke's face. "And you are mighty handsome yourself, cowboy, but we do need to go get ready to dance." She liked that Luke made her feel all woman. "Come on, Sherry, let's go get ready."

Sherry picked up her bag and followed Darlina to the dressing room.

Darlina couldn't help noticing that she was beginning to feel euphoric, and thought about the foolish worrying she'd done over Luke's trip. Now it was time to relax, have a good time, put on a good show and let Luke handle the rest.

Once the girls were in their go-go costumes and walking back into the club, they were greeted with whistles and catcalls from the men nearby.

Johnny jumped up on the table and beat his chest, while making Tarzan like jungle sounds.

As they approached the table, he jumped off, grabbed Sherry and twirled her around.

Luke said teasingly, "Hey, stud, she's on the clock now. Don't handle the merchandise."

He threw a playful punch at Luke, "I'm with the band, asshole. I've got privileges."

"I'll show you privileges, you crazy little bastard," Luke replied.

The mood of everyone in the group was lighthearted and it was time to kick-off the show.

By the time Luke called the girls up to dance, the club was filled to capacity. The response from the crowd was overwhelmingly enthusiastic. Darlina felt as though she was walking on air and the top of her head tingled. She and Sherry danced the way they'd both been taught and the crowd cheered them on, with some of the men even tossing money onto the stage.

During the course of the night, Luke had the girls come on stage and dance four different times. Each time they were eagerly received. Darlina felt that she and Sherry complimented each other. She was tall and willowy with long hair and Sherry was shorter, with shoulder length brunette hair and lots of curves. Because Marketa had taught both of them to dance, they did a lot of similar moves in unison; almost as if it was choreographed.

Soon, Luke was announcing last call and the band played a rousing version of *Pusher Man*. Johnny grabbed both girls and pulled them out on the dance floor with him. They were still dressed in their go-go costumes and people on the dance floor formed a circle around them; clapping and cheering.

Darlina laughed as she threw her head back; tossing her long auburn hair. Sherry gyrated her hips and shimmied her boobs and both girls motioned to everyone around them to join in and dance.

Once the song was finished, Luke stepped up to the mic. "And that one, ladies and gentlemen, you got for free. Thank ya'll for coming out tonight to hear the Rebel Rousers. You don't have to go home, but you do have to leave here. We'll catch you down the road. Be safe."

Sherry and Darlina headed for their dressing room to change back into their street clothes. Darlina looped her arm through Sherry's and the two girls playfully skipped along like two children.

Johnny and Sherry left the club before Luke and Darlina and as they were leaving, Johnny shouted to Luke, "Ya'll just come on in when you get there. The door will be unlocked."

Luke helped the band load up the equipment. Then he collected the money and paid everyone. Darlina noticed Luke and Red standing apart from everyone, talking in very serious tones. She wished she could hear their conversation, but reminded herself that she'd decided not to worry.

Now that the show was over and Darlina knew Luke would be leaving shortly, the apprehension came back full force. She was determined to shake it off and hold on to the euphoric feeling.

Luke's long strides brought him to where she was waiting. "You ready to go, sugar?"

She bravely forced a smile. "Yes, I'm ready."

Sherry lived in an apartment building with four units. When Darlina and Luke arrived, just as Johnny had said, the door was unlocked, so Luke opened it and they went in.

Neither Johnny nor Sherry was anywhere to be seen and Luke called out. "Johnny. Where are ya'll at?"

He replied from the bedroom. "Ya'll make yourselves at home. We'll be out in a minute."

Luke poured himself a drink and offered one to Darlina before they sat on the couch. She curled up next to him and he put his arm around her, holding her tight. They could hear the sounds of love making coming from the bedroom and Luke looked down at her. "Guess ol' Johnny's gettin' a piece of ass before we head to Oklahoma."

She smiled and snuggled closer. "Sure sounds like it. How about you?"

Luke chuckled. "Darlin', I always want you anytime day or night, but I won't disrespect you by making love to you here, on Sherry's couch, with them right in the next room. You don't deserve that."

"Luke, you gotta promise me that you'll come back safe and sound."

"I promise," he said, brushing the top of her head with his lips.

"I took the other half of the pink heart and I won't close my eyes until you're back."

"Okay, sweetheart. Just don't worry." He got up from the couch and thumbed through Sherry's record collection. "Here's a record I want you to listen to while I'm gone. It's Joan Baez and there's two songs on here that are magic songs for me; *Go 'Way From My Window* and *I Still Miss Someone*. You listen to this 'til I get back and it will make good magic for me."

She took the record album from him and noted the two songs he mentioned. "Okay, honey. I will."

Johnny came from the bedroom tucking his shirt in his pants. "You ready to ride, hoss?"

"I've been ready you little bastard. Let's hit the road."

Luke kissed Darlina, Johnny kissed Sherry and then they were gone.

Darlina felt tears come close to spilling, but determined not to cry, she turned to Sherry. "Show me how to work your record player. I want to listen to this record."

Sherry turned the stereo on and loaded the record on the spindle. Soon Joan Baez's soothing voice was coming out of the speakers. "When you get ready to go to sleep, I'll make the couch out for you."

"I won't be going to sleep. I took a pink heart tonight."

"I thought you were high at the club," she grinned. "I had a white cross and I'm not sleepy either. We'll just talk and listen to music until the men get back."

"Johnny sure seems to be crazy about you."

"I'm crazy about him. We really fit together. The only problem I see for us is that Johnny uses drugs with a needle and that scares me."

Darlina had never been around anyone who did drugs with a needle, but it sounded dangerous to her. "Why does he do that?"

"I don't know. He says he got started a year or so ago and now he thinks he needs it. I hope I can help him get off it."

"I hope so too, Sherry. Luke feels really close to Johnny. Wonder if he knows."

"He knows. Johnny told me that Luke made him shoot him up one time. He said he begged Luke not to make him, but he insisted. He said that Luke only did it that one time and never asked him again. Said he just wanted to see what made Johnny like it so much."

"How about you? Have you ever done it with him?"

"Hell no! I don't use needles and if I have anything to do with it, Johnny will quit."

"Well, I sure hope he can."

The record player continued playing and the girls sat talking for hours. The next time Darlina looked out the window, the sun was coming up. She wondered where Luke was now and what he was doing. She trusted him, but at the same time feared that he might be in danger.

There were lots of questions and not many answers. But for now, Darlina listened to the words of the song playing. *"Go 'way from my window. Go 'way from my door. Go 'way from my bedside and bother me no more..."*

Why had Luke wanted her to listen to that song? She understood why he wanted her to listen to *I Still Miss Someone* and she did miss him deep down. The hours seemed to drag by and she was anxious for him to be back. She believed with all her heart that he would return, as he promised, safe and sound. Her world was only right when he was with her. She couldn't bear the thought of something happening to take him away from her.

# Chapter 22

Darlina felt her heart leap inside her chest when Luke and Johnny came bounding through the door, like a couple of school boys, at three o'clock in the afternoon. They were both in high spirits. She jumped to her feet and flew into Luke's arms.

"Oh, baby! I'm so glad you are back. That was the longest night of my life."

Luke planted a searing kiss on her lips. "I'm glad to be back, sweetheart. Let's go home."

The two of them said their goodbyes to Sherry and Johnny and were soon on the road between Abilene and Brownwood. Darlina sat close to Luke and they talked non-stop.

"Did you get all your business tended to?" she asked Luke.

"Sure did and even scared us up a couple of gigs. We're gonna be playing Fort Sill in March. That'll be another great place for you girls to dance."

"That's wonderful! Me and Sherry dance real good together."

"Yes you do. I'm thinkin' I'll make her the other regular go-go girl. What do you think?"

"I love that idea. Hope it doesn't cause problems with Louise, though."

"Sugar, there aren't gonna be any problems. What's between Louise, Johnny and Sherry has nothin' to do with puttin' on a show."

"I know, but I really like Louise and don't want her to be mad at us."

Luke chuckled. "You haven't learned yet...I don't put up with any petty bullshit. She'll be just fine. She's got a good head on her shoulders and is probably glad Sherry's got Johnny occupied, so he'll leave her alone."

"Maybe you're right. Sherry seems to be fallin' in love with him."

"Yeah, he talked about her all the damn way to Oklahoma. I think they've got it bad for each other. I'm just glad to be back beside you."

"Me too, baby. I can't wait to get home. I listened to the Joan Baez record over and over. I think I know all the words to every song on it now."

"You're magic for me, sweetheart. Probably more than you can possibly know."

"I love bein' your magic. I want to be your everything."

Luke kept his arm around her the entire seventy eight miles back to Brownwood, as the car flew down the highway. Darlina glanced at the speedometer and gasped when she realized Luke was driving ninety miles an hour.

"Honey, slow down. I don't want you to get a ticket or wreck us."

Luke laughed. "I'm not going to do either, sweetheart, but I am gonna get us back to Brownwood so I can make love to your sexy little body."

"Oh baby, I want you too, in the worst way. I don't ever want to have to spend another night away from you."

"I'm damn glad we're playin' in Brownwood tonight so we don't have to get right back on the road."

"Me too. Luke, how come you've never danced with me?"

"Sugar, if I ever dance with you, you'll know the answer to that question. I never learned how because I was always makin' the music. I hear a different beat than a normal person and I'd step all over your feet."

"Let's just try sometime. Ok?"

"Alright. It's your feet that'll be in danger."

"I think I can handle the danger. At least I'm willin' to take the risk," Darlina said with a playful smile.

Within minutes, they were pulling into the driveway in Brownwood. They hurried into the house and into each other's arms like two love starved teenagers.

Darlina lay contentedly next to Luke, her head on his chest, listening to the rise and fall of his breath and the beating of his heart. She felt relieved that the Oklahoma trip was over. Whatever he hadn't wanted to tell her, seemed unimportant now that he was back beside her.

He smoothed her hair and kissed the top of her head. "Darlin', we gotta get up from here and get ready to go play some music. Why don't you hop in the shower while I go next door and talk to Red for a minute?"

"Alright." She rose up on one elbow and kissed him gently. "Thank you."

"For what?"

"For coming back to me in one piece."

"I told you I would. You just gotta learn to trust me. I'll never steer you wrong."

"I do, Luke. Really I do."

"Then get your sweet little ass up and let's get ready to go give the ol' Traveller's crowd a show."

As she turned on the water in the shower, she heard the back door close. She hummed a *Joan Baez* tune as the warm water ran over her head and body. She was happy and content and swore to herself that she would never doubt Luke again.

Luke knocked lightly on Red's front door. From inside, Red called out, "Come in."

Luke let himself in and found Red sitting half dressed at his table. He was drinking a warm beer and eating cold left over fried chicken. "You made it back, hoss. Want some chicken?"

"Nah. I'm not hungry. Yeah, I'm back and I got what we needed. Plus, I picked us up a couple of gigs."

"Big Royce has called twice today and I told him I'd let 'em know when you were back. They seem mighty anxious this time."

"Call the fat bastard and set up a meeting tomorrow at the Red Wagon. I don't want 'em comin' here right now."

"Alright. What time tomorrow?"

"Let's say two o'clock."

"I'll call 'em right now while you're here."

Red picked up the phone and dialed. "Royce, is that you? Hey man, Luke's back. Tomorrow at two, he wants to meet at the Red Wagon. That alright with you?"

Luke's voice turned hard and brittle. He was past caring and just wanted to be done with the whole mess. "I don't give a damn if it's alright with them or not. They better be there."

Red held the phone away from his ear so Luke could hear Royce on the other end. "I heard him. Tell the sonofabitch we'll see you tomorrow."

Red hung up the phone and he and Luke sat in silence for a brief minute. Red broke the silence. "You still want out?"

"Yeah, I still want out. I've got a bad feelin'."

"I'm with you. Whatever you want to do, I've got your back."

"I know, stud. If things start to break bad, I want Darlina out of all this. I don't know how I'm gonna do it, but she don't deserve to be drug into this mess."

"I hope you're wrong about shit breakin' bad, but I agree with you, she don't deserve it. I can tell you right now man, that little lady's gonna be hard to shake. She loves you, Luke."

Luke sighed heavily. "I know she does and I love her too. That's why I'll do anything to make sure she doesn't wind up in a bunch of shit because of me."

"Well, let's hope you don't ever have to worry about it."

"Me too. Hey, I'm gonna go get ready to go. We're ridin' with you to the Traveller's."

"Alright, hoss. I'll be ready. Jerry and I cleaned the band trailer out this morning and unloaded all the shit we've been haulin' around that we ain't usin'."

"Thank you, man. See you in a bit."

Luke entered the apartment to the sound of Darlina humming. He walked into the bedroom, where he found her getting dressed. He thought to himself that she was looking thin and made a mental note to make sure she ate more regularly.

She looked up as he came in. "Red alright?"

"Yeah. Sugar, will you polish my brown boots while I shower?"

"Of course."

"After the gig tonight, we're gonna go eat. You're gettin' too skinny."

"I'm not really hungry, Luke, but we probably do need to eat somethin'."

As she finished dressing, she heard him singing from the shower a song she'd never heard.

"*You wanted everything I'm not and I guess that's what you got, but he could never love you half as much as me.*"

When he came back into the bedroom, she questioned. "I've never heard that song before. Is it a new one?"

"It's one I've got rollin' around in my head. Don't have it finished yet."

"I love it. I want to hear the whole thing when you get it done."

She was sitting on the floor polishing his boots and he knelt down behind her, wrapping his arms around her. "You'll hear it, baby. You'll be the first to hear it."

She turned her face toward his and their lips met in a tender kiss. "I love it here with you, Luke."

He sighed. "You make me a very happy man, sweetheart."

The Travellers was packed with the regular Brownwood crowd. Darlina felt more and more at home sitting at the band table, listening to the band and watching Luke perform. He sang several new songs she hadn't heard before and one in particular caught her attention.

"*It's the thirty third of August and I'm finally comin' down. Eight days from Sunday finds me Saturday bound...*"

She pondered over the lyrics and tried to figure out what they meant. She made a mental note to ask Luke and she'd also tell him how good he sounded tonight.

Luke turned to Red on the stage and said something to him. He then sat his guitar down and came to the table where Darlina sat, as Red started singing *Silver Wings*.

Luke stopped in front of her. "Can I have this dance?"

She grinned from ear to ear as she replied, "You certainly can."

Luke was right about one thing. He was no dancer. She loved being in his arms even though she had to constantly move her feet out of the way to keep them from getting stepped on. It warmed her heart that he'd remembered her request. The effort he was putting forth to do something he was no good at, just because she asked, only made her love him more. She nestled her face against his chest as they moved awkwardly on the dance floor.

"If we're gonna try to do this very much, I'll have to buy you a pair of steel toed boots."

Darlina looked up at him and laughed. "I hate to say it, but you might be right. I love you even more for trying though."

"I'd do most anything for you, sweetheart."

"I know. Me too."

He held her close until the song ended; walked her to the table, held the chair for her and got back on stage. He winked at her and she blew him a kiss. She would never forget that he'd tried to dance with her just because she'd asked. She breathed a happy sigh of contentment.

Nothing could take the smile from her face or the song from her heart. It was all because of the rebel of a man she'd accidentally fallen in love with. Every sacrifice ever made was worth it, just to be with him. She knew she'd go to the ends of the earth and back for him and was beginning to believe he would do the same for her. After all, wasn't that what true love was all about?

# Chapter 23

Luke awoke early the next morning. Very quietly, he slipped out of bed and into a pair of faded blue jeans. He moved stealthily so as not to awaken Darlina.

After starting a pot of coffee, he sat down in a chair across from the bed and picked up his guitar. He strummed lightly on the strings, enjoying the feel of them under his fingertips. He'd always said his fingers were never meant to be those of a musician because they were too big and as he played, they would flatten out on the ends. Nevertheless, he loved everything about the guitar and the words that flowed with the melodies from it.

That morning, there was a song he'd dreamed a few nights ago haunting his thoughts. He sang softly as he strummed, "'Til the end of the earth, with a heart that is true, I'll be waiting here, in love land for you..."

He looked at Darlina lying peacefully asleep, her long hair draped across the pillow. He was suddenly filled with a realization that he was being very selfish to think he could have a life with her and to allow her to think the same. He knew he wasn't being fair. It was too late to start over and things were just too tangled to ever get free.

A deep sadness came over him as he accepted what he had to do. He didn't know exactly what, when or where, but he had to do something that would make her want to leave. Playing the part of an asshole came naturally to him, so he had no doubt he could pull it off, but whether or not she'd go for it was another question.

He sighed, took a sip of coffee and continued strumming. He also knew today wasn't the day and so for now, they would continue living this fantasy of having a life together. He vowed to soak up every bit of sweetness and love she showed him for later times when there would be a drought.

She stirred, rubbing her eyes sleepily, then opened them and fixed her gaze on Luke sitting across from the bed. "Mornin', baby."

"Mornin'," he said, as he leaned the guitar against the end table. "I've got some coffee made."

"How long have you been up?" She sat up in the bed, glancing at the clock and saw that it was 10:30.

"Oh for a while. Had a song haunting me that I had to get written down."

She smiled as she swung her long shapely legs over the side of the bed. "I wanna hear it."

"Come here," Luke invited, patting his lap.

She glided across the room, sat on his lap, draped her arms around his neck and nestled her head against his neck. "What, baby?"

"You gotta know I love you, Darlina Flowers."

"I do know, Luke, and I love you too."

"No matter what happens, you've gotta keep that close to your heart and know that everything I do is for your own good."

"Alright, but nothin' is gonna happen. I'm always gonna be here with you."

He sighed. "I'd like that."

"Me too," she replied raising her mouth to meet his.

He patted her on the bottom. "Let's get some breakfast. I'm hungry."

She reluctantly took her arms from around his neck and raised herself up off his lap. While slipping into a pair of jeans and sweatshirt, she said, "How about I make us pancakes, sausage and eggs this morning?"

"Sounds good. I've got a meeting this afternoon with some folks and I'll be gone for a while. Figure I'll run by and see the kids first."

"I think that's an excellent idea. I need to do some laundry, so maybe you could drop me off at the Laundromat."

"I'll just give you the keys to the T-Bird and you can drive it. Red's going with me to the meeting, so he can go with me to see the kids too."

"Okay. I can do a little grocery shopping for us too. Why don't you buzz Red and see if he wants to come eat breakfast with us?"

"Good idea. That way, I can make sure his lazy ass is up."

Luke buzzed the intercom, and then called into the kitchen. "He'll be here, baby."

Luke headed for the shower, while Darlina busied herself in the kitchen making breakfast. He could hear her humming as she fried the sausage, grilled some fluffy pancakes and made eggs over-easy.

By the time she was finished, Luke was out of the shower and there was a light knock on the back door.

She opened the door, gave Red a quick hug, and then the three of them sat down to a steaming hot breakfast.

As soon as they were finished eating, Luke handed Darlina the keys to the T-Bird and two twenty dollar bills. He kissed her and said, "I'll be back after while, sweetheart. Just do whatever you need to, and can you get my clothes ready for the gig tonight? I'm wearin' the brown bolero jacket and pants with the conchos."

"Sure, honey. Bye, Red. See ya'll later."

Once the two men were in the car, Red asked Luke, "Got what we need to take to Butch?"

"Oh shit! Glad you thought to ask me." It's in the glove box of the T-Bird. I'll be right back."

Luke got out of the car, walked over to the T-Bird and came back with a notebook under his arm. "Okay, let's roll, hoss."

When the two men arrived at Joyce's, she seemed relieved to see them. Ignoring Luke, she cordially spoke to Red. "Good to see you, Red. It's been a long time."

"Nice to see you too," Red replied.

As soon as the children heard the men's voices, they all came running with excitement.

"I've gotta be somewhere at two, Joyce, so make sure your ass is back here by then," Luke warned.

"I'll be back," she tossed over her shoulder, as she hurried out the door.

The men played with the children, giving each one of them individual attention. The boys wanted to wrestle and Lexxi wanted to dress up and show them how she'd learned to put on her mama's lipstick.

"You look stupid, Lexxi," Joseph taunted. "Besides, mama's gonna tan your hide for gettin' in her stuff."

Lexxi pouted. "No she won't if you don't tell on me."

Luke broke in, saying to both of them, "Now, don't you kids go tellin' on each other and tryin' to get each other in trouble. You need to stick together and look out for each other."

"Okay, daddy," Joseph promised.

They played Cowboys and Indians, had wrestling contests and ate snacks. Luke made sure the two younger boys didn't get hurt in any of the activities since they were smaller.

Lexxi looked up from playing with her dolls on the floor. "Mama's comin'."

Luke never failed to be amazed at her ability to know ahead of time that Joyce was on her way. Within five minutes, she walked in the door.

The two men said their goodbyes to the children, promising to visit again real soon, and then headed off to the Red Wagon to meet with Butch, Royce and Joe.

Luke and Red arrived first. They chose a table in the back of the restaurant and ordered glasses of iced tea. Luke was seated so that he could see the door and motioned to the three men when they entered.

He stood as they approached the table, feeling the muscles in his jaw tighten. "Royce, Butch, Joe; glad you could make it."

"Of course we made it. You've got something we need." Royce said.

"You guys want something to eat?" Luke offered

"I'll take a hamburger," Royce said.

Butch and Joe declined food but ordered coffee, which the waitress brought right away.

Red looked directly at Butch. "I think ya'll are gonna like what Luke's brought you."

"That's what we wanna hear," Butch said.

"I looked at a bunch of little towns and these two are the very best for what you are wanting. You take the highway out of Wichita Falls toward Lawton and before you get into Lawton, turn off to the right on Highway 53. That'll take you to Walters and Comanche."

"Let's see what you've got." Butch took a sip of his coffee.

Royce was engrossed in wolfing down his hamburger, but pushed it aside as Luke brought out his notebook.

For the next hour, the five men poured over the pages Luke ripped out of his notebook, along with a map Butch spread out on the table.

Luke watched the men, thinking to himself that of the three, he liked Indian Joe the best. He'd seen him in action and knew he always carried a pistol in his boot. He was a man of few words, but when he did speak, folks tended to listen.

Royce was a big overgrown bear of a man who loved living, drinking, dancing, eating and courting women.

Butch was the one he trusted the least, even though he'd never given him any particular reason. He was the one that did all the planning for them.

He'd known the men for years. They all came out to the clubs where he played and over time they'd formed a sort of friendship. It was only within the past year, that they had brought Luke and Red in on their business.

Now, Luke was done and he would make that clear to them today. The foreboding lingered strong inside of him and it continued eating away at him, no matter how hard he tried to get past it.

Finally, Butch spoke. "Luke this is a helluva job and it's gonna be very profitable." He took a stack of hundred dollar bills out of his coat pocket and passed them under the table to Luke. "This is for the last one."

Luke took the money and slipped it into his pocket, unnoticed. "I told you before that this is the last one for me and I still mean it. I'm out."

Royce answered before Butch could reply. "We hear you, Luke. After these two, we're gonna lay low for a while. Joe's headin' back to Tennessee, Butch is going to Angelo and I'm gonna stay in Abilene."

"We'll see if you still feel this way after things cool off," Butch stated.

"I will."

"Okay, man. We'll have some more money for you in a few of weeks."

"I'll have Red come pick it up. Just let us know where and when."

Butch folded the map, gathered Luke's papers then pushed his chair back. "Thank you, Luke. You won't regret this."

"I already do," Luke replied, as he also pushed back his chair.

The five men stood and walked out of the restaurant after paying for their food and drinks.

Once they were out on the sidewalk, they went their separate ways.

Luke was again overcome with the feeling that someone was watching but after looking around in all directions, didn't see anyone or anything out of the ordinary.

As they got back in the car, with Red driving, Luke said, "Red Hoss, stop at Ruby's flower shop before we go home. I want to get Darlina some flowers."

"Alright."

The minute Luke walked into the shop, he knew what he wanted. There was a bouquet of six red roses arranged in a pretty vase, with fresh baby's breath and green fern surrounding them. He held it on his lap, while Red drove back to their apartments.

"She's gonna like those, Luke."

"They are beautiful and sweet just like her. Hoss, I know I'm gonna eventually have to do something to make her leave, but it's the hardest thing I'll ever do."

"What are you thinkin'?"

"I don't know. I just know it has to be done, but not today and not tomorrow. You'll know when and I'll need you to play along with me. It's for her own good."

"I'll do anything you ask."

"I know, Red, and I appreciate it."

Luke didn't see Darlina when he walked into the house, but he heard Johnny Cash's voice coming out of the stereo speakers in the bedroom.

She looked up from the ironing board when Luke walked through the door. Her eyes lit up like a Christmas tree when she saw the flowers. She ran to him, threw her arms around his neck and kissed him. "Oh baby, these are beautiful!"

"Just like you, sweetheart."

"Thank you so much." She took the vase and placed it on the end table beside the big cozy chair in the corner. "Did you have a good time with the kids and how did the meeting go?"

"We had a great time with the kids and the meeting went okay."

"I was just ironing your shirt for tonight. Got the laundry all done and a few groceries bought."

Luke walked up behind her, put his big hands around her slim waist and turned her around to face him. He then gave her a hot, deep searing kiss that he felt all the way down to his toes. He was a foolish man for wishing and wanting a life he couldn't have. A foolish man indeed, but he savored the moment and pushed the thought away that haunted him about having to end it. Not now, he told himself. There was time.

# Chapter 24

Several weeks had passed and it was now mid-February. Luke and Darlina had settled into a comfortable routine and life was good. Luke even dared to think, since his association with Butch, Royce and Joe had ended, the premonitions might have just been a case of nerves.

Darlina felt closer and more bonded to Luke with each passing day. She and Sherry were dancing regularly at Rebel Rouser's shows and things seemed to be good for everyone. She was looking forward to the Saturday night show at Dyess Air Force Base on the 20th, knowing they would be dancing again. Little did she know, it would be the very last time she'd ever dance on stage.

She decided to resurrect her blue go-go costume and add tassels along the bottom of the midriff top and along the top of the white shorts. Once again, she raided Luke's box of fabric decorations and found what she was looking for. The tassels were white, with blue sparkles interwoven through them. Once she had them sewn, she tried on the outfit for Luke's approval.

"What do you think baby?"

"Looks good to me. I think you oughta' wear it for the show at Dyess."

"That's what I had in mind. I wanted something a little different and I've worn the leather one the last two times. Glad you like it."

"I do like it. You girls sure have added a lot to our shows."

"It's been wonderful for me. Sometimes when I'm on stage dancing, I have to pinch myself to make sure I'm awake and not just dreamin'."

"Sweetheart, you've come a long way in the past few months. I've watched you blossom from an insecure girl into a confident woman. I'm very proud of you."

And so it went for the next few days. Things were good and there didn't seem to be anything that could cause it to change.

On February 19th, Luke Stone awoke in the early hours of morning, drenched with sweat and trembling from the disturbing dream he'd been in the midst of.

His grandmother had always told him he had the gift of "knowing". He'd often wondered if it was a gift or a curse. Whatever it was, he knew it was very real. He was shaken to the core and the premonition of a brewing storm bigger than anyone could imagine was revealed to him. He knew it was time.

As sleep evaded him, he carefully slipped out of their warm bed. He locked himself away in his office for several hours while he battled with the distasteful task he knew was at hand. No matter what, Darlina could not be caught with him in this storm. It was coming and there was no power on heaven or earth that could stop it.

As the sun rose and the day came alive, he still wasn't sure how he would do what needed to be done, but he did know it was time.

The phone rang at two o'clock in the afternoon. It was Johnny calling Luke.

"Hey, man. I'm sorry to have to tell you this, but Sherry's sick and can't dance for you tonight."

"Shit, I hate to hear that. Tell her to get well and I'll figure out something."

Darlina hearing the conversation, asked, "What's the problem, baby?"

"Sherry's sick and can't work tonight. I'll call Louise."

He picked up the phone and dialed. Darlina could tell from his end of the conversation that Louise was already committed for the night.

"Guess I'll call Dee Dee and see if she's available," he said to Darlina.

"That's a good idea. Hope she can do it."

He thumbed through his phone book and then dialed her number. "Hey sugar, it's Luke. You busy tonight?"

Again, Darlina could only hear his side of the conversation, but by the time he hung up the phone, she knew she'd be dancing with Dee Dee that night.

She didn't know Dee Dee well, but had no problem dancing with her. She trusted Luke and knew it would be alright.

Luke's mood through the remainder of the day deteriorated and by five o'clock he had begun to drink heavily. He chose to wear all black to the show and Darlina ironed his shirt and polished his boots for him.

By the time they left Brownwood to head to Abilene, he'd grown sullen and withdrawn from everyone. Darlina didn't know what was going on, but she stayed quietly by his side. She was confident that whatever was bothering Luke, would pass.

Once they reached the club, Luke seemed to purposely distance himself even further from her. She needed some answers. She caught Red by himself and questioned, "Red, do you know what's wrong with Luke tonight?"

"No, I just figured maybe you two had a spat or something."

"We didn't. Everything seemed fine until Sherry couldn't dance with me tonight and he had to call Dee Dee."

"Well, don't worry. He'll be alright." He patted her reassuringly on the arm.

She hoped he was right and re-focused her attention on helping to put on a show for the soldiers.

She and Dee Dee shared a small dressing room to change into their costumes. Dee Dee gushed with excitement, "I can't believe I'm gonna get to dance with the Rebel Rousers. I was so excited when Luke called me."

"Well, we're glad you were available tonight, otherwise I'd be trying to do it all by myself."

The girls took their places and waited for their cue to go on stage. They were met with the same enthusiastic response from this crowd that Darlina had seen everywhere they'd danced. She was pleased and hoped Luke would be happy too.

When the band took their first break, Luke came to the table where the girls sat. He seemed to purposely ignore Darlina and praised Dee Dee for doing a good job. She sat quietly, thinking he was just being a good boss and trying to make the new girl feel comfortable.

As the night wore on, Luke drank heavier and became more distant from Darlina. On the other hand, he gave Dee Dee a lot of attention. Darlina began to get agitated. She considered saying something, but thought Luke must have a reason for what he was doing, so she remained quiet. After all, he'd asked her to trust him, so that was what she was going to do.

When the show was over and the girls had changed back into their street clothes, Luke pulled Dee Dee aside and spoke to her privately.

As he talked to her, Darlina could see Dee Dee looking towards her, as if questioning him. Luke appeared to be persuading her about something and finally, Dee Dee agreed.

Darlina approached the two of them. "Hey, baby. Is everything alright?"

"Sure. We're about ready to head back to Brownwood." He put his arm familiarly around Dee Dee's waist.

Darlina was confused. What did Luke mean? Was Dee Dee coming back to Brownwood with them? She didn't know, but suddenly felt like an outsider and wished Luke would just talk to her.

When it came time to get in the car, Luke and Dee Dee got in the front seat together, leaving Darlina standing in total confusion. It became painfully clear to her what Luke's intention was and although somewhat reluctant and embarrassed, she got into the back seat.

She questioned Luke, but he wouldn't turn around or even acknowledge that he heard her. How could he do this? What had changed in a few short hours?

All the way to Brownwood, she heard Dee Dee giggling and could see that they were fooling around under the blanket. Tears coursed down her face and her heart felt as though it was being stabbed with a hot spear; over and over again.

She tried talking to Red, but he looked straight ahead while he drove, and ignored her. His stoic and expressionless face told her nothing.

She finally curled herself up in a ball in the corner of the back seat and cried silent tears. She knew she didn't deserve to be treated like this and began to try to figure out what she should do. Maybe she should think about going back to her sister's house, but that thought left her with another stabbing pain in her heart.

She was faced with something she never saw coming. All of Luke's words came flooding back. Did he mean any of them or had he just been playing a game? How could she have let herself believe he truly loved her? Right now, his actions spoke louder than all of the words he'd ever said.

By the time they reached Brownwood, her face was streaked with mascara and she felt completely humiliated. She reluctantly followed Luke and Dee Dee up to the door.

To everyone's surprise, a visitor sat on the doorstep waiting for Luke to get home. Shank Patterson was an old time friend of Luke's and a fellow musician. When he wasn't playing music, he worked on a turkey farm at Goldthwaite.

Luke greeted him. "Shank! What in the hell are you doing here?"

"Shit man, I was coming through Brownwood and thought I'd drop by. I brought you some turkey eggs."

"Well, come on in. It's good to see you brother." He accepted the box Shank handed him.

They all entered the house. Luke immediately put the box in the refrigerator. "Shank, make yourself at home. I've got a little business to tend to, but Darlina can keep you company. Thanks for the turkey eggs man."

Luke guided Dee Dee into his office and closed the door.

Darlina glanced at the stranger standing in front of her. "Look, I don't know who you are, but you're obviously a friend of Luke's. You'll have to excuse me, but I'm not in the mood for entertaining any visitors. Like Luke said, make yourself at home."

The man pulled his boots off and stretched out on Luke and Darlina's bed. She didn't care what he did as long as he didn't talk to her.

She shivered uncontrollably with a cold that came from the inside. She got a blanket and pillow and curled up in front of the Dearborn heater on the floor.

Her sobs came in great heaves and she didn't care who heard. Nothing mattered except that Luke had forsaken her and why? What had made him turn to another woman? She fingered the little gold necklace around her neck and wondered if she'd been crazy for putting her faith in him.

She searched her mind over and over for some answers but got none. Maybe when morning came, she would call Norma and ask if she could come pick her up. She only knew she was not going to tolerate being treated the way Luke was treating her tonight. No excuse on earth could justify it.

The night dragged on and eventually Darlina cried herself to sleep. She was awakened the next morning by footsteps on the floor and voices. She sat up, hugging the blanket close around her.

The door to the office flew open and Luke and Dee Dee emerged. Darlina avoided looking at either of them.

Dee Dee knelt on the floor in front of Darlina. "Sweetie, I don't know what kind of mojo you've put on Luke, but he sure must love you because he couldn't do a thing with me all night."

Luke avoided Darlina's gaze and instead walked over to their bed. He started shaking the man that lay sleeping there. "Shank, wake up man."

Shank stirred and rolled over.

Luke grabbed him by the shoulder and rolled him back over. "Shank! Wake up you sonofabitch."

Shank sat up on the bed. "What the hell, Luke?"

"Wake up. I need you to drive Dee Dee home for me."

Shank mumbled under his breath, but pulled his boots on and got off of the bed.

Luke handed him a twenty dollar bill. "She lives in Abilene."

"Shit, I don't wanna drive to Abilene right now."

"Well, do it anyway. There's money for gas and coffee."

Shank and Dee Dee made their way out the door and Luke and Darlina were now alone.

Darlina continued to sit wrapped in the blanket on the floor. She could feel that her eyes were swollen and stinging. She didn't give a thought about what she must look like.

Luke came to her, gently picked her up and laid her on the bed.

The tears came flowing again and her voice shook. "Luke, please tell me why you brought Dee Dee here?"

Luke didn't answer her. Instead he held her tightly and stroked her hair. How could he have thought that bringing Dee Dee home with him would drive her away? Was he hoping to come out of the office and find her in bed with Shank, so he could demand she leave? He didn't know. All he knew was that his plan had backfired and the only thing he'd succeeded in doing was hurt her and him.

With each tear that fell, his heart broke into a million pieces. He wished it didn't have to be this way. He wished he could wipe the slate clean and start anew with this sweet girl. But he knew it was too late. He'd been warned in the dream.

There was only one other answer. It wasn't one he'd wanted to consider, but he seemed to be left with no choice. The only decent thing he could do at this point was to make sure he got Darlina out of the way before the sky fell in. There was no doubt in his mind it was gonna fall hard and soon.

# Chapter 25

The two of them lay like that for thirty minutes or more, Darlina sobbed, as Luke tried to decide his next move.

A tear trickled down Luke's cheek and he brushed it away angrily with the back of his hand.

Finally, he broke the silence, speaking slowly and softly. "Darlina, you've gotta know I'm no good for you. As much as I wanna try to lie to both of us, I know I'm no good for you."

"How can you say that, Luke? How could you do what you just did? I thought you loved me."

Suddenly, Luke pushed Darlina away from him and got up off the bed. "Did you not hear me?" His voice grew harsh and bitter. "I'm a rotten, lowdown, no good sonofabitch. I'm no good for you and you should know that you deserve better."

With a crackle in her voice, Darlina replied, "But I love you Luke, and I could never see you that way. I see you as the most handsome and talented man in the world."

Luke sat back down on the bed with his back to Darlina. "I'm so sorry. I never meant to hurt you."

Dammit it all to hell! Luke realized he'd screwed up in his effort to drive Darlina away. He felt ashamed at how badly he'd hurt her. Still he knew that the only decent thing he could do was to get her away from him. The storm was quickly descending upon him. What was he going to do now?

"Then why, Luke? Why did you feel like you needed to have sex with Dee Dee? Why wouldn't you just talk to me?"

"I've never been a man that was satisfied with just one woman, but you heard her. I wasn't able to do anything. It wouldn't get hard for her." He laughed somewhat sarcastically. "I thought I was puttin' a mojo on you with the garlic and all the while, you've been layin' your own mojo on me."

Darlina sat up behind him, rubbing his shoulders, as tears continued to flow. "I just love you. It's that simple. I'm glad you couldn't do anything with her, but it sure did hurt me to be cast aside. I don't understand how you can flip like that."

Luke sighed and turned around to face her. "I thought if I showed you what a sorry bastard of a man I am, you'd want to leave."

"I don't, and I don't ever want you to do that to me again, no matter what."

Luke took his handkerchief from his pocket and wiped her tears away, gently kissing her swollen eyelids. Then making his way to her still pouting lips, he laid her back on the bed and joined her.

She wrapped her arms tightly around him and managed to stop the flow of the tears. "Luke, promise me you'll never do anything like that again."

"I promise baby. I thought it would be for your own good in the long run."

"Well, it wasn't. If you think you have to be with another woman please just tell me, so I can deal with it head on."

"Alright. Please forgive me for hurting you."

"I already have. Make love to me, Luke."

They slowly undressed each other; touching, caressing and kissing until their passions melted together, bringing them both to a shuddering crescendo that left them spent.

The emotional and physical exhaustion took over and they fell asleep wrapped in each other's arms.

They were awakened by a loud knock on the back door. Luke jumped up and slipped into his blue jeans.

When he opened the door, Shank was back. "Alright you sonofabitch, I got your meskin whore delivered back to Abilene. She gives pretty damn good head."

Luke chuckled. "Yeah, she does. Thanks man. I owe you."

"You sure as hell do. It's time to do some drinkin' and play some music."

"You got any whiskey or beer?"

"Hell no, I came to drink yours man."

Luke handed him money. "Holler at Red and you two run to the liquor store. We'll get dressed while you're gone. Get a bottle of Beam."

Shank took the money. "Be back in a few minutes. I do love drinkin' on your dime." He laughed, as Luke shot him the finger.

Luke went back to the bedroom to find Darlina awake and getting out of bed. "Shank's back. We're gonna do some pickin'."

"Okay, I'll get dressed." She walked over to Luke, wrapped her arms around his neck and kissed him. "I love you."

"I know, baby. I'm sorry again for last night."

"I've already forgotten it."

By the time Darlina was dressed, Shank and Red were back with the liquor. They'd bought a bottle of whiskey and a case of Lone Star. Luke carried chairs from the kitchen into the bedroom and Red went next door to get his bass guitar.

Darlina helped Shank put the beer in the refrigerator. "Let's start over again. I'm Darlina and I apologize for the mess last night."

"You already know I'm Shank and I'm never surprised at what I find going on at Luke's place. No apology necessary, but I damned sure don't know what you see in the big ugly bastard," he said, with a wide grin that revealed a missing front tooth.

Shank was tall and lanky with brown shoulder length hair. He smoked one cigarette after the other, lighting a new one before the one he was smoking went out. As soon as the beer was put away, he hurried out to his car and returned with his guitar.

He opened a beer just as Luke walked into the kitchen. "Darlina, would you mind fixing me a Beam and Coke?"

"Of course not."

Both men went back into the bedroom just as Red walked in carrying his guitar.

"Would you like a drink, Red?" she asked.

"I'll get myself a beer," he said, avoiding looking her in the eye. "You alright, sugar?"

"Yeah, I'm alright."

He patted her on the shoulder, took his beer and joined the other two men in the next room.

Darlina made herself a cup of coffee. She then took Luke his drink and sat down on the outside of their picking circle to listen. The ache in her heart was beginning to subside, but there were still ragged edges. She was happy to have the distraction of some music.

From the conversation that flowed back and forth between them, she learned that Shank played lead guitar for Augie Meyers, a hippie band out of Austin. Luke referred to him as *Augie Doggie*.

He and Red had plugged their guitars into the amplifiers that Luke had brought out of the office. Luke played his acoustic Martin.

Shank's raspy voice contrasted with Luke's smooth baritone and Red was somewhere in between the two. They took turns around the circle playing and singing.

She loved listening to the music and finally, her heart felt contented again. She tried not to think about what had transpired last night and decided to wipe it from her memory as if it were only a bad dream. It made her smile inwardly knowing that Luke hadn't been able to perform with Dee Dee. Maybe she had put a mojo on him.

After three hours of playing guitars, singing and drinking, Luke stood up. "Boys, we gotta get ready to go play tonight. Why don't you come along Shank? You can sit in with us."

"I would Luke, but I've gotta get on down the road. We're playing tonight at the Broken Spoke in Austin."

"It's been a while since we've played there. Tell ol' White he needs to book the Rebel Rousers back in."

"Will do. Man it was good to see you guys." Shank stood and shook their hands. "It was nice to meet you, little lady."

"You too, Shank, and thank you for the turkey eggs."

"Speaking of those turkey eggs, how about you cook us up a mess while we get ready for the gig baby?"

"Alright. Sure you don't want to stay and eat with us Shank?"

"No, I'm gonna head on down the road. Ya'll take care."

"Come back anytime you are down this way brother," Luke invited.

Shank left, but not before taking another six pack of Lone Star out of the refrigerator.

Red went back to his apartment to get cleaned up for the gig and Luke hit the shower.

Darlina went into the kitchen and opened the box of turkey eggs. She'd never seen such big eggs in her life. They were at least three times the size of a chicken egg.

She got out the skillet and turned on the fire. She picked up the first egg and tried to crack it on the side of the pan. The egg bounced off without even making a dent. She banged it a little harder on the edge of the cabinet, with the same result; no cracked egg.

How on earth was she supposed to break open these eggs?

She tried hitting the egg on the edge of the table but it bounced out of her hand and rolled across the floor. She found herself giggling as she chased the egg. Finally, she got a knife and meat mallet. She put the egg in a bowl, held the knife downward on the egg and hit it with the mallet. At last, there was a tiny crack. She kept pounding away on it until the shell broke open.

When she dropped the turkey egg into the skillet, it almost covered the entire bottom of the pan. While the first egg sizzled, she began trying to crack the next one.

By the time Luke and Red were cleaned up and dressed, she had managed to break open and cook four of the turkey eggs along with sausage and biscuits.

Luke brought the chairs back into the kitchen and put the amplifiers back in the office. He then joined Darlina and Red at the table to feast on the giant eggs.

The two men talked shop through the meal. Luke had some new songs he wanted the band to learn and they talked about setting up practice sessions.

"We used to practice every week," Red reminded Luke.

"Yeah I know. I guess I just lost interest and we already knew all the songs we were playing."

"Some new material couldn't hurt."

"I want you to start doing more of the singing Red. You've got a good voice. Pick out some more Haggard songs you'd like to do."

"I will, but you're the one people want to hear."

"Yeah, well we might as well start weanin' 'em."

"What about the go-go girls? Are you still gonna have them?"

"I think we'll give that a rest for a little while," Luke said, reaching across the table to take Darlina's hand.

"You know I love dancin' for you Luke."

"Yeah, I know, sugar. I just need to do some thinkin' about it all. I'm not takin' you with me to the gig tonight."

"But, I want to go. I can get ready fast."

"You need some rest. I'm gonna pop a couple of those ol' pills to keep me goin' for a few more hours. Want some, Red?"

"Sure, hoss. We've got a few miles to make tonight."

Luke pushed his plate back and got up from the table. He returned with a pill bottle and shook some out in Red's hand, while he swallowed some himself.

"Let's roll, stud. Angelo ain't gonna come to us."

"I'll go get the car ready," Red said, as he stood to leave. "Thanks for the grub Darlina."

"You're welcome. Ya'll be safe tonight."

Once Red was gone, Luke took Darlina's hand, pulling her to her feet. "You just keep the home fires burning, darlin'."

"I always do," she said, standing on her tiptoes to kiss his lips.

He let go of her, grabbed his guitar and then was gone.

She sat down at the table and put her head in her hands. What had just happened over the past twenty four hours? Thoughts whirled in her head and she suddenly felt physically and emotionally drained.

She forced herself to move on legs that felt wooden and heavy, as she gathered their dirty dishes and made quick work of cleaning the kitchen. She fell into bed, exhausted. Even though she hated not going with Luke, she felt relieved to be alone. She needed to sort out the chaos in her mind.

She could almost hear her mother's voice warning her that she'd be sorry for taking up with Luke and that he'd only hurt her. Maybe mama was right.

All she knew for sure was that she idolized this rebel of a man and that she'd forgive him over and over again if need be.

The last thought she had before she fell into the abyss of sleep, was that the past twenty four hours had aged her beyond her mere nineteen years. Little by little, the naiveté was being stripped away. She was no longer the innocent little girl that had fallen in love with Luke.

Instead, she was a woman who was still in love with him. She knew she would be until the day she died.

## Chapter 26

At four o'clock in the morning, Luke came stumbling loudly through the bedroom, instantly waking Darlina.

Sleepily, she asked, "Everything go alright, baby?"

"Yeah, just a long night. Go back to sleep. I'm too wired to go to bed." He took his guitar and bottle of whiskey into the office and closed the door.

Lying back down, she was soon enveloped in the blackness of sleep again. The next time she opened her eyes, it was ten o'clock in the morning. She was shocked to realize she'd slept for twelve hours. The pillow beside her was still vacant and she knew Luke had never come to bed.

Slipping into her robe, she walked softly to the office door. All was quiet, so she lightly knocked. When she got no response, she opened the door and shivered, as the frigid air hit her.

Luke sat slumped in a chair his head lying on top of the desk. The empty bottle of Beam perched precariously on one corner. She couldn't tell if he was asleep or passed out, but she propped the door open between the office and bedroom to let some of the warmth from the Dearborn in. She got a blanket and draped over him, then left him alone.

Looking at her reflection in the bathroom mirror, she was pleased to see the swelling was gone from her eyelids. She was even able to smile at herself.

Opening the medicine cabinet, she reached for her birth control pills. As she looked at them, she strongly considered throwing them away. At least if she got pregnant with Luke's child, she would have a part of him that no one could ever take away. She popped one out and swallowed it, knowing he'd be furious if she didn't.

Turning on steaming hot water in the tub, she poured lavender scented bubbles in and enjoyed a relaxing bath. Then, taking great pains to fix her hair and put on makeup, she resolved to look her best when Luke awoke.

With a growling stomach, she made herself a peanut butter sandwich. Then she settled down in the big chair to finish reading the book about *Sam Bass* that she'd started several weeks ago.

After reading for a while, she went to check on Luke again. Nothing had changed. She cleaned up the bedroom, kitchen and bathroom. In the kitchen, she took inventory of the contents of the refrigerator and the cupboards. It was definitely time to buy some more groceries, as the shelves were looking very bare.

It was getting on into mid-afternoon, when she sat back down in the chair and picked up the book again. Before she knew it, she'd dozed off.

At five o'clock in the afternoon, she jumped out of the chair when she heard a crash. She frantically ran to the doorway between the bedroom and the office. She saw that the Jim Beam bottle had fallen to the floor. Luke was stirring restlessly, knocking papers and pencils off the desk.

She went to him and shook him. "Luke, honey...wake up."

He groggily sat up in the chair. "What?"

"Wake up, baby. You've been sittin' in this chair for hours."

He pushed himself up and stiffly stood. "What time is it?"

"Five o'clock."

"Shit! I've gotta get ready for the gig."

"Why don't you get in the shower while I make you some coffee?"

"Pick me out some clothes to wear tonight, please," he called over his shoulder, as he staggered into the bathroom.

Darlina first put the coffee on to brew and then went to the closet and picked out Luke's clothes. She felt determined to go with him tonight and was dressed and ready.

She picked out his brown striped pants with a matching vest along, with a tan silk shirt. Then, she polished his brown boots, as had become her routine.

When Luke came out of the shower, he immediately went to his clothes neatly laid out on the bed. "Thank you, honey."

"You're welcome. Got some coffee for you."

"Thank you again." He slipped into his clothes, grabbed a cup of coffee and headed toward the door.

"Luke, I wannna' go with you tonight. I'm dressed and ready."

"That you are and lookin' damn fine too. Let's go. We're gonna be late." He grumbled as they walked. "Red shoulda' woke me up."

"I would've woke you, but I didn't know."

"Shit! This coffee ain't gonna get it. I need a drink."

When they got to the car, Red was just coming out of his apartment. Luke called to him. "Let's roll, stud. We're gonna be late."

"Sorry man. I just woke up a few minutes ago."

"We need to stop at the liquor store before we leave town. I need a drink."

Darlina felt a little anxious about the sudden heavy drinking, but knew it wasn't her place to say anything. She sure didn't want to start any kind of fight with him, especially in the mood he was in. She was thankful she was getting to go along, although she didn't know where they were headed.

Once they were on the road, Red stopped at the J & J Liquor Store and Luke went in. He returned in five minutes with a bottle of Beam, a six pack of Coke and a cup of ice.

Before the city limits of Brownwood was behind them, he had poured himself a stiff drink.

"Are you okay, baby?" Darlina asked, as she tucked the blanket around them. She wondered why they didn't just get the heater fixed.

"Just got a lot of shit goin' on in my head."

"Wanna talk about it."

"Nope. I wanna drink and get this damn gig over. Want a drink Red?"

"Hell yes. I need something to get me going."

Darlina wondered where Preacher was. "Is Preacher riding with Jerry and Rita?"

"Preacher's gone to Tennessee for a few days. We've got a sit-in drummer that's meetin' us at the club," Luke explained.

Red turned south out of Brownwood on Highway 84 and headed toward Goldthwaite. The weather had turned bitterly cold and even under the blanket, Darlina shivered.

Luke felt her shiver and put his arm around her. "Get up close to the fat man, baby. He'll keep you warm."

She smiled up at him. "You are always warm."

Red drove over the speed limit the entire way to Goldthwaite. Darlina worried that they might get pulled over and since he was drinking, that could be bad. She breathed a sigh of relief when they made it without any problems.

The gig was at a small night club on the outskirts of Goldthwaite and there wasn't much of a crowd. Luke continued to drink heavily all night and only got up on stage to sing for fifteen minutes out of the entire show. The rest of the time Red sang as the band performed.

He sat at the table with Darlina, withdrawing farther from her the more he downed the whiskey. There was something eating at him, but unless he was willing to talk to her about it, she knew all she could do was be there.

By the time the night was over, both Luke and Red were drunk. Darlina volunteered to drive them home.

"Can you pull the band trailer?" Red asked.

"As long as I'm going straight, I can pull it."

Red laughed. "Well, then here's the keys." He got into the backseat and Luke rode on the passenger's side.

She drove carefully, especially watching for deer. She did not want a repeat of what had taken place on their way back from Junction.

The car was quiet, except for the radio. Luke rested his head against the window with his eyes closed and Red was stretched out in the back seat.

She drove them back to Brownwood safely and was happy to turn onto Cottage Street and see their apartments ahead. Once she parked the car, she woke both men and she and Luke went into their apartment.

He took his boots off and sprawled out on the bed, fully clothed, and was snoring within minutes.

After covering Luke with a blanket, Darlina got undressed and crawled under the covers. She hoped this was not a new trend for

Luke. Even though he was there, he wasn't. Maybe things could never be the same for them after Dee Dee, but she was going to try and hoped he would too.

She tossed and turned for a while before sleep overtook her. At least Luke was beside her in the bed tonight, even if he wasn't under the covers and holding her close.

The next week brought more of the same. Luke continued disappearing into the bottle, taking pills and withdrawing from everyone around him. Darlina stayed close by and hoped that this would soon pass.

Sometimes he acknowledged her presence. He would stop to kiss her or ask her to do something for him, but there were no conversations. It left her to wonder what was eating at him.

Saturday night, after they'd played at the Deuces Wild Club in Abilene, Luke seemed particularly sullen, downing drink after drink.

As they got in the car to leave the club, Red said, "Hey Luke is it alright with you if we go to the truck stop for a bite to eat? I'm as hungry as a horse."

"I don't give a shit. I'm not hungry, but you can stop."

Darlina was happy they were stopping. Her stomach was growling because she'd been eating hit and miss for the past few days.

They sat in a booth near the front and Luke, as always, faced the door. He looked up as a four men walked in, then let out a growl. "Shit!"

Red turned to look and the color drained from his face. "Maybe they won't start nothin', hoss."

Darlina looked the four men over and then gasped, as she recognized the one who had asked her to dance at the Christmas Eve party. He had gotten his face carved up with Luke's knife. She could see deep red scars healing in various crisscrosses on his face.

When he saw Luke and Red, he walked directly to their table.

Luke looked up at him, his jaws clenched and muscles rippling on his arms. "What do you want asshole?"

"Let's go outside and I'll show you what I want," he replied cockily.

"Looks like you didn't learn a damn thing. Guess you want your worthless throat cut this time."

"I've got something in my boot that'll take care of you, sonofabitch."

Red interrupted him, "Come on man. You don't wanna do this. Luke'll cut your damn throat just like he said."

"We'll see about that. Come outside, or I'll blow your brains out right here in this booth."

"Go ahead, if you think you're man enough," Luke barked with a sneer on his face.

"Too big of a coward to go outside with me, huh?"

"No. I ain't stupid either. There are four of you and two of us."

"There were two of you and one of me when you carved my face up. I think these are pretty good odds, unless you're scared."

The manager of the restaurant approached the men. "Is there a problem here?"

Luke responded. "Damn sure is. We came in here to peacefully eat a meal and these bastards are trying to start some shit."

The manager turned to the four men. "Get the hell out of my restaurant. I mean it. Get out, or I'm callin' the law."

The men turned to leave, but Scarface warned over his shoulder, "We'll be waiting, you sonofabitch. I'll catch you somewhere. Just remember that."

Once they were gone, Luke said, "Ya'll eat up. Let's get out of this dump."

Red and Darlina quickly finished their meal and they left the restaurant. Luke looked over his shoulder, to the left and right, as they approached their car.

Just before Red opened the door to get in, he exclaimed, "Shit! Man, they've cut our damn tires."

Sure enough, the tires on the Rebel Rouser's band trailer had been sliced. It was apparent they weren't going anywhere.

Cursing under his breath, Luke went back into the restaurant and asked to use the phone.

"Johnny, this is Luke. Can you come out to the Beacon Truck stop and help us out? Some bastards cut our band trailer tires."

"Sure. I'll be right there."

Red unlocked the car and he and Darlina were inside when Luke returned. He opened the door and got in. "Johnny will be here in a few minutes."

"That's good. I figure that little coward's sitting around the corner somewhere laughing his ass off."

Luke angrily slammed his fist on the dash. "I'll kill him next time I see him."

Darlina flinched at his outburst. "Calm down, baby. It'll be alright."

He turned, eyes flashing, and warned, "Don't you ever tell me to calm down. I'll damn well be pissed off when and where I want to."

"Sorry Luke, I was just trying to help."

"I don't need no damned help. I just need the damn trailer tires fixed." He reached under the seat, bringing up the whiskey bottle. He drew a long drink out of it and passed it to Red.

Red motioned it away. "I don't need any more tonight, Luke."

Luke grumbled. "Fine then...that just leaves more for me."

After ten minutes, Johnny arrived with a tire repair truck that belonged to his father. "I'll have 'em fixed in no time. Who did you piss off this time, Luke?"

"Some little coward bastard that won't fight like a man."

"Well, looks like he got even."

Luke growled, "Just wait 'til I see that asshole again. I'm gonna cut his worthless throat."

"You're in a mood. Wanna come to the house for a little while?"

"No, I wanna get the hell back to Brownwood."

Darlina noticed that Luke's mood didn't change or soften, even towards his friend. Something was definitely eating away at him and he continued to distance himself farther from everyone that gave a damn.

He seemed to be caught in some kind of living hell from which there was no escape. Not only that, but as long as he was in this hell, she was right there with him. She felt helpless and wished there was something she could do. She would stick with him; keep loving him and hope this would all pass soon. She was beginning to feel doubtful things would ever be the same between them.

Nevertheless, she loved this man through good and bad times. She had no intention of abandoning him just because things had turned bad. She believed if she stood by him, he would eventually return to her. That was what she wanted most. She would be patient and wait.

# Chapter 27

By the time the tires on the band trailer were fixed and they had driven back to Brownwood, it was close to four a.m. With each mile they drove, Luke became more depressed and distant. As was beginning to be customary, the music from the radio was the only sound inside the car.

The weather had turned bitterly cold for an early West Texas March. Darlina was thankful to get inside the apartment and warm herself by the Dearborn heater.

Luke had followed her in and without a glance in her direction, barricaded himself in the office. She flinched as he slammed the door. She wished she knew what was wrong. Somehow, she believed if only she knew, she could help fix it, but Luke had locked her and everyone else out.

After a few minutes, she knocked on the door.

"What?" Luke bellowed from the other side.

"Baby, can I come in?"

"Suit yourself."

She opened the door to find Luke sitting with his back to the door and staring into nothingness. She approached him from behind, wrapping her arms around him and laying her cheek next to his.

"Honey, please talk to me."

"Whatcha' wanna talk about?"

"What's bothering you so bad? Maybe if I knew what it was, I could help."

He took her arms from around his neck, while leaning forward in the chair. "How many times do I have to tell you that you can't fix this? No one can. There's really nothing else to say."

"Will you please come to bed with me?"

"I'm not sleepy. Go on and lay down."

"I'll leave the door open so you won't freeze in here. If you change your mind, there'll be a warm spot for you beside me in the bed. I love you, Luke."

"Go lay down and don't worry about me. I've just gotta sort some shit out in my head."

Once she was gone, Luke leaned back in the chair; stretching his legs out in front of him. He hated locking her out. He hated the choices he was forced to make right now. More than anything, he wanted the impending doom to go away and let him get back to living. But, he knew that no matter how much he willed it to go away, it was coming straight for him, and fast.

The only preparation he was concerned with making, was getting Darlina away from it. As he thought about her soft warm body lying in their bed, he ached to go to her, hold her and make love to her. The stark ugly truth of it all gnawed at his gut.

He made up his mind. They were playing in Abilene again that night and he would take Darlina and her things back to Norma's house. What would he tell her? He knew if he told her it was for her own good, she wouldn't buy it. He had to be convincing. As the plan formed in his mind, he hated himself and everything that was about to transpire. He stared at the open bottle of Jim Beam, wishing he could drink enough to drown the guilt and sorrow he felt.

Darlina lay alone in their bed, restless and worried. She tossed and turned as she tried to think of how she could get through to Luke and bring him back to her. With no answers, she finally drifted off into a troubled sleep; filled with haunting dreams of losing him.

When she awoke, it was noon. Even though she'd slept, she didn't feel rested. Worry lay heavy on her mind. She slipped out of bed and went looking for Luke. He was nowhere to be found. When she peeked out the window, she saw that the T-Bird was gone. Maybe he'd gone to see his kids.

Rummaging through the cupboards in the kitchen, she managed to find one can of corn and half a package of crackers. She opened the corn and ate it cold. When Luke got back, she'd remind him that they needed to buy some groceries.

Several hours passed and still Luke did not return. Her worry turned into fear. She went to the intercom box and pressed the button.

Red's voice responded, "Whatcha' need?"

"Red, it's Darlina. Luke was gone when I woke up and he's not back yet. Do you know where he went?"

"No, I sure don't, darlin'. But, he'll be back in time for the gig."

"Okay. I was just worried about him."

"Don't worry. He's a big boy."

"I know. Thanks, Red."

"No problem."

Standing under the warm water in the shower, she began to feel a dread that started in the pit of her stomach and made its way up to her throat. Maybe the storm that Luke kept talking about was here.

He was still not back when she'd finished dressing, fixing her hair and putting on her makeup. It was getting close to the time to leave. It wasn't like Luke to be late for a gig. Red had assured her that he'd be back and yet he was not there.

Just when she'd given up hope, she heard the back door fly open. She ran to the kitchen to greet Luke and found him looking disheveled and bleary eyed.

"Luke, where have you been? I was so worried."

He didn't smile nor try to reassure her. He just looked at her and said, "I've been fishin'."

"In this weather? You're gonna catch your death of cold."

He muttered under his breath as he made his way into the bedroom, tracking mud as he went, "That'd be the easy way out."

He closed the door to the bathroom and Darlina heard the shower running. She decided to get clothes laid out for him to wear, since there was no time to waste. They had to get on the road and soon.

When he came out of the bathroom, he went straight to the clothes that were lying neatly on the bed. As he was putting on his pants, he turned to Darlina. "I want you to get your bags and pack your things."

"What?" Her voice trembled.

"You heard me. Get your shit packed. I'm leaving you in Abilene tonight."

Tears came to her eyes. "But...Luke...why?"

"It don't make a damn why. It's just the way it is. Whatever you don't have packed by the time I'm dressed, I'll throw away. Get movin'. We've gotta roll."

She turned away from him as tears streamed down her face. Retrieving her bags from the closet, she began tossing her things into them out as fast as she could. Her heart felt as though it was caught in a vise. So, this was it. This was what it had all come down to. All the love, all the joy, all the happiness, whittled down to a few harsh words and a couple of hastily packed bags.

Each time she turned around to say something to Luke, he had his back to her. "Darlina, don't make this any harder than it has to be. And for God's sake, would you stop bawling."

"No, I won't," she said, with a quivering lip. "I can't."

Luke threw up his hands. "I'm going next door to see if Red's ready to roll. You've got five minutes."

She blindly continued flinging her things into her bags. She couldn't imagine that her heart could ever hurt any worse than it did when Luke brought Dee Dee home with them, but she was wrong. She felt as though she might die from the pain and didn't care if she did. How could a person still live and breathe, when their heart was being ripped out?

Just as she was gathering her things from the bathroom, Luke came back in the door. "Come on. We're leaving."

She tossed what she had in her hands into the open bag and clicked it shut. Luke grabbed it almost before she finished and headed out the door. She threw on her coat, grabbed the other bag and followed him.

At the car, he held the front door open for her and tossed her bags into the backseat, while Red took his place in the driver's seat. When she got in, he closed the door and climbed into the backseat with the bags.

She turned around. "Luke, please don't do this."

He looked blankly out the window and didn't answer.

"Can't you hear me?" She raised her voice. "Please don't take me back to Abilene. Would you at least talk to me?"

"Red, turn up the radio and let's get gone," he said, never looking at Darlina. He continued staring out the window.

She slowly turned around, put her head in her hands and wept. It was obvious to her that Luke wasn't going to answer her and there was nothing she could do about it.

As they flew down the road, the radio blasted out one sad country song after another. In record time, they were in Abilene and Luke directed Red to Norma's house.

Red stopped the car at the curb. Luke opened his door, set her bags out and then opened her door. "Come on, Darlina. Get out."

"I don't want to get out."

"Look kid, it's been fun and all, but I'm tired of playing kid games. I'm ready for a real woman, not a little girl."

His words stung all the way to her core. She slowly moved her legs and forced them to make her stand. The minute she was out of the car, Luke jumped in and they left.

She stood on the curb watching the tail lights disappear until she could no longer see them. Tears coursed down her face like rivers and she felt as though she might be sick. Her legs wouldn't move to take her up to the house. She stood motionless; her body wracked with sobs.

The front door of the house loudly banged as it closed and Norma ran out to her. "Darlina! What is going on?"

Darlina couldn't form words between sobs. "Luke."

"What about Luke? Come on, let's get in the house." Picking up one of the bags, she looped her arm through Darlina's and slowly walked her up the sidewalk and into the house.

Once inside, Darlina collapsed in a heap on the sofa. She wept as she curled up in a fetal position, rocking back and forth.

Norma sat down on the sofa beside her. "Darlina, please tell me what's going on."

Darlina lifted her head. "Luke made me leave." The sobbing renewed itself. "He doesn't want me anymore."

"Okay. What happened?"

"I don't know. He just said he was tired of a kid and wanted a real woman. Norma, I tried my best. I really did."

Norma put her arms around her sister. "I'm sure you did. Please don't cry."

"I can't help it. It hurts."

"Let's take your things into the bedroom. Why don't you wash your face while I make you some hot chocolate?"

Darlina stood on shaky limbs and followed her sister numbly. Her head ached and her heart was shattered into a million pieces. All she could hear was the echo of Luke's last words.

Norma sat the bag down on the floor. "I'll go bring in your other bag and we can unpack tomorrow. For now, just get your face cleaned up and I'll get us something warm to drink."

"I'm not unpacking. I know he'll change his mind and come back for me."

"Okay. You don't have to unpack. Wash up and then come into the kitchen."

Once Norma left the room, Darlina sat down on the edge of the bed and stared ahead with unseeing eyes. No matter how hard she tried, she couldn't comprehend what had happened during the past few days.

She despised Dee Dee with a seething hatred. Suddenly, her heart froze. Maybe Luke was replacing her with Dee Dee. Nauseated, she ran to the bathroom and abruptly heaved into the toilet. Once there was nothing left to throw up, she sat on the floor, with her head resting on the bathtub.

That was the way Norma found her when she came back to check on her. She got a washcloth from the cabinet, wet it and washed Darlina's face. "Honey, you've got to pull yourself together." She helped her stand. Darlina leaned on her as they walked into the kitchen.

They sat at the kitchen table and Norma placed a steaming cup of chocolate in her shaking hands. The warmth felt good and Darlina gripped the cup.

"Drink up," Norma encouraged.

Darlina gradually raised the cup to her lips and managed a small sip. The tears had dried up for now and she felt only a cold numbness that came from deep inside.

"What am I going to do, Norma?"

"I don't know what you're going to do, but you don't have to figure that out tonight."

Darlina looked into her sister's eyes. "I love him. I'll never stop loving him."

"You don't have to. This is not something you are going to be able to work through tonight. It's going to take time."

"But I don't want time. I want Luke."

"Let's not talk about it anymore right now. Do you want something to eat?"

"No. I couldn't get a bite of anything past this lump in my throat."

"Well, just drink the warm chocolate and go lay down. We can talk about it tomorrow. I'm going out for a little while, if you'll be alright. Greg is coming to pick me up."

"I'll be fine. Go ahead. I'm so sorry to have just barged in like this. I had no choice."

"Don't be silly. You know you're always welcome here. Just promise me you won't do anything rash while I'm gone."

"I won't. I promise. I'm going to go lie down and try to figure all this out." Darlina got up from the table, hugged her sister and stumbled back to her bedroom. Once she closed the door, she fell across the bed and allowed the tears to flow again.

How could Luke have done this? How could he profess his undying love and then just turn it off like a light switch? She had no answers; only a million questions and a heart that was shattered beyond repair.

The vision of Luke with Dee Dee kept coming into her mind and she angrily tried to brush it away. Why did her happiness have to be torn away, like ripping a band-aid off of tender skin?

The questions, doubts, fears, loneliness and hurt took over every fiber of her being. Without Luke, she would never be happy again. She'd never feel love again and right at this moment, she didn't care if she drew another breath again.

Exhausted and drained in every way possible, Darlina finally fell asleep. Maybe she would be lucky and not wake up or maybe she'd wake up and find this had all been a bad dream.

Luke had thrown her and their love away without any regard to what they'd shared. She felt tossed away like a broken toy.

Her life was over just as it was getting started. And there was absolutely nothing she could do about it.

## Chapter 28

As the car pulled away from the curb, where Darlina had been left standing, Luke slammed his fist against the dash. "Dammit to hell, Red. I didn't wanna have to do that."

"I know, Luke. She's a sweet girl. I sure did hate to see her cry so much."

"Me too...man, I need to tell you something. If you wanna hightail it to Mexico for a while, I've got some money and you can have this car. Stay as long as you want," he said, as he stared blindly at the street ahead.

"Nah. I'll just stick around here. Mexico's no place I wanna be right now."

"I'm just offering. I don't know exactly what's coming down or when, but I do know it's coming soon."

"It'll be alright. There's nowhere I wanna go."

"Preacher and Indian Joe will be back from Tennessee in a couple of weeks. I figure that's when the shit will hit the fan."

"Maybe so...guess we'll just have to wait and see. Don't worry about Darlina. Her family will help her."

Luke sighed deeply. "I sure as hell hope so. That was the hardest thing I've ever had to do in my whole life."

"She'll be okay and someday she'll thank you."

"I don't know about that. I do know she was the best thing to happen to me in a very long time. She saw something in me that I didn't see in myself anymore, and dammit, it was all too late."

"Let's go play some music and drink some whiskey."

"Yeah, let's do."

Luke found himself unable to erase the picture from his mind, of Darlina standing desolately on the curb. He had to be the sorriest human being alive to have hurt her so badly. He cursed the choice he had to make. He only hoped that maybe one day he'd be able to explain why. For now, he knew she was devastated and her heart irreparably broken. For now, there was nothing he could do about any of it.

His heart was not into playing music anymore. It wasn't into drinking his fill of whiskey and most definitely not into finding another woman. No, his heart was with the sweet girl he'd left standing on the curb and it would always be. She just didn't know it.

He walked into the familiar night club feeling empty and very much alone.

Darlina awoke with a start, at three a.m. She wasn't exactly sure where she was. She lay very still, trying to gather her thoughts. Slowly, she turned half expecting to see Luke lying beside her but instead saw only an empty pillow. Suddenly, it all came flooding back. All the hurt, pain and sorrow washed over her like a giant tidal wave.

She got up from the bed and went to sit beside the window; gazing out at the blackness. She could picture Luke getting home from the gig. Every detail was etched in her mind. She ached with loneliness and hurt that could not be described in mere words. Her hope, that he'd come back to get her after the gig, was gone. He wasn't coming back. Not tonight. Not tomorrow. Not ever.

She sat staring out the window until the sun started to break over the horizon. She had a lot of thinking to do and a lot of plans to make. First of all, she'd need a job. Second of all, she'd need to get a car.

The reality of her situation hit her and she was suddenly very thankful for her family and the generosity of her sister to take her back in. The truth was that she had nowhere else to go. She'd gladly and willingly given up everything for Luke and look where it had gotten her. She was still having trouble comprehending what had taken place.

Being Sunday morning, the house remained quiet as the morning came to life. Darlina went into the kitchen, made herself a cup of coffee and took it back to her bedroom. She began to unpack her things and put them away. She sighed heavily. It felt as if there was a large brick sitting on her chest, directly in the vicinity of her heart. Now she understood the term, *a heavy heart.*

Once she heard her sister moving around, she joined her in the kitchen, thankful that the tears were at bay for the moment.

"Good morning," Norma said cheerfully. "How are you this morning?"

"I suppose I'm as okay as I can be. I've just got a lot to figure out. Is there any chance I can get my old job back at the boiler factory?"

"We hired a new girl a week after you left and she's still there."

"I'll get a newspaper tomorrow and start job hunting. That's got to be my first priority."

"I'll go get a Sunday paper after breakfast and we'll look at it together. Are you hungry?"

"Not really, but I know I should eat. It's been a while."

Norma stirred up pancake batter and fried bacon and eggs. Once Darlina smelled the food, her stomach responded with a loud growl.

After they'd eaten, Norma was leaving to buy a newspaper and suggested to Darlina, "Why don't you give Leann a call and see if she can come over for a while?"

"I'd like that."

The minute she picked up the phone to dial Leann's number, she felt the tears start to flow.

"Hello," Leann answered.

"Leann, its Darlina." With that, the damn broke and tears flooded her eyes.

"What's wrong, little sister?"

"Oh, Leann, I really need to talk to you. Can you come over to Norma's today?"

"Yes, but tell me what's wrong. Why are you at Norma's?"

"Luke left me here last night with all my stuff." In between sobs, she continued. "He doesn't want me anymore. He said he was tired of playing kid games and needed a real woman."

"That asshole! Please don't cry Darlina. I'll be over in a little bit and we can try to figure everything out."

"Thank you. I love you so much. I don't know what I'd do without my family."

"I love you too. I'll see you in a bit."

She hung up the phone and sobbed into her hands. Where did the millions of tears keep coming from? Would they never dry up?

She went into the bathroom and turned on the shower. Standing under the warm stream of water, she hoped it would wash away some her sorrow. Unfortunately, it didn't, but she did feel some better. By the time Norma was back with the newspaper, she was dressed.

They spread the newspaper across the kitchen table and sat side by side, poring over the classifieds.

Finally, Darlina looked up. "Here's an ad for assembly line workers at Timex. That's close to the boiler factory and maybe we could ride together until I get a car. I'll apply tomorrow."

"That sounds like a good idea. I drop you off in the morning on my way to work."

"Thank you again Norma. I don't know what I'd do without you."

"Oh, don't mention it. This is what family's for." She gave her sister a quick hug. "You'll be back on your feet again in no time."

"How did you handle it when Ray left?"

"I just got up every day and tried to make the most out of it. Eventually, it didn't hurt so much anymore."

Darlina said ruefully, "I don't think I'll ever feel whole again."

"Just give it time."

There was a knock on the door and Norma went to open it. Leann came rushing in. She went straight to Darlina and hugged her. "I'm so sorry Darlina. Tell me everything. I'll help you in any way I can."

Darlina sat between her two sisters and amidst bouts of crying, recounted everything that had happened during the past seven days, ending with the details of Luke bringing her back to Norma's.

"That just pisses me off," Leann exclaimed. "For two cents, I'd drive to Brownwood and give him a piece of my mind. He didn't deserve you."

"I don't think a piece of your mind would make one bit of difference. I just wish I could understand what changed. Everything was so wonderful and we'd grown so close until he brought Dee Dee home. After that, it went from bad to worse."

"You should've called me the night he did that and I would've came and got you," Norma said.

"I thought about calling you, but I really wanted him to tell me what was going on. He did apologize. He kept repeating over and over that a storm was coming and he had to get me to safety."

"Well, I don't know what kind of storm he's talking about, but you're better off here with us. I was so afraid he would wind up hurting you and it looks like he did a good job of that." Leann fidgeted and picked at a loose thread on the hem of her blouse.

"Does anybody want a coke?" Norma offered.

"I'll take one," Leann replied.

Darlina shook her head. "I don't want anything."

"What are you gonna do now?" Leann asked Darlina, as Norma left the room.

"The first thing I've gotta do is get a job. We found an ad in the newspaper today for assembly line workers at Timex. I'll apply there tomorrow and hope they hire me. Then, I need to get a car."

"I'm so sorry, Darlina."

"Me too," she sighed heavily. "I still love him and if he came back for me today, I'd go with him in a heartbeat."

"How can you say that after everything that's happened?"

"Because it's the truth." Her eyes clouded with tears again and one trickled down her cheek.

Leann wrapped her arms around her sister. "Please don't cry. Everything's going to be okay."

"I don't think things will ever be alright again. It doesn't feel like it anyway."

Norma returned with the cokes. "It just feels like that right now because it's all so fresh. Give it some time and slowly but surely the hurt will lessen."

"I don't see how. I love him with all my heart and soul and that's not something I can turn off like a water faucet."

The sisters sat visiting and taking turns comforting Darlina. They tried to assure her that she could get back on her feet again in time. She didn't know what she'd do without them.

Finally, Leann stood. "I've got to get back home, but Darlina, you call me anytime day or night if you need me. If you get the job at Timex, maybe I can come and get you for lunch every day. It would be nice to have company for lunch again."

"I'll let you know how it goes and I'd love having lunch with you again. I feel bad that you'd have to come get me. I'll get a car as soon as I can."

"I know. I don't mind picking you up until you do get one. I'll talk to Wayne and see if he knows anyone with a good car for sale."

"I have absolutely no money. It might be a little while before I can get enough saved up to buy one, but I guess it wouldn't hurt to put the word out. Thank you so much for coming over, Leann."

"Don't worry about our little sister. I'll take good care of her," Norma assured Leann. "Tell Wayne hello for me."

"Me too." Darlina stood and hugged her sister tightly. "Thank you again. I love you."

"I love you too. Please try not to cry anymore. It's all gonna be okay."

After Leann left, Norma busied herself with household chores and Darlina was once again alone with her thoughts.

She wondered what Luke was doing and if he felt the same aching sadness that gripped her. The memories of their love flooded her mind. The words he'd said echoed over and over again. *"You gotta know I love you Darlina and no matter what happens, I always will."*

If only she could believe that, but right now it didn't feel true. Once again, there were a thousand questions and no answers. She walked to her room and lay down on the bed, covering her eyes with her arm. Regardless of how strongly she resolved not to cry anymore, the tears kept coming.

She could clearly hear her mama's voice admonishing her. *"You've made your bed, now lay in it."* That's exactly what her mama would say to her right now.

But, she also knew that you don't love someone with all your heart and then suddenly stop. That's just not the way it works.

Love is supposed to be forever and that's the kind of love she had for Luke.

In spite of all his hurtful words and actions towards her, she longed to have his arms around her and feel his kisses on her eyelids and mouth.

But, it was all over and no matter how hard she tried, she couldn't make sense of any of it.

## Chapter 29

Bright and early Monday morning, Darlina was dressed and ready to go with Norma, as she left for work. Her heart wasn't in it but she hoped Timex would hire her so she wouldn't have to keep looking.

She knew she had to make some money and fast. She'd put on very little makeup and pulled her hair back. She didn't give much thought about how she looked. She wasn't out to impress anyone. She just needed a job.

As Norma stopped in front of the Timex factory office, she said, "When you get finished, walk on over to the boiler factory. If they hire you and put you to work on the spot, just give me a call."

"I will. Thanks, Norma. Wish me luck."

"Good luck, honey."

Darlina found herself in a line with ten other people. A balding man walked down the line, handing each person an application and pen to fill it out with.

She found a seat and made quick work of completing the application. She then approached the window and handed it to a young woman.

"Thank you, Ms. Flowers. Mr. Bradley will be with you shortly."

Within the next hour, Darlina had been hired, issued a light green paper like gown, hat, shoes and rubber gloves. Mr. Bradley explained to her that these were necessary to keep any particles of hair or lint from clothing, out of the delicate watch parts. She was then taken into the assembly line room.

The room was made up of several rows of tables, stools and hundreds of workers, who were all dressed in the same green gowns, hats and shoes. No one looked up as she entered and the young girl, who had been asked to take her into the factory, led her to a stern looking gray haired lady.

"Mrs. Crouch, this your new-hire, Darlina Flowers. Ms. Flowers, this is your supervisor, Mrs. Crouch. She'll get you started. Welcome to Timex."

Darlina smiled at the young girl, "Thank you." Then she turned to her supervisor and said, "Nice to meet you, Mrs. Crouch. I am wondering if I could possibly make one quick phone call before you put me to work."

"Yes, but make it quick," she said tersely.

Darlina walked briskly to the phone on the wall. She called Norma to let her know she'd been hired and then went straight back to her supervisor.

"Are you ready to go to work now?" Mrs. Crouch asked.

"Yes ma'am. I'm ready."

"I'm going to put you at work station forty-nine. You will receive full trays of watches that have been assembled with all the working parts. You are to take each one from the tray, wind it using the machine, put it back in the tray and send it on to the testing station. The faster you wind them, the more quickly you'll be able to reach your quota. Don't fall behind or you'll never catch up. Any questions?"

"No ma'am," she said, as she took her place on the tall stool at her work station.

Mrs. Crouch handed her the first tray of the small watches. This is going to be easy, Darlina thought to herself. She picked up the first watch. It had no cover or face on it. All the tiny gears were exposed and as she wound it, her glove caught in it.

"Be careful," Mrs. Crouch warned. You've got to keep your fingers away from the gears. Hold it by the outside edge only."

"Okay," Darlina replied, as she picked up the next watch. She managed to successfully wind it and put it back in the tray. Mrs. Crouch moved on down the line and left her to the endless task of winding half-made watches.

She'd been winding the watches for two hours, when a loud bell rang. All the workers got up off their stools and moved towards the door.

Mrs. Crouch suddenly appeared beside her. "It's lunch break. You get thirty minutes. There's a lunchroom across the street in the building where you filled out your application. Don't be late getting back."

"I won't." She got up and followed the other workers to the door, where each one hung their gowns, hats, shoes and gloves on a peg with their name above it.

In the lunchroom, it appeared to her that everyone had brought their own lunch. There were a few vending machines against one wall, but she had no money and didn't feel hungry anyway. She found a telephone and called first Norma, then Leann.

She filled both of her sisters in on her job. Leann was disappointed that she'd only be getting a thirty minute lunch break each day and wouldn't be able to eat with her like they had done in the past.

Before she knew it, the whistle blew and everyone filed back across the street. They claimed their work gear and returned to their work stations.

By mid-afternoon, Darlina's neck and shoulders ached from being in one position for so long without moving. She tried to ignore the pain and let her mind wander, as she wound the endless backlog of half-made watches.

It was mindless work, but not as easy as she had first thought. She was happy when the whistle blew at four o'clock, announcing the end of her first day.

Once she hung up her work gear, she walked the two short blocks to the boiler factory. Norma would get off work at five.

She dreaded returning to the office where she'd worked before she left to move in with Luke. What would she say to the questions people would ask?

Luckily, the girl at the receptionist desk didn't know her, so she simply introduced herself as Norma's sister. She then went straight to Norma's office.

Norma was out in the plant, so she made herself comfortable as she waited for her. She couldn't ignore the loud growling sounds her stomach was making. Tomorrow she'd pack a lunch.

It was close to five o'clock before Norma came back into her office. "Hi, working girl. How was your first day?"

"It was alright, but I haven't eaten all day. Tomorrow I'll pack a lunch. I have to be at work at 7:30 in the morning. I'll just ride the bus, if you can loan me a couple of dollars for bus fare, until I get my first check."

"I sure hate for you to have to do that, but of course I'll give you some money."

"It's no problem. There's a bus stop on the corner by the house. They're paying me $1.75 an hour, so that's not bad and my hours are 7:30 to 4:00."

"I have a candy bar in my purse if you want it. I've got a couple more things to do and then we'll get out of here."

Darlina eagerly accepted the candy. "I'm gonna go wait outside for you. I really don't want to have to answer a bunch of questions from people here if they see me."

"I understand. Here are the car keys. I'll be out in a little bit."

Darlina munched on the Snickers bar and waited for her sister. Her mind drifted to the day that Luke had shown up at the boiler factory with the beautiful gold and diamond heart necklace. She remembered the bargain he'd made with her if she'd have dinner with him. He'd kept his end of the bargain by never asking her to share their bed with another woman. She thought sadly that it seemed like a lifetime ago instead of only a few short months.

Her thoughts were interrupted by Norma opening the car door. "Let's pick up some hamburgers and go home."

"Sounds good to me. In a few weeks, I'll have some money to pay you back for all of this."

"Would you quit worrying? I'm glad you got hired today and that's not a bad wage."

"Nope, not bad...it's monotonous work and I'll be surprised if I ever make my quota. But, it's a paycheck."

By Wednesday, Darlina had her routine down. She was at the bus stop by seven each morning and had decided to ride the bus back home each day, instead of going to Norma's office. The thought of having to explain her presence there was overwhelming and she found it simpler to avoid it.

She liked that she could get lost amongst the many other workers at Timex. No one knew her, so she didn't have to explain anything about herself. It gave her the anonymity she needed.

She'd just gotten off work on Friday afternoon and was making her way to the bus stop, when she heard a car honk and someone calling her name. She turned to look and Sherry was waving at her.

She walked slowly over to the car and leaned down to talk through the open window. "What are you doing here?"

"I finally found you. I knew your sister worked at the boiler factory so I went there and she told me you were working here. Get in."

"I really don't feel like talking, Sherry."

"You don't have to talk. Just get in."

Darlina opened the car door and slid in the passenger seat. "Please don't tell me you told me so."

"Oh honey, I would never do that. I saw Luke last night and was shocked when you weren't with him."

Darlina looked out the window, as tears suddenly clouded her eyes. She asked in a hushed whisper, "Who was with him?"

"You mean besides the band?"

"Yes, besides the band."

"Mary."

Darlina was silent for a long moment. The tears she'd been holding back for days flooded like a dam that had burst at the seams.

"Oh Darlina, I didn't mean to make you cry. Please stop."

"Oh God, Sherry, I just wanna die," she said as she sobbed.

Sherry reached across the seat, placing a comforting hand on her friend's shoulder. "You don't mean that. You're just hurting."

"You can't begin to imagine how much I'm hurting. I love Luke with all my heart." The sobs increased. "I'm so lost and I don't know what went wrong."

"There, there. Let's go to my house and we can talk."

"I don't wanna see Johnny."

Sherry laughed sarcastically. "You won't see Johnny. He's gone back to Louise."

"I'm so sorry. Aren't we a fine pair?"

Sherry handed Darlina a Kleenex. "Yep, a fine pair..."

Once they got to Sherry's apartment, Darlina remembered her sister. "Did you tell Norma you were picking me up?"

"Yes. She said she was glad and that you needed a friend."

Darlina wiped her eyes again. "I don't need a friend. I need Luke."

"Well, honey. You're stuck with me. Now tell me everything."

"Do you have anything to drink?"

"Why don't you go fix your face and I'll make us a pitcher of Margaritas."

Darlina went into the bathroom and looked in the mirror at the mascara streaks running down her face. She took a tissue and wiped them off. Ruefully she thought that it was probably a futile effort. When she returned, Sherry handed her a tall frosty glass.

They sat at Sherry's kitchen table and Darlina began unfolding the events that led up to Luke bringing her back to Abilene, just one short week ago.

She finished by saying, "Everything seemed fine until he decided to bring Dee Dee home with us. And he kept talking about a storm that was coming. Guess it got here."

"I'm so very sorry Darlina. I don't really know what to say. And don't worry, I'm not gonna say I told you so."

"You can if you want to. You tried to warn me, but I swear Luke loved me. I know he did and I still love him. I always will."

"I know it seems like that now, but in time, you'll feel differently."

"I don't think so, but that's what Norma tells me." Darlina finished off her drink, gulping down the last swallow. She liked that she was beginning to feel numbness instead of the searing pain.

Sherry refilled their glasses. "I thought I was falling in love with Johnny, but it didn't really hurt too much when he decided to go back to his wife. I guess it wasn't true love. I was running out of patience with his drug problem anyway."

"Maybe there really isn't such a thing as true love. Maybe it's all just a fantasy. I thought I'd found it and it would last forever but look at me now. I'm a mess."

"I have something that will make us feel better if you want it."

"What?"

"It's a capsule called Psilocybin. It's all natural made from mushrooms. A friend of mine gave me a couple and I haven't taken any yet. She said it made her feel wonderful."

"I'd love to feel wonderful again, but I don't think any pill is going to take away the hurt and pain I feel."

"Let's just try it. We don't have to leave the apartment and maybe it will make us both feel good."

"Guess it couldn't hurt. I just don't think anything is going to make me feel alright again until I'm back with Luke."

The girls swallowed the capsules with a drink of their margarita. Sherry started thumbing through her record collection. "What do you want to hear?"

"I don't care as long as it isn't Joan Baez."

Darlina moved to the sofa, leaned her head back and closed her eyes. She was thankful for a friend like Sherry. She wondered where Luke might be and what he might be doing. Somehow, she felt oddly comforted that he was with Mary.

Tears trickled down her cheeks as she envisioned Luke's arms around her. She could almost feel his kisses on her face and neck. Nothing would ever complete her like he did.

She began to feel slightly euphoric and the vise grip on her heart loosened just a little. She breathed out a heavy sigh, opened her eyes and took another sip of her frosty drink.

For the moment, she'd pass some time with her friend and enjoy the temporary reprieve, from the horrible wrenching pain, that had become her constant companion.

Luke just had to come back for her. Maybe after his storm passed. But, what if he didn't? She wasn't sure she'd want to keep living without him. He'd shown her the path to the stars and taught her how to fly. How could she ever be satisfied with anything less?

# Chapter 30

A few short hours later, Darlina found herself laughing hysterically one minute and then sobbing uncontrollably the next. The room took on a liquid appearance, with the walls undulating in brilliant colors. She didn't understand what was happening, but she also didn't feel scared.

At times when she looked at Sherry, her face looked grotesquely like the Joker. Her thinking process had become totally disconnected.

There was no concept of time. As she became more and more in the grips of the drug, she lost all sense of reality.

Suddenly, everything came flooding back. Luke! The amplified searing pain took over again with ferocity beyond anything she'd ever experienced.

Between bouts of laughing and crying, she insistently told Sherry, "I have to go where Luke is."

"We can't go anywhere, Darlina. I'm too screwed up to drive."

"Where are they playing tonight?"

"The Four Aces, but I honestly don't need to be driving like this."

"You have to take me there. If you don't drive me, I swear I'll walk. I have to see him."

"Darlina, you don't want to see him like this. We are both too messed up to leave this apartment."

Darlina got off the sofa, picked up her purse and headed for the door. "I'm going, whether you take me or not."

"Wait! If you go walking across town like this, you'll wind up in jail."

"I don't give a shit. I have to see Luke." Adamantly, she opened the door.

Sherry grabbed her by the arm and pulled her back. "Just a minute...let me see if I can pull myself together and I'll take you. Please sit down."

Darlina sat back down on the sofa, still clutching her purse.

Sherry went into the kitchen and attempted to make coffee. After an hour of serious concentration, she finally succeeded in producing a steaming pot of the brown liquid.

Darlina had settled down but was lost inside her head with distorted thoughts. When Sherry handed her a cup of coffee, she sat with it between her hands and marveled at the brilliant colors in the rising steam.

"Drink it," Sherry encouraged.

Darlina looked up at Sherry. "Aren't these colors beautiful?"

"I don't know what you're seeing, but I'm seeing bright orange, blue and yellow."

"Oh no, there's red! Brilliant red..."

The girls sat engrossed in the steam off the coffee until it began to dissipate. "Oh yeah," said Sherry. "We're supposed to drink it."

Darlina took a sip. "Ew, that tastes awful."

"Well drink it anyway. We've got to get straight if I'm going to take you to see Luke."

"Oh, Luke...I almost forgot. Let's go now."

"Drink your coffee first, then I'll take you."

With the cups of coffee downed, they headed to the car. As Sherry drove very slowly across town, Darlina looked in wonderment at the lights they were passing. Each one left a trail of brightly colored vapors.

For now, there was quiet inside the car. Finally, the blinking neon sign came into view. All the raw emotion, at the prospect of seeing Luke, unleashed itself again.

She found herself sobbing so hard that she could barely breathe.

"You need to pull yourself together. Luke ain't gonna want you going in the club like this."

"I don't care. I can't help it."

"I'm going to let you out and then I'm leaving."

"Alright. Luke will take care of me. I know he will."

"Call me, Darlina."

Darlina was already out of the car before Sherry could get another word out.

The older gray haired lady, working the door, appeared to recognize Darlina instantly.

"Wait here. I'll go get Luke," she said, as she hurried off. She left Darlina standing by the door.

Darlina could hear the music and had the urge to go running into Luke's arms, but did as the lady asked.

In what seemed like a flash, Luke stood angrily in front of her. "What the hell are you doing Darlina? And what in the hell kind of drug did you take?"

She flung herself against his chest, wrapping her arms around him. "Oh Luke! I just had to see you. I've missed you so much."

"Let's go outside."

He extracted himself from her grasp, took her arm and led her to the car. He opened the passenger side door and gently pushed her inside. He then went around to the driver's side and got inside the car with her.

She shivered from the cool night air. He picked the blanket up off the seat and wrapped it around her shoulders.

Darlina could not stop the sobs and when she did, she laughed hysterically. "Luke, please let me come back home."

"I don't know what you've taken, but you are screwed up. I sure can't let you go in the club like this."

She gasped for breath. "I'll be good Luke. I promise I will."

"You stay here. I'm going to lock the doors and I'll send Mary out to sit with you until I can get this gig finished and then I'll figure out what to do with you."

"Mary?"

"Yes, Mary. Stay here."

Luke got out of the car, locked all the doors and went back inside the club.

Darlina sat staring out of the car window at the wondrous colors of the car lights passing by. For a moment she forgot where she was. Then out of nowhere, a parade of cut-out gingerbread men, with hands joined, began to dance across her line of vision. She watched as they started on the left and danced across to the right until they were out of sight. Then they started all over again.

She was barely aware when Mary opened the door and got in the car with her. She thought Mary said something, but couldn't make the words out. When she looked at her, she saw bright red glittering eyes and a crimson mouth. Then the gingerbread men would take over again.

She had no idea how long she sat in the car with Mary, crying and laughing; watching the endless trail of gingerbread men over and over again.

Then, Mary was gone and Luke was back in the car. The car was moving and she didn't care where they were going as long as he was with her. Then the gingerbread men came back. If Luke spoke to her, she didn't hear him. She was trapped in the clutches of the drug.

Once the car stopped moving, she realized they were in Brownwood, at Luke's apartment. For a moment, her heart soared. He was taking her back!

"Come on," Luke coaxed, as he opened her car door.

She could feel her legs moving, but didn't think her feet were touching the ground. Everything was altered, yet oddly familiar.

Inside the apartment, Luke seated her at the kitchen table, while opening a bag of hamburgers. "You need to eat, Darlina."

She wondered where those had magically appeared from. She hadn't been aware that they'd stopped anywhere. "I don't want to eat, Luke. I'm not hungry."

"I know you aren't, but you're gonna eat if I have to shove it in your mouth. I don't know what in the hell you've taken, but you need food to help bring you back down."

"It was a capsule that Sherry gave me. She called it sillycibin or something like that. I've been seeing lots of colors and little gingerbread men."

"Dammit! That's a psychedelic drug. Darlina, you can't just swallow anything anyone hands you. You'll wind up hurting yourself."

"I don't care Luke. If I can't be with you, I don't give a shit what I do to myself."

"Just eat and drink this milk. We've got to get you back down somehow."

Darlina sat at the table and attempted to swallow the food Luke pushed towards her. Obediently, she opened her mouth and put it in, even though the texture of the food made her gag. The smell of it made her stomach reel and yet she continued putting bite after bite into her mouth because Luke wanted her to. The milk wasn't so bad and it didn't make her gag.

Gradually, the walls began to appear normal again and the prismatic colors off the lights began to subside.

All the while, Luke sat the table. He wasn't eating or talking, except to coax her to eat a little more.

As the sun was beginning to peek over the horizon, Luke took Darlina by the hand and led her into the bedroom, gently laid her on the bed and then lay beside her. They were both fully clothed.

"I'm sorry Luke."

"Shh...don't talk. Close your eyes and try to rest."

"I love you."

"Shh..."

Darlina closed her eyes, content to have Luke beside her. She didn't think she could fall asleep and with her eyes closed, the brilliant flashes of color began again, this time behind her eyelids. She instinctively turned towards Luke; draping one arm across his chest.

Luke didn't try to move her arm but he also didn't bring her up close to him nor wrap his arms around her the way he longed to do. When he heard her soft even breathing, he let out a sigh of relief.

As he stared up at the ceiling, a thousand thoughts flew through his mind. What next? He knew he had to take her back to Abilene. He didn't have the heart to be mean or cruel to her again. He'd have to be firm but he wouldn't be mean. He hated what loving him had done to this beautiful, sweet girl.

He turned to gaze at her tear streaked face and thought she looked angelic. He couldn't resist reaching up and brushing a strand of auburn hair from across her eyes.

Over and over again, he wished he could undo the tangles in his life. He cursed fate. He cursed the bad choices he'd made; knowing full well it was too late to undo them.

She stirred beside him and her eyelids fluttered open to meet his gaze. "Make love to me, Luke," she murmured.

"No, Darlina. Go back to sleep."

"Please."

"No, just rest."

She closed her eyes again and sighed deeply.

Once she had drifted off into a deep sleep, Luke quietly slipped off the bed. He sat in the big chair in the corner of the room where Darlina had spent countless hours keeping watch through his fever a couple of months back. He put his head in his hands and a feeling of helplessness washed over him.

He wanted nothing more than to have Darlina with him, but if he couldn't have her without destroying her, then he simply had to send her away forever.

Luke Stone had screwed up a lot in his life but this was the one time he was determined to do the right thing. She had her whole life ahead of her and deserved only good and wonderful things; not the tattered, tangled baggage of a broken down musician.

With resolve, he went back to the bed and lay beside her. Once she was okay, he would take her back to Abilene where he knew she would be taken care of by her family.

Somehow he had to make her promise not to do anything foolish like this again. He knew that if she made a promise, she'd keep it.

He couldn't stand the thought of her hurting herself, or someone else hurting her even though he was powerless to protect her.

It had been many years since he'd uttered a prayer, but he closed his eyes and silently prayed to God to take care of this precious girl. "Not for me God, but for her." Then he prayed for forgiveness.

He didn't know if God would pay any attention to him, but surely he would to her. With that, he closed his eyes and let the tiredness wash over him. At least with her beside him, he knew for the moment she was safe. In a few hours she'd be gone again. No matter how hard he wished it could be different, the die had been cast.

# Chapter 31

When Darlina opened her eyes again, it was four o'clock in the afternoon. Her stomach churned and she was disoriented. She looked around the room, knowing where she was, but not quite sure how she got there.

She could hear the water in the shower running and knew Luke was getting ready for the next gig. It was all too painfully familiar.

Every detail of the past twenty four hours came flooding back. She felt ashamed of herself for showing up at the club messed up on a crazy drug. She wanted more than anything to be back by Luke's side, but this was certainly no way to do it.

She reached up and brushed her hair out of her eyes. She must look a mess. She wished she had a hair brush, toothbrush and some mascara. When she blinked, her eyelids felt puffy.

Luke came out of the shower, drying his hair with a towel.

Darlina sat up on the side of the bed and hid her face in her hands. "Luke, I'm so very sorry."

He sat down beside her on the bed. "Darlina, you've got to promise me you won't ever do anything like that again. Taking a drug that you don't know anything about can really hurt you, dammit."

"I know. I just wanted to feel better and stop hurting. Sherry said the pill would help."

"I'd be pissed at Sherry, except you're a grown woman and I know she didn't force you to take it." He fastened his watch around his wrist. "I have to take you back to Abilene."

"Why does it have to be this way, Luke?"

"I've explained it over and over and all I can do is repeat myself. It's for your own good."

"It sure doesn't feel like it. I can't just stop loving you Luke. My heart isn't made that way."

"Look, we can hash this out 'til the cows come home and it's not gonna change a thing. The cards are dealt and I can't un-deal 'em. Why don't you go get washed up a little and as soon as I'm dressed, I'll take you back to Norma's?"

Darlina slowly got off the bed and went into the bathroom. She was shocked when she looked at her face in the mirror. There were black streaks of mascara down both cheeks. Her eyes were swollen and red and her hair was a tangled mess. She did what she could to clean up, while dreading walking back into the bedroom. She knew what was waiting for her and it was a trip back to Abilene.

The radio played softly in the car, as Luke drove. Darlina was grateful that Luke was taking her in his T-Bird. She couldn't bear the thought of riding in the band car with everyone and the humiliation she'd feel.

She suddenly had a memory flash. "What happened to Mary last night? I remember her being in the car with me."

"I asked Red to take her home."

"Are you back with her?"

"Nah. She just showed up at the club."

"Well, I appreciate her babysitting me. Would you tell her?"

"If I see her, I'll tell her."

Luke was turning from Sayles Boulevard onto Seventh Street when Buck Owens' voice rang out from the radio, *"Together again. My tears have stopped falling. The long lonely nights are now at an end..."*

Darlina had been holding back her tears but as the words of the song resonated in her ears, they began falling so fast and hard that she could barely catch her breath. "I don't know why you're so determined that we be apart. It just doesn't seem fair."

"Sweetheart, there's nothing fair in life and the sooner you figure that out, the better off you'll be. I can't change what is."

"You could take me back home with you if you really wanted to."

"No, I can't, and you need to get that through your head."

Luke pulled the car into Norma's driveway and turned off the engine.

"Please don't make me get out," Darlina begged, through her tears.

Luke sighed heavily taking Darlina's hands in his own and looking into her tear-filled eyes. "You have to get out, but you have to promise me that you won't take another drug that you know nothing about."

Darlina sobbed.

"Promise me," Luke said sternly.

"Okay, I promise. But I won't ever stop loving you, so don't ask me to do that because I can't."

"Another thing...I don't want you coming around the clubs where I'm playing. I'm dead serious. I don't want to see you anywhere I'm playing."

"Alright," she reluctantly agreed. "I'll do what you ask, but I don't like it and I never will."

"Goodbye, Darlina." He touched her cheek gently with his fingertips.

She opened the car door, turning to look at Luke one last time. "Goodbye, Luke. Never forget that I love you with all my heart."

Luke turned his face away from her and stared out the window until he heard the door close. He started the engine and backed out of the driveway without taking another look back.

Darlina walked up the sidewalk into her sister's house. Her tears fell like big wet raindrops, splashing down the front of her blouse. The house was empty when she let herself in and she was very thankful that she didn't have to explain things to Norma just yet.

She went straight to her bedroom, stripped off her dirty clothes and stood under the hot steamy shower. She let the water run over her head, then scrubbed her body from head to toe, as if to wash away the past few hours of her life.

Every time she thought about what she'd done, wave after wave of humiliation washed over her. How could she have let herself be so stupid? She'd only wanted the pain to stop. If she could only go backwards, she'd choose not to take the drug that left her so out of control.

By the time Norma got home, Darlina had managed to pull herself together. She was truthful and explained exactly what happened.

"Oh, little sister, that is so dangerous. You can't be doing things like that."

"I know and I'm really sorry. Luke was very disappointed in me and I don't blame him. I'm disappointed in myself."

"Don't spend time beating yourself up. We all mess up from time to time. All we can do is make sure that we don't repeat our mistakes."

"I need to call Sherry and let her know I'm alright. I don't blame her for any of it. She had no idea I'd react the way I did."

"I think that's very mature not to blame someone else. You did what you did willingly and you learned from it."

"I wish I could get a do-over, but I know that's not possible."

"Well, the main thing is that you're alright and you learned a very important lesson. Do call Sherry and let her know you're okay."

Once Darlina hung up the phone, after talking to Sherry, she felt emotionally and physically drained.

Norma had to get ready for a date with Greg and Darlina was glad for the quiet darkness of her bedroom, where she could be alone with her thoughts.

It seemed that life was throwing some hard lessons her way and she felt very inadequate to deal with any of them.

Monday morning found her back at Timex, at her workstation, winding the endless trays of watches. At times, she got lost in the repetition and other times, her neck and shoulders hurt so much, she could only count the hours until the day was over.

Friday she would get a paycheck and that was the motivation she needed to get up every day and do it all over again.

Luke had made it clear that he was done with her and it was totally up to her to try to put her life back together. There was a huge gaping hole in her heart that nothing could ever fill. She was convinced of that fact.

Two weeks had passed since the fateful night Darlina took the drug and wound up on Luke's doorstep. She'd settled into a routine of working, going home and then doing it all over again. She had no desire to socialize with anyone and certainly didn't want to hit the club scene alone, especially without Luke.

Tuesday morning, Norma burst into Darlina's bedroom, as she was getting ready for work.

"Darlina! You've got to turn on the radio and listen to the news." Norma's voice shook in her excitement.

"Okay, but why?"

"Luke's been arrested for bank robbery."

Darlina's legs buckled and she sank to the bed. "What?"

"I just heard it on the radio. They said that he and two other band members were arrested yesterday, along with some other men that weren't in the band, for robbing banks."

"Oh my God! How could that be?"

"I don't know, honey, but I'm damn sure glad you were out of there before they arrested him."

"Poor Luke. I can't even imagine him being locked up in jail. I need to leave a little early so I can pick up a newspaper."

"I knew you'd want to know. Are you okay?"

"Yeah, I guess. I just feel numb."

She quickly finished getting dressed for work and ran to the bus stop. She couldn't believe what Norma had told her. Luke would never rob a bank. Surely there was some mistake.

The headlines of the newspaper blared, *"Popular Local Musician Arrested for Bank Robbery"*.

So, it was true. She pored over the newspaper article. It gave specific details of the arrest and stated that the Texas Rangers had been involved in the investigation for almost a year. Luke, Red, Royce, Butch and Joe were accused of robbing a bank in Rising Star and one in Bangs. She sat looking ahead, unseeing with a jumble of thoughts running through her head.

She thought about the three men who had come to the apartment and how Luke quickly ushered them next door to Red's. Then she remembered them showing up at the club and how Luke had reacted. Somehow, she just knew they had something to do with all of this. Maybe they had set Luke up.

Her heart went out to Luke. Suddenly, she thought of his children and Joyce. The children would never understand and must be terrified. She wished she could somehow offer some comfort to them, but knew that was impossible. Then her thoughts turned to Mr. and Mrs. Stone and to Bobby. So many people were going to be hurt by this.

It had to be a huge mistake. She hoped with all her heart that was the case. Surely Luke would be able to clear his name.

As she sat at her workstation, numb and in a daze, her thoughts continued to be filled with Luke and this crazy new development. She realized that he walked a little outside the line, but robbing a bank? She couldn't picture him doing anything that bizarre.

More than anything, she wished that she could go to him and assure him that everything would be alright. After all, in America, you are innocent until proven guilty.

The buzz in the lunchroom that day swirled around her and everyone was talking about the arrest. They all seemed to either know Luke personally, or know of him. This was big news for Abilene, Texas.

She remained quiet and did not share in their conversation. Not only did she know him better than any of them, but she loved him and would remain loyal, no matter what the newspaper and all the people were saying.

Perhaps this was the price he was forced to pay for being a rebel. She didn't know, but she did know that her heart belonged to him and it would for as long as she continued to draw a breath.

Even then, she was sure it would continue beyond the grave. Her love for Luke Stone was eternal.

# Chapter 32

Over the next several weeks, Darlina picked up a newspaper every morning on her way to work and scanned through it, looking for any news about Luke.

One article referred to the men as the *Thursday Bandits* since the robberies had taken place on Thursdays. Another article called Luke the head of the *Dixie Mafia* and they used words like *Kingpin* and *Gang leader*.

It seemed that the newspapers were convicting Luke before he ever went to trial. She cut out every article covering Luke's arrest she could find. She felt that each piece of paper helped her stay connected to him in some odd way.

She also began spending time regularly with Leann and it appeared that her sister had troubles of her own. On this particular Wednesday afternoon, she'd taken the bus to Leann's house instead of going home. The two sisters sat on the sofa sipping Cokes, while the radio crooned one country hit after another.

With spring arriving, Leann had bought two Easter lily plants and they sat cheerily on tables at each end of the sofa.

"Look at today's newspaper article." Darlina pulled the piece of newspaper from her purse.

"I can't believe all of this is happening. I know he had his faults, but this is just wild," Leann replied.

"I know. I really wish I could go and see him. I've got a little money saved up now and I'm ready to start looking for a car."

"I'll tell Wayne. He might know somebody that has one for sale. That is if he can stay sober long enough."

"Leann, I'm so sorry you're having troubles."

"Wayne is drinking heavier all the time. I don't know what to do. It looks like we just need to get the hell out of Abilene." Leann nervously twisted a lock of hair between her thumb and finger.

"Where would you go?"

"I don't know for sure, but I've been talking to our brother and he told me that he'd give Wayne a job at his meat market in Hobbs if we want to go there."

"Shit! I'd rather take a beating than to move back to Hobbs."

"Yeah, me too, but we have to do something. I need to get Wayne away from his drinkin' buddies here. Mama said we could live in our old house until we found a place. Besides that, I've been waiting to be sure before I told anyone, but I'm pregnant."

Darlina excitedly jumped up and threw her arms around her sister. "Oh my God! I'm so happy for you. I'm gonna be an aunt. How far along are you?"

"Well, if my guess is right, the baby will be due in November."

"Does Wayne know?"

"I haven't told him yet. That's another reason why I need to get him out of Abilene. If we are going to be parents, he can't stay drunk all the time."

"That's very true, but maybe he wouldn't drink so much if he knew he was going to be a father. Oh, this is so exciting. I needed some good news to come along about now."

"Guess we could both use a little good news, huh?"

"Yep. I better get to the bus stop and get home. I'll see you again soon though."

"You better."

"I love you and you take really good care of yourself. You've got a little one growing inside of you now."

Leann laughed. "I will and I love you too. Come back tomorrow if you can."

"Okay. Let me know if Wayne hears about any car possibilities."

"I will. Tell Norma I said hi but don't tell her about the baby yet."

"My lips are sealed. I'll try to see you tomorrow."

Darlina's steps were a little lighter as she walked to the bus stop. There was going to be a new addition to the family. She thought about how often she'd wished she had Luke's baby inside her, but realized now that it was a blessing that she didn't. That would surely make her life more difficult than it already was.

It had been a month since Luke's arrest and the newspaper finally reported that a trial date had been set. He would face trial in Eastland, on July 12th. Darlina's heart ached to be there in the courtroom. Luke's last words echoed in her mind when he insisted that she stay away from him. It was probably good that she didn't have a car because she knew she'd be tempted to miss work and go sit in on the trial.

Again, she thought about how awful it must be for Luke to be locked up and even more devastating, the pain it must be causing for his family.

She also began to feel the need to find a place of her own and get out of her sister's house. She searched the newspaper for something she could afford on her Timex salary and was thrilled when she found an apartment near Hendricks Medical Center for seventy five dollars a month.

To make it even better, there was a bus stop right on the corner next to the apartment.

"Norma, will you go with me to look at an apartment on Saturday?" she asked her sister, as they sat eating supper.

"Sure. But, you know you don't have to move out. You're welcome to stay here as long as you like."

"I know and I appreciate that more than you'll ever know, but I think it's time I got out on my own. Lord knows you've done enough."

"Well then, we'll go look at it and I'll help you get set up as far as household stuff."

Darlina sighed. "You're the best sister in the world. Between you and Leann, I have all the family support I could hope for. Of course, I would love to have mama and daddy back in my life, but that's something they've chosen."

"They'll come around eventually. You'll see."

"I sure hope so. I miss them terribly."

"Hey, why don't you and me go out and get a drink somewhere?" Norma picked up their plates and put them in the sink.

"Like where?"

"We could go to the Silver Spur."

"No. I can't bear the thought of seeing people that I knew with Luke and having to answer questions or listen to things they are saying. I'm not ready for that."

"How about we go to the Oasis then? You haven't been anywhere outside this house but to work and back. You've got to get out and start living again."

"I don't feel ready, Norma. I'm afraid."

"Afraid? Of what?"

"People can be downright mean and even though Luke had lots of friends, he had some enemies too."

"Look, we only have to stay long enough to get one drink. You don't have to talk to anyone if you don't want to. Come on, go with me."

"I don't know."

"Oh, just get ready and let's go. I insist," Norma impatiently prodded.

Darlina got up from the table, gathered the rest of their dishes and loaded them into the dishwasher. "Alright, but if I freak out, promise me you'll bring me back home."

"I promise."

Two hours later, the girls entered the darkened but lively Oasis club. The laughter, smoke and dim lights brought back familiar but painful memories of Luke for Darlina. She stayed close to her sister's side, not daring to make eye contact with anyone.

They sat in a booth at the back of the club. There wasn't a live band, but *Merle Haggard* blasted *Silver Wings* from the jukebox. Darlina felt a tug at her heart as she remembered Red singing that song many times.

They had barely sat down when Darlina heard a familiar voice. "Darlina! Where have you been? I've been so worried about you."

She looked up to see Louise approaching their table. "Hi Louise. I've been hibernating. I guess you've heard about Luke."

"Yeah, me and everyone else in Abilene. It's a crazy, messed up, bunch of shit."

"Yes it is. Louise this is my sister, Norma."

"Hello. Nice to meet you," Norma warmly said, motioning to the waitress who walked by.

"Mind if I sit down?" Louise asked, as she slid in the booth beside Darlina.

"Of course not. It's good to see you. I've been so torn up over Luke. I've just been working and going home."

Louise put her arm around Darlina's shoulders. "Honey, I don't know if you realize it or not, but you were the best thing that had happened to Luke in a very long time."

"I truly loved him," Darlina said, feeling hot tears gathering and praying that she wouldn't break down in public. "I don't believe for a minute any of the bogus charges filed against him."

"I know. Me either. He was a real friend to me and Johnny."

"I'm glad you and Johnny are back together. You belong."

Louise laughed. "Don't know for how long, because he's a pain in the ass, but we'll see how it goes."

"Would you like a drink Louise? What do you want Darlina?" Norma asked as the waitress approached their table.

"I'm fine," said Louise. "I've got a Daiquiri over at my table."

"I'll take a scotch and soda," Darlina said, then turned to Louise. "Are you dancing anywhere?"

"Yeah, still over at the Silver Spur. It pays good."

Their conversation was interrupted by a small group of men who approached them.

The apparent leader of the group sneered, "So, looks like Luke's woman is out on the town, while his sorry ass rots in jail."

Louise confronted him. "Bill, you don't know what the hell you're talking about and you're drunk. Leave Darlina alone!"

"Come on, sugar. Why don't you come with me and I'll show you what a real man can do for you?" he said, motioning to Darlina.

Louise slid out of the booth, facing him. "I told you to leave her the hell alone, Bill and I mean it. If Luke walked into this club right now, all of you assholes would tuck your tails between your legs and hide under a table. You're not men, you're pieces of shit."

Darlina couldn't stop the tears from spilling. "It's alright Louise. You don't have to fight my battles for me." She slid out of the booth and looked squarely at the men who were antagonizing her. "Not one of you is man enough to fill Luke Stone's boots and Louise is right. If he walked in here right now, you'd all shit down both legs."

Bill sneered at her. "You just don't know what a real man is."

"I know more about a real man than you will ever dream about knowing. I think you just need to get the hell away from our table."

Norma stood up beside Darlina, putting her arm through hers. "Come on, sister. Let's go."

The men parted to let the girls through.

Darlina turned and hugged Louise. "Thank you for sticking up for Luke. I'll see you around sometime."

Louise returned her hug. "Sweetie, take care of yourself and if you ever need anything, please let me know."

"Thank you so much. We're gonna go now."

Norma turned to Louise. "It was nice to meet you, and thank you for taking up for my little sister."

"You're quite welcome. It was nice to meet you too. Ya'll come over to the Silver Spur sometime and I'll buy you a drink."

Norma laughed. "I had to twist Darlina's arm to get her out here tonight and I have a feeling it will be a while before I get her out again, but thanks anyway. Would you mind telling the waitress we had to go when she brings the drinks?"

"Sure, I'll go tell her now. Ya'll take care."

"Tell Johnny I said hi," Darlina said, as she and Norma turned to leave the club.

In the car, Darlina's tears increased. "I told you, Norma. These people who sat at Luke's table and drank his liquor have turned on him and act like he's some kind of monster."

"I'm sorry, honey. I shouldn't have talked you into coming out with me."

"It's okay. It's just something I'm going to have to get used to dealing with. Maybe next time I'll be more prepared."

"Those men were just drunk and obviously jealous of Luke. Don't let them bother you."

"It's kinda' hard not to" Darlina said quietly. "I just wish Luke would've told me what to expect. All he kept saying over and over was that a storm was coming."

"I think the storm got here. I don't care what you think, I'm just glad you weren't there when they arrested him. They could have tried to drag you into it too."

"Yes, I know. Luke did his best to look out for me."

"He did, and I appreciate that very much."

"Let's just go home. I'm suddenly very tired," Darlina leaned her head back on the car seat, closing her eyes.

In the quiet darkness of her room, Darlina thought about the arrogance of the men and how Louise stood up to them. If she ever got the chance, she would tell Luke. He would have been very proud of Louise. Tonight she proved that she is a true friend.

She pictured Luke in his jail cell and could only imagine the despair, anger, betrayal and loneliness he must feel. She wished she could reach out to him, caress his face and assure him that everything was going to be alright.

But was it? She wished she could be sure of that herself. With Luke locked away in jail and facing very serious charges, she couldn't be certain. The outcome looked bleak indeed.

For the first time in a very long time, she whispered a fervent prayer. "Please God, watch over Luke, his family and please make everything be okay."

As she drifted off to sleep, she dreamed she was safe and secure in Luke's arms and that everything else had just been a nightmare. She hoped that when she awoke, she'd find that to be true.

She felt the coolness of the little gold heart necklace around her throat and fell asleep with it nestled between her fingers.

# Chapter 33

The hardness of the small bunk he lay on, in the Eastland County jail, pressed into his back, as Luke Stone lay wide awake in the early morning darkness.

The Texas Rangers and local police had surrounded his and Red's apartments early on a Monday morning and arrested them. He was thankful that they hadn't arrested him while on stage.

His attorney, Bob Church, had assured him that the evidence they had against him was circumstantial and the odds of a conviction were slim.

That was good, because he hadn't done what he was accused of. He had to believe that a man couldn't be hanged for a crime he didn't commit.

He shared a four-man cell with Red, a young kid who'd been arrested for possession of marijuana and an older man they all called Bud who was in for cattle rustling.

Since their snores rattled the bars, he knew the men were sound asleep. He quietly sat up on the side of his bunk. He found it hard to believe he'd been in jail for three months.

The faces of his children flashed before his eyes, and his heart broke for them. Joyce had come to visit once since he'd gotten locked up. She was so full of anger and bitterness that all she could do was scream at him. The Texas Rangers had questioned her and searched the house. She was humiliated and scared.

He felt a huge guilt for abandoning them, but reminded himself that he hadn't voluntarily disappeared. There had been a little help from the Texas Rangers and apparently a few other so-called friends, who made up stories and lies to save their own asses.

At least there was now a trial date, so maybe soon, this nightmare would be over.

He thought about his mom and dad and how they'd stood beside him throughout this ordeal. He knew this was terribly hard on them, but they tried not to show it and kept the faith that he'd be free soon.

His brother, Bobby, had come to the jail to visit him two weeks ago. He brought news that he was moving his family to Alaska, where his wife's parents lived. He was glad that Bobby hadn't been dragged into this, although he'd been questioned several times.

He vowed that when he got out of this mess, he was through with the honky-tonk life. He'd go back to work in the oilfield or get a job doing carpentry work. As much as he loved the music, the lifestyle that came with it had damn near destroyed everything he cherished.

Daylight began to break through the small window at the top of the cell.

The jailer walked through the hallway banging his night stick on the bars. "Time to rise and shine, ladies."

Luke heard moans and groans from up and down the hallway as the men arose from their bunks. Everything was regimented. Each inmate wore the same orange coveralls that had *Eastland County Jail* emblazoned across the back. Food was brought to their cell three times a day. It was the same food every day and most days, Luke left his plate untouched.

The eggs were runny, the toast burnt and a spoonful of canned peaches plopped down in the middle of it all. Lunch consisted of dry bologna sandwiches and more peaches. Supper was the only meal that changed. Sometimes it was meatloaf and other times it was some sort of chopped bar-b-que. All-in-all, there was nothing appetizing about any of it.

Luke leaned against the bars. "Hey Lefty, are we gonna get the same runny eggs this morning?"

"I don't what know you're talking about Stone. My wife cooks every single one of these meals and she's a damned good cook."

"If you say so, hoss."

"Besides that, this ain't no damned country club. This is jail."

"You sure got that one right," Luke congenially replied.

As part of the daily routine, if it wasn't raining, the men were allowed to exercise outside in a small fenced area. It was secured with razor wire that was wrapped around the top. Luke liked feeling the sunshine on his face and looked forward to the one hour when he was out of his cell.

A week before his trial the jailer came to his cell. "Stone, you've got a visitor. Come with me."

Luke followed the jailer wondering who had come to see him. He'd seen his attorney the day before and his mom and dad had visited a couple of days ago.

Once seated in the small visiting room, he looked at the man across the table from him. The man had piercing blue eyes, ruddy complexion and wore an Irish herringbone plaid cap. Luke did not recognize him. "Do I know you?"

"Aye, sir. Yer 'av lads who sent me."

Luke looked furtively around to make sure the jailer was out of earshot. "You're with the Irish Republican Army?"

"Aye. We 'av an offer ter make ter yer."

"Okay. Let's hear it."

"You've been a mucker ter de IRA. Ah've been sent ter tell yer dat we can git yer oyt av 'ere an' git yer ter Oirlan' wha' you'll be safe."

"You're offering to bust me out of here and take me to Ireland?"

"Aye. Yer an yisser partner."

"Me and Red? What's the catch?"

"Yer 'av to break al' ties wi' family an' lads. Naw contact at al'."

"What about my kids."

"Naw contact at al'."

The Irishman paused to light a cigarette, offering one to Luke.

Luke accepted the cigarette, before answering. "I've believed in and supported your cause for a long time, but hell man, I can't leave my folks and kids here and not have any more contact with them ever. Please tell my Irish brothers I appreciate this offer very much, but I have to decline."

"Gran so, Paddy. "Tis yisser choice. De offer won't be made again."

"I understand, and as I said, I appreciate it very much, but I can't leave my family and never contact them again."

The man stood, extending his hand. "Gran' luk to yer den."

"Thank you, my friend. God speed...our day will come."

"Aye, Brah'der." The man crushed out his cigarette and knocked on the door, signaling to the jailer he was done with the visit.

Luke stood and waited for his escort back to the jail cell.

The jailer commented as they walked down that hall. "That was a weird sort of a feller."

"I reckon to somebody who lives in Eastland, Texas, he would be. He was a friend of mine," Luke informed him.

"Well, I didn't mean nothin' by it. Just an observation."

"I understand."

Luke found the young kid gone when he got back to his jail cell, and Bud was stretched out, asleep on his bunk. He and Red spoke in soft tones in the corner of the cell.

"What was that all about?" Red asked. He'd gotten even skinnier since they'd been locked up and when he spoke, his Adam's apple bobbed up and down.

"The IRA sent a man who offered to bust us out of here and take us to Ireland."

"What did you say?"

"What could I say, Red? He told me we would have to sever all ties with family as part of the deal and I just can't do that."

"No, I reckon not."

"So, I thanked him and told him we still support the cause, but that we'd stay here."

"Did Lefty suspect anything?"

"Nah. He commented on what a weird dude he was, but poor ol' Lefty ain't got much to work with in the brain department."

Red chuckled. "You sure got that right. What do you think is gonna happen to us, Luke?"

"I don't know, hoss. I don't see how a man can be convicted for something he didn't do. Guess we'll just have to ride this train and see where it takes us."

"I sure do want out of here."

"I know. Me too."

Just then the jailer escorted the young kid back into the cell. Once the cell door closed behind him, the boy collapsed on his bunk, sobbing.

Luke moved over to him, putting a hand on his shoulder. "Hey, kid. What's the matter."

"I got five years in the State Penitentiary for possession of less than an ounce of marijuana."

"Shit! That's a bad break, son."

"I can't survive in prison."

"Sure you can. Don't start thinking like that."

"Well, boy. Looks like I got you five years to do." Luke looked up to see the District Attorney peering smugly through the bars. He had his thumbs tucked in his vest pockets and his chest thrust out.

Luke rose to his feet and walked over to the bars separating them. He was at least a foot taller than the D.A., who wore a brocade vest and bowtie. "Hey, man. Why do you wanna pick on this kid? Can't you see that he's already tore up?"

The smaller man growled, "Why don't you mind your own business, Stone. Mess with me and I'll get him another five for intent to sell."

"Why don't you come on in here and lets me and you talk about it," Luke said, narrowing his eyes.

The man patted his vest pocket. "I've got something in here that would take care of you, Stone."

Luke lost his temper. "You sawed off little piece of shit. You're nothing but a chicken shit little man. Come on in here and I'll stick that derringer up your ass sideways."

"Don't worry, Stone," he taunted. "I'll take care of you in court."

Luke slammed his fist against the bars. "You've got nothin' on me, asshole."

The District Attorney had already turned and walked back down the hall without any other reply.

Luke turned back to the boy. "Don't cry, son. You can always appeal."

The boy sat on the side of his bunk. "It won't do no good. Mr. Walton's got it in for me. Said he was gonna make an example out of me."

"Emory Walton is a sorry piece of chicken shit, but he does have power and that's a dangerous thing for a little man with a big ego to have."

The boy lay down on his bunk and turned his back to the other men.

Luke sat down on his own bunk. Perhaps he'd been too hasty in turning down the offer made by the IRA. He couldn't bear the thought of having no contact with his kids, parents or brother ever again. He also knew that part of the offer wasn't up for negotiation.

He picked up the tablet and pencil that he'd asked the jailer for several weeks back. He thumbed through the pages he'd already written on. His thoughts turned to Darlina as he wrote. He could almost smell her sweetly scented hair and feel her soft skin.

For once in his life he'd done the right thing by sending her away. She hadn't deserved to be dragged into this mess of shit. He closed his eyes and remembered the feel of her under him. He ached with a deep loneliness that ate a hole in his gut.

He wrote.

*"Since skies were blue, I have loved you.*
*Long before nights faded into day*
*Longer than tomorrows have been new*
*Before children learned to play.*
*I loved you before buttercups painted meadows yellow*
*Leaves whispered wind refrains*
*Before colors and songs came gay and mellow*
*And roses were kissed by gentle rains.*
*Even before stars thought to shine*
*Cool springs flowed to the rippling stream*
*The master designer made you mine*
*To love forever, my little dream."*

He sighed deeply and lay back on the hard bunk, draping his arm across his eyes.

If only fate had allowed him to meet Darlina before his life had gotten so off track and tangled. Her sweet warmth filled his thoughts and wherever she was and whatever she was doing, he wished her only good and wonderful things. He hoped that he'd taught her enough about the world that she might face it more squarely with open eyes.

He wished he could let her know how much he loved her, but that wouldn't accomplish anything. He'd keep that locked inside his own heart; tender memories tucked away to recall whenever he needed a reminder of her sweet love.

He had a feeling those memories would become more precious in the days and months to come.

# Chapter 34

Darlina began to feel more apprehensive, as Luke's trial date drew closer. It was now one week away. She kept reminding herself that you can't be convicted of a crime you did not commit.

The hot Texas July summer days became almost unbearable. Inside the Timex factory, there was very little air circulation. As Darlina sat at her workstation winding the endless trays of watches, the room around her began to spin.

She stood and took a deep breath.

Her prune-faced supervisor walked up behind her. "Just where are you going, Ms. Flowers?"

Darlina turned around to face Mrs. Crouch. "I don't feel well. I think I'm going to faint."

As soon as the words came out of her mouth, she crumpled to the floor.

When she opened her eyes, she was lying on a worn sofa in Mrs. Crouch's office. Her supervisor and another worker knelt over her. One of them washed her face with a damp towel and the other one shook her.

"What happened?" she asked.

"Apparently, you fainted," Mrs. Crouch said. "Are you pregnant?"

"No ma'am."

"Have you eaten today?"

"A little."

"Well, I think you need to go home for the rest of the day."

Darlina sat up and immediately felt lightheaded again. "I think so too." She shakily stood, as she removed her work gear. "Would you mind hanging these up for me? I'll be back tomorrow."

She walked out the door on wobbly legs to her recently purchased car. Leaning her head back on the seat, she sat for a few minutes to make sure she was okay to drive.

The green 1964 Chevrolet wasn't much to look at, but it only cost two hundred dollars and at least it ran. Norma had a new boyfriend who worked at a used car lot and he'd gotten her a deal.

She started the engine and drove slowly toward the small apartment she'd rented almost two months ago. It felt good to be independent.

The entrance to the apartment was up a steep flight of stairs on the outside of the two story brick building. Most of the time she didn't mind, but today she was dreading the climb.

The apartment was sparsely furnished, although Norma had given her a few pieces of furniture.

Darlina owned an antique dome-top trunk that had once belonged to her grandmother, who passed away years before she was born. It was her one prized possession. Norma had given it to her when she turned sixteen. She'd painstakingly sanded, painted, and re-lined the inside of it, including the removable tray.

She then began accumulating things like towels, bed linens, dishes, pots and pans, silverware and kitchen towels. She called the trunk her Hope Chest, and as she placed each item in it over the years, she had such high hopes for how and when they'd be useful to her.

Now that she was in her own place, she had put all of those things to good use. Because the building was brick, it always felt cool inside, even in the hot Texas summer.

Besides the steep stairs, it had one other flaw. At night, she would occasionally see a long centipede crawling up the wall. The first time she saw one, she panicked and ran out of the apartment screaming.

A neighbor had come to see what had frightened her and assured her they wouldn't kill her. If one bit her, it would feel much like a bee sting. Nevertheless, she kept a can of bug spray on hand, in case one made an appearance.

She was a couple of blocks away from the apartment building when she suddenly had the urge to go to Leann's house instead. She knew Leann would be packing, since she and Wayne had made the decision to move to Hobbs.

Darlina felt a heavy sadness that her sister was moving away. Leann's pregnant tummy was starting to show a little and Darlina hated to miss sharing the experience with her.

Leann looked up in surprise when Darlina came through the door. "Hey, little sister; why aren't you at work?"

"I fainted and the supervisor told me to go home for the day."

"You fainted?"

"Yes."

"What happened? Why?"

"I don't know. It was so hot in there. I felt a tingling at the base of my spine and the room started spinning. I stood up thinking I just needed to catch my breath and then I keeled over."

"Oh no! Well, lay down here on the couch. Let me get you some water or tea or something."

"I feel alright now, I'm just a little shaky. A cold glass of tea would be good though." Darlina sat on the couch and took her shoes off. "Can you stop packing and sit with me for a few minutes?"

"Of course, just relax. I'll be right back." Leann was back in a flash with two glasses of iced tea.

"Thanks. I don't really know what happened. I just know that job is turning out to be unbearable and I'm going to have to do something else. I've been there for four months and haven't made my quota. I go as fast as I can go all day."

"I think you're right. Maybe you should find another office job, like the one you had at the boiler factory." Leann kicked her shoes off and propped her swollen feet up on the coffee table. "Remember when I worked at Timex right after Wayne and I got married? I never made my quota either."

"I remember. Look at your feet. Are they supposed to be swollen like that?"

"The doctor says it's normal for being pregnant in the summer. It helps if I sit down and prop them up. I've been packing all day, trying to get ready for this move."

Darlina swirled the ice around in her glass. "I know it's probably the best thing for you and Wayne to get out of Abilene, but I sure hate to see you go."

"I know and I don't care much for the idea of going back to Hobbs, but we have to do something. Wayne hasn't been drinking nearly as much since I told him I was pregnant." Leann picked up a magazine and fanned her flushed face.

"That's good. I really do hope it all works out for you. I'm just being selfish, wanting you to be here so I can share the whole pregnancy experience with you."

"We've pretty much shared everything throughout our whole lives. Guess it's time for us to be grown ups and make our own separate ways."

"I suppose so, but I feel sad. With you leaving and Luke in jail facing trial, it's all very depressing. It feels like a part of me has died."

"Have you heard anything new about him? Are you going to go to the trial?"

"No. He told me to stay away so I will. The newspapers quieted down after the dust settled, but I'm sure they'll cover the trial. I just hope he gets it all straightened out. Sometimes at night I dream about him and always wake up crying because he's not with me."

"Darlina, I know how much you love him, but you really need to try to get back to living. Even if he gets out of this mess, he may not come back to you."

"I know. I'm just not ready to start going out in public yet. Sherry's hanging around with a hot new band and wants me to go hear them. I get nauseated when I think about having to see people that knew me and Luke when we were together." Darlina absentmindedly played with a strand of hair that had gotten loose.

"You're gonna have to get over that. It's been over three months. Surely people won't still talk about him."

"Maybe you're right. I'm just not ready. I am ready for a new job though."

"I agree with that. I can't believe in less than a week, I'll be living back in Hobbs."

Darlina laughed. "Who would have thought it? Hey, at least you know where everything is, so it won't be like moving to a strange place."

"That's for sure. I'll miss you though." Leann reached over for her sister's hand and gave it a squeeze.

"I'll miss you too." Darlina looked away as she felt tears stinging her eyelids. "Thank you for the tea. Guess I better get on home and let you do your packing."

"I'm glad you came but you've got to take better care of yourself. Do you even have any food at your apartment?"

"Yeah, I've got some peanut butter and bread."

"Why don't you stay and eat supper with me and Wayne? You can help me pack," Leann offered.

"I don't mind helping you pack, but I don't want to be in the way."

"Oh please. When have you ever been in my way?"

"I don't know. There must have been some time or another."

Leann got up from the couch, slipping her shoes back on her swollen feet. "Come on. I'll put you to work. I'm packing up the dishes in the kitchen and you can help me wrap everything."

"Okay," Darlina said, following her sister into the kitchen.

Leann turned the radio dial to a new station she'd discovered. "Let's listen to some rock music today. Country songs are too depressing."

"I like rock 'n roll. That's what we used to listen to when mama wasn't around. Remember KOMA?"

Leann laughed. "Of course I remember. We got pretty good at hiding our transistor radios under our pillow when we heard her coming."

"I miss mama and daddy. I'd like to see them, but I know she's still really mad and hurt. Do they know about the baby?"

"Yes, and she's at least talking to me. They have decided to put the house up for sale. We'll have to look for another place after we get there, but they said we can live in it for a while."

"It all seems so strange. I feel very alone. I'd give anything to be back with Luke and making him a real part of our family. Guess that's just wishful thinking, but I can't help it."

"Dreams are okay, but at some point you have to start living in reality. That's always been a problem for you."

"I like dreams. They're a lot nicer than reality. If we're packing up all of your dishes what are we gonna eat supper on?" Darlina finished one box, taped it shut and started on another.

"I bought some paper plates. Guess I better get supper started. I've got some pork chops. How does that sound?"

"Yummy. Much better than peanut butter. I get paid Friday and I'll go buy some groceries."

"You better. Wanna peel some potatoes for me?"

"Sure."

The two sisters worked side by side, at times stopping to sing along with a song on the radio. Darlina loved being with her sister and every time she thought about her moving away, she became filled with gloom.

She was thankful she still had Norma, but it wasn't the same closeness she shared with Leann. Life for Darlina had become rather bleak.

A constant glimmer of hope remained alive in her heart. In her daydreams, Luke was cleared of all the bogus charges; returned for her and they lived happily ever after. That was what she wanted more than anything in the world.

She longed to be Mrs. Luke Stone. Nothing else really seemed important.

# Chapter 35

The headlines of the July 14, 1971 Abilene Reporter News, screamed out; *Brownwood Musician Given 50 Years In Bank Robbery*. Shock rippled through Darlina making it hard to force the next breath. In the parking lot of the Timex factory, she sat dumbfounded. Surely this was a mistake.

She read through the article twice before the newspaper fell from her hands, landing on the seat beside her. Visions of Luke flashed through her mind. She saw his crooked grin, handsome face, how he would wink at her from the stage, but most of all, how he made such gentle sweet love to her. Hot tears trickled down her face.

The article gave details of the trial. Mary had been called to testify, but she had cried hysterically on the witness stand, and said she couldn't testify because she loved Luke.

Preacher's testimony, however, was the most damning. He described Luke and Butch as the ringleaders of the robberies and gave details as to how Luke planned and staged them. Preacher had been arrested along with everyone else, but, in exchange for his testimony, he was granted leniency.

So, her gut instinct about him had been right all along. Preacher was a snake-in-the-grass and would tell any kind of lie to save his own ass. He gave a statement to the authorities saying Luke had forced him to commit various crimes in Texas and Tennessee, while describing him as a Kingpin. The end of the article reported that Red, who had already faced trial for the same crime, had received a fifty year sentence as well.

To Darlina, fifty years was a lifetime. The newspaper stated that Luke was being transferred to San Angelo, to stand trial in Federal court, for the Bangs bank robbery. She knew she had to see him.

She dried her tears, got out of the car, and walked straight to her supervisor's office. "Mrs. Crouch, may I speak with you for a moment?"

Mrs. Crouch looked up from her paperwork with a frown. "Make it quick, Ms. Flowers. I've got work to do."

"I need to ask for a few hours off this morning. Something has come up that I have to tend to."

"Well, you do know these watches can't wind themselves, don't you?" She asked in a curt tone.

"Yes ma'am. I can be back by noon."

"Alright then...go on. Just make sure you're at your work station by 12:30 and no later."

"Yes ma'am. Thank you."

Mrs. Crouch looked back at her paperwork; dismissing Darlina with a wave of her hand.

Walking quickly back to her car, Darlina wondered how far away Eastland was. It must be fairly close by. She had to see Luke, in spite of his warning to stay away. This was serious.

She stopped at the first gas station she came to and asked the attendant how to get to Eastland. As soon as he finished filling her tank, she headed east on highway 80.

Thoughts randomly ran through her head, as she drove, and in an hour she found herself in the city limits of Eastland. She followed signs that took her to the downtown area and the Eastland County Jail.

The minute she walked through the door of the jail, she felt prickles up and down her spine. This had been Luke's home for the past four months. She'd never seen the inside of a jail before and her eyes were wide with curiosity.

An older man sitting behind a desk looked up as she approached. "May I help you?"

"Yes sir, I'd like to see Luke Stone please."

He peered up at her. "Are you kin?"

"No sir. I'm a friend."

"What's your name?"

"Darlina Flowers."

He shuffled through some papers and ran his finger down a list. "I don't see your name on his list of approved visitors."

"I'm sorry. I didn't know I had to be on a list," she said innocently.

The man grumbled. "Wait here and let me see what I can do."

Darlina sat in a straight-back wooden chair and folded her hands in her lap. Her heart raced inside her chest. She prayed that she would be allowed to see Luke. Suddenly she felt panic. What was she going to say to him? He'd made it plain that he didn't want to see her when he left her at Norma's house. She hoped he wouldn't be angry at her for coming.

She probably should have told Norma she was leaving town. No one knew where she was.

Her racing thoughts were interrupted when the man came back through the door. "The Sheriff said you can see Luke, but we have visiting rules. You are not to touch each other; no hugs, no holding hands, no kissing and you are not to give him anything. You will sit at a table across from him and if you violate any of the rules, the visit will be terminated immediately. Any questions?"

"No sir," Darlina said standing.

"You will have to be searched for contraband. Come with me."

Darlina followed the jailer. Her heart was beating so loud that she was quite sure he could hear it.

He asked her to wait in a very small room that was hardly bigger than a closet. She stood quietly and waited.

A matronly woman opened the door and stepped into the small room with Darlina. "Give me your purse ma'am."

Darlina handed her purse to the lady.

"Turn around."

She turned around and faced the wall. She felt the woman's hands running over her body lightly.

"Alright, Ms. Flowers, I'm going to take your purse to the front desk and you can pick it up on the way out. The jailer will come get you in a few minutes."

"Okay. Thank you." Darlina felt her legs begin to tremble. Even though she wasn't sure of his reaction, she felt ecstatic that she was being allowed to see Luke.

After what seemed like an eternity but was actually only five minutes, the door opened and the jailer motioned to her. She walked down a narrow hallway and into another room, where one wooden table and two chairs sat. The chairs faced each other across the table.

"Have a seat." The jailer motioned to one of the chairs.

Darlina sat down and wiped her sweaty palms on her jeans. She must not allow the hot tears stinging behind her eyelids, to escape. She fought to push them back and keep control.

She jumped when the door opened and there stood Luke, with the jailer behind him.

"Darlina! What in the hell are you doing here?" He sat down in the chair across from her frowning slightly.

She was shocked at the gauntness in his face. "Hello, Luke. I know you told me to stay away, but I had to come see you. I've been reading about this whole crazy mess in the newspapers. I can't believe what's happened."

Luke put both his hands on the table in front of him. "You think you can't believe it. Try it from this side. Preacher sure fixed my ass good."

"Luke, please tell me if any of this true?"

"No, darlin', it ain't. I'm bein' railroaded for somethin' I didn't do. My lawyer's filing an appeal."

"Oh Luke! I'm so sorry. Are you mad at me for coming to see you?"

"No, princess, I'm not. In fact, I'm glad you're here. There are some things I need to tell you and I want you to listen real good."

"There are some things I need to tell you too, but you go first."

Luke leaned back in his chair, running his hands through his hair. "I hope now you understand why I had to get you away from me."

"Yes, but I still don't agree with it. I would like to have been with you through this nightmare."

"There wasn't a single thing you could've done and they most likely would've tried to drag you off into it too. I couldn't let that happen."

"Luke, I miss you so much. I've been trying to get my life back, but without you, there doesn't seem to be much purpose."

"That's what you need to understand, baby. Hell, I'm thirty five years old, with a fifty year prison sentence. You do the math. It may be a very long time before I'm a free man again, if ever. You've got your whole life ahead of you. You're young and beautiful and you'll make some man a damned good wife."

The tears she'd been holding back began to silently trickle down her cheeks. "But, that's just it, Luke. I don't want to be someone else's damned good wife. I want to be yours."

"Sweetheart, there is nothing on this earth I'd like better, but it just can't happen. You have to promise me that you'll go on and forget about me."

"I'll never forget about you, Luke and I'll never stop loving you; no matter if you're locked away for a hundred years."

Luke sighed. "I know you think that now, but you'll meet someone else and before you know it, you'll be married with a baby hanging off your hip. That's what I want you to do, Darlina."

"Norma talked me into going out with her for a drink a few weeks ago and it was a disaster. I saw Louise and that was good, but there were some men that knew you and apparently knew me. They were so mean and said horrible things about you. I have to tell you that Louise stood in the middle of all of them and told them what cowards they were. She took up for you good, Luke."

He laughed quietly. "Louise has a little fire in her. If you see her again, tell her I said thank you. But, she, you or anyone else doesn't have to stand up for me. I stand up for myself."

"I know, but it made me feel good for her to do that. We never got the drink. We just left. I haven't been back out anywhere since. I can't stand the thought of listening to what everyone's saying behind your back."

"Those same sonsofbitches sat at my table and drank my liquor without any problem," Luke growled.

"That's right and I don't want to listen to any of their bullshit, so I just go to work and home every day."

"Did you get your job back at the boiler factory?"

"No. They hired a girl to replace me after I quit and she's still there, but I got a job at Timex working on the assembly line."

"Shit! That sucks."

"It does, but it's a paycheck. I rented an apartment over by Hendricks but I'm about ready to find something else. There are centipedes that crawl out on the walls at night and the warmer the weather gets, the more often I see them. They give me the willies."

"Sugar, I think you definitely need to find another place to live. However, I bet it's a helluva lot better than where I'm livin' right now."

"I can't imagine what it's been like for you and for your family. I often think about your kids, your parents and Bobby."

"Yeah, it's been rough on everybody. Joyce has had to go to work and it's pretty hard on the kids. Mom and dad have stuck with me all the way. Dad even mortgaged the place at the lake to pay my attorney."

"Have you gotten to see the kids since they locked you up?"

"Hell no. Joyce won't let 'em anywhere near me. I want to see 'em, but not like this. They damn sure wouldn't understand."

"Luke, is there anything at all I can do for you?"

"Oh sugar, there's a lot you could do for me, but the poor ol' jailer would have a heart attack and they'd throw you outta' here."

Darlina smiled through the tears. "You are so bad, Luke Stone. I miss you so very much."

"I miss you too, sweetheart. Hell, I miss everything about living. This ain't living here; it's barely existing. I sure ain't lookin' forward to being in the state penitentiary."

"I'm so sorry. I would change it all if I could."

"I know you would. That's the kind of person you are. Darlina, I want you to stop talking and listen to me. I need you to hear me."

"Okay, Luke. What?"

Luke spoke slowly, "You've got to promise me that you'll go back to living. You don't need to be moping around your apartment all the time. You have your whole life ahead of you. Go live it!"

"How, Luke? How do I turn off the love I have for you? How do I do that? The thought of being with someone else nauseates me."

Luke tapped his fingers on the table. "I can't tell you how. I can only tell you that it's what you have to do and you must promise me you'll at least try."

The jailer knocked on the door and yelled, "Five minutes."

"Promise me, Darlina."

"Okay, Luke. I'll try, but that's all I can promise."

"That's good enough. All anyone can do is try. I'm glad you came to see me today, baby. Please take care of your sweet self."

"I'll do my best. Can I write to you or visit again?"

"No. They're transferring me to San Angelo next week and I have no idea how long it'll be until they give me a trial date over there or where I'll wind up. Please just get out, start living and forget about me."

"I'll never forget about you if I live to be a thousand years old. I love you."

"I've gotta go, sweetheart. Remember what I said." He stood and the jailer escorted him out the door. He turned to look at her one last time, winked and pursed his lips to form a kiss; then he was gone.

Darlina sat with silent tears running down her face until the woman who'd patted her down appeared in the doorway. "It's time to go, Ms. Flowers."

She stood and walked on wooden legs, following the woman down the hall, back to the front desk where she retrieved her purse.

She sat in her car for an hour, not moving, just sobbing uncontrollably. How could she possibly go on living as Luke had made her promise? Her heart belonged to him, even if he was locked behind bars forever.

Her life was over at the young age of nineteen.

"Why, God? Why did Luke have to be taken away?"

There was no answer to her question; only an aching heart and empty life ahead of her. How was she supposed to go on living, when everything inside her was dead?

All her hopes and dreams were locked inside the jail with her blue-eyed rebel and his gentle touch.

# Chapter 36

Darlina didn't remember seeing the road on the drive back to Abilene. She replayed the conversation with Luke over and over in her mind.

His words echoed. "You have to promise me you'll go on living."

She didn't have a clue how to do that. The finality of the long prison sentence and Luke's words weighed heavy on her heart and mind.

As she'd assured Mrs. Crouch, she was back at her work station, dressed in her work gear, winding watches by noon.

Today there was a feeling of thankfulness for the repetitious work, as it gave her mind free rein to roam. The two things she knew for sure that needed to be changed right away were her job and the apartment.

Norma might have some ideas, so a visit to her this evening seemed in order. She already missed Leann terribly and they'd moved only a week ago. The distance between them made her feel sad, but she'd decided to save all of her dimes so she could call Leann once a week. This week she had a lot to tell her.

The four o'clock whistle blew announcing the end of another work day at Timex. Darlina suddenly realized she'd not eaten a bite of food all day. Her stomach growled in protest.

Inside her car, she dumped the contents of her purse out on the seat, hoping to find enough money to get a hamburger. By the time she counted all of her change, except for the dimes, there was a whole two dollars. She headed to Casey's Drive Inn.

As she munched on the hamburger, she wondered what Luke would be eating for supper tonight. She shook her head, as if to rid herself of the image. How could she possibly go back to living, when thoughts of Luke consumed her day and night?

It was something she didn't know how to do. She'd just have to stay busy with things she could do, like finding a new job and an apartment.

By the time she'd devoured the hamburger, she knew Norma would be getting home from work. She had some things to talk over with her older sister.

She knocked lightly on Norma's door and then let herself in.

Norma sat on the sofa thumbing through the day's mail when Darlina walked through the door. "Hey, Darlina. I was going to head over to your apartment as soon as I finished supper. I think I may have some good news for you," she said lightly.

Darlina sat down on the sofa. "We must be on the same wavelength, because I needed to talk to you, too. I saw Luke today, but tell me your news first."

Norma turned to face her. "Well, the girl we hired after you left resigned today. She gave a two week notice. But, I want to hear about you going to see Luke."

"Oh Wow! That's better than good news. That's great news! Do you think I can get my job back?"

"You most definitely can, if you want it."

"If I want it? That was one of the things I was coming to talk to you about. Timex has become unbearable and I was going to ask you for suggestions about where I could apply."

"Are you serious?"

"As a heart attack! This is unbelievably good timing. If you think for sure I can get it back, I'll turn in my two week notice at Timex tomorrow."

"It's a sure thing. All I need to know is if you want it."

"I do! More than you know."

"Then come by the office when you get off tomorrow, and we'll do the paperwork. Now what else is on your mind? Tell me about seeing Luke."

"Well, I don't know if you saw the newspaper this morning, but he was found guilty of bank robbery and sentenced to fifty years in the state prison. When I read that along with how they were going to be transferring him from Eastland to San Angelo for the federal trial, I knew I had to go see him."

"I didn't see the newspaper, but I did hear it on the radio. That was another reason I was coming to see you tonight. I knew you'd be upset." Norma got up to go to the kitchen. "Can I fix you a scotch and soda?"

"I would love a drink. Thank you."

Norma returned shortly with two iced drinks. "Okay. Now tell me everything. You didn't tell me you were going."

"I know and I thought about that when I was sitting in Eastland waiting to see him. I didn't think about a thing but going to see him after I read the newspaper."

"So tell me about it."

"Well, he wasn't angry at me for coming. He was glad I was there because he had some things to tell me. He said he hoped that now I understood why he sent me away."

"I hope you do too. But, go on."

"Then he told me he was thirty five years old, with a fifty year prison sentence and I should do the math; get on with my life and forget about him."

"What did you say to that?"

"I said that I didn't know how to forget about him and that I loved him and always would."

"Honey, I know you do, but what he was telling you is the truth. You're young and your whole life is ahead of you."

"That may be true, but it feels pretty empty without Luke."

"I understand you feel that way now, but if you'll just allow yourself to get out of your hibernation and start being around people again, you'll see that it is possible."

"I suppose you're right." Darlina took a sip of her drink. "But, I just can't imagine being with anyone else."

"What was the other thing you wanted to talk to me about?" Norma ran her finger around the top of her glass.

"I have to find another place to live. The centipedes are driving me crazy. Since the weather is warmer, they are coming out more and I'm having trouble sleeping because I'm afraid that one is going to crawl on me."

"Well, let's start looking for another place. That isn't the only apartment in Abilene. Besides, you'll be making more money once you start back at the boiler factory."

"Oh, I didn't think about that. More money will certainly be nice. I've decided to save all my dimes so I can call Leann once a week."

"Why don't you come over here and call her? I surely don't mind."

"I hate to run up your phone bill and the only way I'd do that is if you'll let me give you some money."

"You don't have to, but whatever makes you happy. We need to find you another apartment soon though."

"I'll pick up a newspaper on Sunday and come over, so we can go look at some places." Darlina stood and walked into the kitchen with her empty glass and Norma followed.

"I love you little sister and I want to see you smiling and happy again." Norma gave Darlina a hug.

"I love you too and you'll never know how much I appreciate you." Darlina returned the hug and then walked to the front door. "I'm gonna go by Sherry's place before I go home tonight."

"That's a good idea. You've got to do what Luke asked."

Darlina laughed wryly. "Like I told him, I'll try, but I don't see how it's possible. I'll see you tomorrow after work."

"Okay. Sleep good tonight and we'll find you a new apartment soon."

"Thank you, Norma. I don't know what I'd do without you."

"You won't have to find out. Drive safe."

Darlina drove to Sherry's apartment hoping to find her at home since it was early and a week night. She spotted her car as she parked in front of the apartment building.

"Come in." Sherry's voice came from the other side of the door when Darlina knocked.

Darlina opened the door and went in. "Hi, Sherry."

"Darlina! I've been thinkin' about you today. What are you up to?"

"I want to talk. I went to see Luke today."

"I heard about the guilty verdict and sentence on the radio. That's why I was thinkin' about you."

"Are you busy? I don't want to interrupt what you're doing."

"Oh bullshit. I'm not busy. Sit down and talk to me." Sherry sat on the sofa and patted the seat beside her. "Can I get you something to drink?"

"No, I'm alright...just wanna talk." Darlina sat down, kicking her shoes off. She shared every detail of her trip to see Luke, including not being on the visitors list and getting patted down.

Sherry folded her legs up under her on the couch. "Oh my, I'd love to have seen your face when you got patted down. How did Luke look?"

"His face looked drawn and he'd lost weight. It looks really bad for him with all of this bullshit. He said Preacher turned on him and told a bunch of lies to save his own hide."

"Good ol' Preach," she said sarcastically.

Darlina sighed and looked down at her hands resting in her lap. "Luke is thirty five years old, with a fifty year prison sentence. He told me to do the math, get on with my life and forget about him."

"He's right, you know. You need to come out of hibernation and start living again."

Darlina looked up at her friend, eyes brimming with tears. "I don't have a clue how to do that. How do I just stop loving Luke? I can't."

"Honey, you don't have to stop loving him. You can love him all you want, but you need to be around people again. Why don't you come back to the Faded Rose? Marketa would love that."

"I really do love Marketa, but I don't wanna dance anymore. I have no desire to be up on stage again, with men lookin' at me."

"What in the world am I gonna do with you, Darlina? You've gotta do something."

"You know how much I love music. I'll go with you sometime soon to hear this new band you keep talking about, but first I have to find a new apartment. Oh yeah, the other thing I wanted to tell you is that I'm gettin' my old job back at the boiler factory."

Sherry clapped her hands. "Hurrah for you! That's good. I know you haven't been too happy working at Timex."

"I was ready to quit, so was really good timing. Once I get moved into a new place I'll go out with you. What's the name of this band?"

"Wait here. I've got a picture of them. They're called The Sensations and they're really good. I know you're gonna enjoy listening to them. I'm dating Ken, the bass player." She jumped up and returned with an eight by ten glossy photo.

"What kind of music do they play?" Darlina looked at the photo.

"They play mostly Charlie Rich type songs but they play a little bit of everything. They aren't country."

"That's probably good for me. Country music makes me really sad and depressed right now. I've been listening to a new radio station and really like the music on it. Have you heard of KNIT?"

Sherry turned excitedly toward Darlina. "You're kiddin' me? The lead singer and piano player for The Sensations is a DJ at that station."

"Really? Well then, I'm sure I've heard him. So, once I get moved and settled, I'll go with you to see them."

"Great!" Sherry clapped her hands again. "It's time for you to come out of your shell."

"Don't expect too much. I truly don't feel ready to do this, but since Luke insisted, I'll at least try."

"That's the spirit. Just go with me. You won't have to say a word to anyone if you don't want to."

"Alright. I better get going. I've got some busy days ahead of me. Thank you for being my friend and for listening to me."

Sherry hugged Darlina. "Oh bullshit...you've listened to me plenty of times. See ya' soon."

Darlina drove to her apartment and walked up the steep flight of stairs feeling a little lighter. She was very glad she'd gone to see Luke. In the dark quietness of her temporary home, she lay on the bed and re-lived every word, facial expression, motion and gesture Luke had made.

She especially lingered on the wink and air kiss he'd given as he was being led out the door.

She reached for the tiny gold heart necklace that lay beside her bed and drifted off to sleep, clutching it tightly in her hand. Images of Luke Stone drifted through her head. These images were all she had left. After today, she realized she might not see the man she loved, with all her heart, ever again.

# Chapter 37

The third apartment Darlina and Norma looked at, on that hot July Sunday afternoon, immediately felt like home to her. It was a one bedroom duplex with covered parking for her car and best of all, no stairs.

From her Friday paycheck, she put a fifty dollar deposit down to hold the apartment until the first of August, when she could pay the rent and move in.

She was also returning to work at the boiler factory, on the first Monday in August. She'd happily given her two week notice at Timex.

Things were looking up for Darlina. She continued to spend many of her waking and sleeping hours thinking and dreaming about Luke, although the pain of the separation was lessening as time went by.

She hated to admit that Norma was right, but an older sister knows things.

"Let me take you out to eat this afternoon," Norma proposed.

"Oh that would be fun. Let's go to Farolito's for some Mexican food and a margarita," Darlina said happily.

"I'm sure glad to see you in better spirits. I've been worried about you."

"I know and I'm sorry. I was just so depressed and everything felt hopeless. Now the horrible pain has eased up a tiny bit."

"I told you so. You need to listen to your big sister more often." Norma laughed as she drove.

"I tell everyone that you and Luke have taught me everything I know." Darlina glanced at her reflection in her compact mirror, putting a stray hair in place.

Laughing, Norma said, "I don't know if that's good or bad."

"I think it's good. I've learned a whole lot over the past year. I'm gonna go with Sherry after I get moved, to hear The Sensations. I promised her I'd give it a try."

"Good for you Darlina. That's exactly what you need to do. You will love that band."

The two sisters continued talking and laughing through the meal and Darlina was beginning to feel like there might be a small chance of enjoying life again, even without Luke.

The next two weeks flew by. Darlina stayed busy working and packing boxes, preparing to move her belongings. Before she knew it, the weekend had arrived. She put in her last few hours at Timex, and now it was time to claim her new apartment.

Her excitement was more than obvious when she paid the first month's rent and the landlord handed the keys to the apartment to her. She immediately went to look at it again.

A quick inspection told her that it needed a thorough cleaning before her things would be placed in it the next day. She hummed to herself as she drove back to the apartment that she was moving out of. She gathered all of her cleaning products, a broom and mop. She loved that she felt excited about something again.

As an afterthought, she grabbed her small radio on the way out the door. Soon, she was busily scrubbing and listening to music. It wasn't so bad being alone.

The next thought to enter her mind was about Luke. A sudden flood of memories of their time together flowed through her mind. Her thoughts turned to the time when Luke got sick with the strange fever and was out of his head for days. What would happen to him in prison if that occurred again? Who would take care of him? Would they think he'd gone crazy? Would he get to have his guitar in prison? What would happen to all the songs he'd written, all of his dreams, hopes and wishes? Would he die an old man, locked away in some prison cell?

With that thought, her breath caught in her throat and a river of tears broke loose. As she scrubbed, the tears mixed in with the Spic and Span. By the time she the floors were shining, she also felt cleansed on the inside as well.

Her heart would always belong to Luke, no matter who else came into her life, and that fact she understood. The time they'd spent together had intensely bonded them forever on a level beyond human and would never be replaced.

A few hours later, she locked the door to her shiny new apartment. At Norma's insistence, she drove to her house for supper. Once again, she was very thankful for her big sister. Not only had she borrowed a friend's pickup to move Darlina the next day, but had also recruited two men from the boiler factory to help.

As she parked her car in Norma's driveway, she noticed another car she'd never seen before parked at the curb. She wondered who else Norma had invited for dinner.

After knocking lightly on the front door, she let herself in. She was greeted with music blaring loudly from the stereo and the sound of conversation and laughter coming from the kitchen.

"Hello," she said, as she walked into the kitchen.

Norma ran to greet her with a hug. "Darlina, so glad you made it." She turned Darlina to face two men standing beside the table. "Darlina, this is my friend, Charles and his friend, Will. Ya'll, this is my little sister, Darlina."

Darlina extended her hand to the men. "So nice to meet you."

"Same here," Charles said, shaking her hand.

Will's hand lingered on hers a little too long to suit her. "Good to meet you, Darlina."

Darlina looked accusingly at her sister. She'd set her up on a blind date and hadn't even given her a clue. "Please forgive the way I look. I've been scrubbing floors in my new apartment and I'm a mess." She consciously smoothed down her hair and straightened her clothes.

"Oh, you look just fine," Norma assured. "How about a drink?"

"Sure. Looks like I need to catch up with you guys."

Will pulled a chair out from the table. "Have a seat, Darlina."

"Okay, but let me run to the little girls room first and freshen up." She quickly walked out of the room, stopping to take a deep breath. How could Norma do that to her without asking?

In the bathroom, she could hear the chatter of conversation and an occasional laugh coming from the kitchen. She leaned against the counter and looked at her reflection in the mirror. She got a tissue and patted her face to remove the last traces of her tears and ran her hands through her hair. Well, this was just what they were getting. She didn't really care whether or not she impressed anyone and felt a tad bit angry at Norma for putting her in this situation. Obviously, Will was there for her and she'd be nice, but aloof.

Back in the kitchen, she took the chair Will had pulled out, picked up the drink waiting for her, and then turned to look at him. "I apologize for my appearance. Norma didn't tell me she'd invited company and I really have been cleaning on my new apartment all afternoon."

"Stop apologizing. Charles didn't tell me Norma had a little sister either, so I guess we're both in the same boat. Where is your new apartment?"

"It's on North Twelfth, not too far off Mockingbird. It's a huge improvement over the place I'm moving out of."

"Yeah, Norma told me about the centipedes and the stairs that she fell down," Charles said, draping his arm over Norma's shoulders.

Norma added, "I'm sure glad I won't have to climb those steep stairs anymore after tomorrow. I hadn't even had a drink the night I fell down them. Who's hungry?"

"I'm hungry enough to eat a horse," Charles said playfully.

"I'm not quite that hungry," added Will, "but, I could eat."

"Me too." Darlina twirled the ice in her glass. "Can I help you with anything Norma?"

"Nope. I've got it. Just sit there and enjoy your drink." She went to the oven and took out a roast with potatoes, carrots and all the trimmings; along with warm rolls.

"Yum! That smells delicious." Darlina's mouth watered. "I didn't realize I was hungry 'til I smelled it."

"Certainly smells better than a horse." Charles laughed.

Soon, they all had heaping plates of food and Darlina was grateful for the excuse not to have to talk. She dared a closer look at Will out of the corner of her eye. She was sure he was nice enough, but the shoulder length blonde hair, sharp nose and high forehead just weren't her type. He was of medium build and she'd always been attracted to taller men. She couldn't help comparing him to Luke and he came up short. She had a feeling that would be the case with anyone new she met.

As the plates began to empty, conversation started again.

"Norma tells me you're starting to work at the boiler factory on Monday," Charles said, looking at Darlina.

"Yes, and I'm very happy about that. I've been at Timex for the past four months and I'm more than ready for a change." Darlina finished the last of her drink. "Where do you work Will?"

"I'm a carpenter's helper right now. I work for a guy that has his own business. My goal is to go into business for myself."

Norma stood and took the remaining food off the table. "Let's move into the living room."

"You and Charles go ahead. I'll clean up. It's the least I can do after you did all the cooking," Darlina offered.

"I'll help you," Will said, pushing his chair back.

"Alright. Come on Charles." Norma and Charles walked from the room hand in hand.

Darlina began gathering up the dishes and Will clumsily tried to help. Finally, he gave up and stood at the counter watching.

Darlina turned to face him. "Look, Will; I'm sure you're a very nice person, but I'm just coming out of a very intense relationship and I'm not looking for anyone. I apologize for my sister trying to set us up."

Will laughed. "I'm just as uncomfortable as you are. How about I give you a call and we'll go to a movie sometime."

"I don't have a phone yet and I really don't want to go out on a date, but thank you anyway."

Will's face reddened. "Well, just in case you change your mind, I'll give you my number and you can call me."

"Okay. That's a deal. Let's talk about something else. What do you like to do when you aren't working or being set up on blind dates?"

Will's eyes brightened. "I have a Harley Davidson motorcycle and I love to ride around on country roads."

"Now there's something I'd truly enjoy doing. I'd love to go riding out in the country on a Harley."

"Okay then. Can I come pick you up next Sunday afternoon and take you riding?"

"Yes you can." Darlina wrote her address on a piece of a napkin lying on the countertop.

Will stuffed it in his pocket. "Whew, now that's over, let's just talk."

Darlina made small talk with Will as she cleaned up the dishes and put the food away. Once she was done, she excused herself. "I'm really beat and got a big moving day tomorrow, so I'm going to head home. It was nice to meet you, Will."

"You too."

The two of them walked into the living room where Darlina said her goodbyes to Norma and Charles, and then escaped out the door. She knew Norma was just trying to help, but she would tell her tomorrow not to fix her up on any more blind dates.

Darlina had been living in her new apartment for a week and now she had to keep her promise to go with Sherry to hear *The Sensations*. She almost wished she hadn't agreed to go.

As she was getting dressed, her stomach turned upside down at the thought of having to be out in public with people who might have known Luke. She hoped there wouldn't be a repeat of what had happened at The Oasis.

Sherry assured her that this band drew a different type of crowd.

Darlina hoped that was true because one more bad experience might just send her into hibernation for good.

Sherry's knuckles rapped on the door as she was putting on the finishing touches of her makeup. She gave herself one last glance in the mirror.

"Come in, sweetie. I'm just about ready to go," Darlina said as she opened the door.

"No rush. We've got plenty of time. You look nice, and I love your new apartment."

"I do too. I'm very nervous about going out tonight. You do know that, don't you?"

"I know, but trust me, everything's gonna be alright. You'll see. I brought something to help you relax before we go. Have you ever smoked pot?"

"No, but I don't think I want to after my last experience with you and drugs." Darlina remembered the promise she'd made to Luke not to try any drug she wasn't familiar with.

Sherry laughed. "This is totally different. Pot just mellows you out and makes you relax."

Darlina pulled out a chair from the kitchen table. "Have a seat. Go ahead and smoke whatever you want, but I'm gonna stay straight."

"Sure you don't mind? I hate to smoke by myself," Sherry said, as she sat in the chair.

"Suit yourself, but I'm not going to do it with you." She watched as Sherry took what looked like a hand rolled cigarette out of her purse and lit it.

"Just take one little puff. It will make the nerves in your stomach settle down," Sherry prodded, as she sucked hard on the marijuana cigarette.

"It does smell good, but I really don't want to, Sherry. Please don't try to make me do something I don't want to do." Darlina sat in the other chair facing her friend.

"I'm sorry. I just want you to feel good." Sherry went to the sink and crushed out the joint. "Let's go, if you're ready."

"I'm ready. I just need to get my purse. Are you sure I look okay?" Darlina picked up her purse off the end of the counter.

"Honey, you look just fine, although you could've worn a lower cut blouse."

Darlina laughed. "Exactly what I'd expect you to say. I'm not interested in displaying my wares tonight. I'm just going to hear some live music."

Sherry linked her arm through Darlina's. "Let's go have some fun."

The *Southern Hills Club* was new to Darlina. It was one she'd never been to with Luke. She was relieved not to be going back into familiar surroundings without him by her side.

Her mind was strongly focused on Luke, as they parked in front of the club. She could hear the music before they got to the door and her stomach did flip flops. She wondered what Luke was doing right now and her heart wrenched at the thought of him sitting in a darkened jail cell.

She felt guilty to be enjoying life again. She knew he'd give anything to be a free man enjoying his own life, but there was nothing she could do to fix that for him. After all, she'd promised him that she would to try to move on.

She took a deep breath and walked through the door of the darkened club. She had the comfort of carrying Luke in her heart wherever she went and that was something that would never change.

# Chapter 38

Once inside, Darlina began to feel her insides relax. The true love she had for live music hadn't changed and she quickly became caught up in its magnetic energy. She realized how much she'd missed it.

Behind the piano, a nice looking man, with a smooth baritone voice, sang *"Hey, did you happen to see the most beautiful girl in the world, and if you did, was she crying crying?"*

Sherry leaned in towards her. "That's the lead singer and the guy I told you is a DJ at KNIT. His name is Henry Michaels."

"He's got a very good voice and not bad to look at either." Darlina swayed to the music.

"When they take a break, I'll introduce you to everyone. Ken is the one playing bass. He's married, but we're really hitting it off."

A waitress approached the girls' table. "What can I get you ladies to drink tonight?"

"I'll have a Coke please," Darlina requested.

"I'll have a whiskey sour," Sherry added.

"I'll be right back with those drinks." The waitress turned and walked toward the bar.

"You could have ordered a drink if you wanted one." Sherry reached for her purse.

"I know, but I just want a Coke."

"Honey, you've got to loosen up a little. You're way too tense about everything."

"I'm alright. Let's just listen to the music."

The girls soon had their drinks and listened intently to the music; tapping toes and swaying to the rhythm. For a three-piece band, they were making a lot of good music and Darlina suddenly felt happy to be there.

After an hour, the band took a break and Ken walked directly to their table. Sherry stood as they hugged and kissed. Then she turned to Darlina. "This is my very best friend, Darlina Flowers. Darlina, this is Ken Hughes."

Darlina extended her hand. "Very nice to meet you, Ken. I'm really enjoying your music."

"Thank you so much. We love playing. Hey, I'm gonna go get a drink and take care of some business, but I'll be back in a couple of minutes." He kissed Sherry, and then walked toward the restrooms.

"He seems nice."

"He is very nice and he's older than any guy I've ever dated. Maybe there is something about older men, huh?"

Darlina felt a sudden pang of sadness engulf her heart. "Yeah, there's something about older men."

"Oh Honey, I'm sorry. I didn't mean to say anything to make you think about Luke."

"Nothing ever has to be said to make me think about Luke. I think about him twenty-four seven."

Sherry stood and motioned to the other two band members that were walking by. "Henry, Pete, come here. I want you to meet someone."

The two men walked up greeting Sherry. "How are you, sugar?" Henry asked.

"I'm good. Henry, Pete, this is my best friend, Darlina Flowers. I brought her out to hear you guys play tonight."

"Very nice to meet you Darlina," Henry said. "You look very familiar to me. Have I met you somewhere?"

"No, I don't think so. I used to work at The Faded Rose. Maybe you saw me there."

"No, that wasn't it. Oh, I remember." He paused raising his hand slightly. "I saw you with Luke Stone and his band at The Silver Spur one night."

"That's entirely possible. Sorry, I don't remember seeing you."

"Hey, I'm glad you girls came out tonight," Pete said. "I'm gonna get a drink. Ya'll have fun." Pete turned and walked toward the bar.

"Yeah, ya'll have a good time tonight and it's nice to meet you Darlina. Stick around for the whole show. I'd like to talk to you some more."

"We'll be here," Sherry assured.

"Nice to meet you too, Henry. I'm really enjoying your music."

Henry walked away, stopping to talk with several other people. Darlina watched him, remembering how Luke worked the crowds in much the same way.

"Well, what do you think?" Sherry asked.

"About what?"

"About anything...are you glad you came out?"

"I love the music and I don't see a single soul I know so that makes it even better."

Ken returned, pulling up a chair. He put his arm around Sherry's waist familiarly. "So, Darlina, are you enjoying yourself?"

"I am. The music's good and I'm enjoying listening to it."

"Well, thank you, sweetheart."

"How long have you guys all been together?" Darlina inquired.

"We've all known each other most of our lives and have played together off and on for years. We've been back playing steady for the past six months."

"Ya'll are great," Sherry interjected. "But, I may be a little biased. Hey, ya'll should think about adding go-go dancers to your show. Darlina used to dance with me at The Faded Rose and we both danced for Luke Stone and The Rebel Rousers."

Just then Henry walked back toward their table. Ken motioned to him. "Henry, come here and listen to what Sherry is telling me."

Henry pulled up a chair and sat down. "What is Sherry telling you?"

"She said that she and Darlina used to go-go dance together at The Faded Rose and that they also danced for Luke Stone."

"Is that so? Well, we just might have to ask for a private show."

Darlina blushed. "I don't dance on stage anymore. Guess Sherry will have to demonstrate by herself."

"Aw, come on now. Don't be that way. If you'd dance for the likes of Luke, surely you'd dance for The Sensations."

Sherry jumped in quickly. "I think we need to change the subject. Are you singing any new songs tonight?"

Henry looked directly at Darlina as he spoke. "We're going to do a couple I wrote and I'd love to hear your opinion about them after the show."

"Okay. I'll be listening for them." Darlina slightly blushed under his gaze.

Henry stood up. "Come on, Ken. We've gotta get back to work. You girls don't run off."

"We'll be here." Sherry kissed Ken lightly on the lips before he got up.

Once the group returned to the stage, Darlina turned to Sherry. "Well, that was very weird."

"I'm so sorry Luke and the dancing got brought up the way it did. Don't be mad. Just let it go and enjoy the music."

"I'm not mad. I just find it very strange the way Henry was talking and looking at me."

"He's interested."

"I'm not."

"Just relax, honey. Please, let me order you a drink."

"Oh okay, fine. Order me a whiskey and Coke."

Sherry motioned to the waitress and placed the order, getting herself another drink as well.

The relaxed atmosphere was good medicine for Darlina, as she got lost in the music, Henry's smooth voice, and the songs he sang. Occasionally when the band played an upbeat rock tune, she and Sherry got out on the dance floor together.

Darlina found herself throwing her head back and actually laughing for the first time in months. The girls fed off of each other, in a complimentary way, when they danced together.

Henry, Pete and Ken had gravitated to their table during breaks and the conversation remained light and easy.

Pete praised the girls. "You girls weren't lying about knowing how to dance."

Ken hugged Sherry up close to him. "That's my girl."

Henry turned toward Darlina. "We'll be finished with this gig in the next hour. Would you consider hanging out with me and talking for a while? I get so wound up doing a show that I don't sleep for hours."

"I don't know," Darlina hesitated.

"I promise I won't touch you if that's what you're afraid of. I just want some company."

Darlina looked at Sherry. "Oh, go on Darlina. He won't bite."

Henry laughed. "I've had my rabies shots, I promise."

Darlina finally agreed, "Only if you'll take me home when I'm ready. No questions asked."

"Deal." Henry said, smiling triumphantly.

Outside the club, in Henry's 1967 cream colored Cadillac DeVille, Darlina listened to him talk about his life.

"I really don't like working the club circuit. I want to play the big stages and have my songs recorded by other artists. That's my dream."

"There's nothing wrong with that dream and I truly hope you get it. You're good and the two songs you sang tonight, *He'll Have to Go* and *Just Hold My Hand*, are both commercial songs, in my opinion."

"Well, those are my dreams. Now, tell me how did a sweet, nice, pretty young girl like you wind up with a sorry, no good bastard like Luke Stone?"

The hair on the back of Darlina's neck prickled. She turned to face Henry, eyes filling with tears. "I fell in love. It's that simple and he's not like everyone thinks."

"Sorry, I didn't mean to upset you, but I can't pretend to have any love for the man. I've watched him and his brother strut around Abilene for years, being bad-ass, belligerent assholes, not caring who they hurt or how many people they destroyed along the way."

"I never saw him that way. I saw a talented songwriter and musician that had his own way of doing things."

"Looks like he really did a number on you."

"A number on me? I don't think so. I still love him and always will. So, if that offends you, feel free to take me home."

"Whoa. I didn't mean any harm. I was just expressing my own opinion."

"He didn't do what he's accused of."

"Maybe he did and maybe he didn't. It's not for me to say. All I know is what I saw with my own eyes and he brought every bit of this shit on himself."

"I really don't want to talk about Luke, and I'm feeling tired. Would you please take me home now?"

Henry started the car and followed Darlina's directions to her apartment. The silence inside the car was only interrupted by the radio playing softly in the background.

When he stopped in front of her apartment he reached across the seat, gently taking her hand. "Darlina, I think you're a really sweet girl and I'm glad Sherry talked you into coming out and hearing us play. I do hope you'll do that again."

"I'm sure I will. It's just hard for me to make myself get out in public and face people who knew Luke."

"I'm sorry if I upset you. It was strictly my opinion."

"I know. No hard feelings. I only wish everyone could have known him like I did."

"Yeah...well sweetheart, I seriously doubt very many people around here had the same view of him that you did. He is a lucky man to have you in his corner."

"Bye, Henry." She opened the door to get out of the car.

Henry pulled her back toward him, giving her a light peck on the cheek. "Bye, Darlina. I'll see you again?"

"Yeah, you'll see me again." With that, she got out of the car, closed the door and watched as the tail lights disappeared.

As she let herself into the darkened apartment, her mind whirled with thoughts. She hated that Luke had made such a bad name for himself through his actions over the years.

Maybe that's why he never made it big in the music world. He had the talent and the voice, so maybe it was the attitude that had held him back. She didn't know, but did know was he was now locked away in a jail cell, facing a very long prison sentence. She wondered if he was in San Angelo by now and when the next trial would take place.

It was funny how the newspapers had suddenly dropped the story after his conviction. It seemed that no one cared about Luke Stone anymore, except if they had bad things to say about him. Tears filled her eyes and silently trickled down her cheeks.

How could she possibly open herself up to any kind of new relationship with anyone, when she was still so completely occupied by Luke?

Her thoughts turned to Henry. He was handsome and definitely a good musician. She sensed he had a superior attitude about him and that didn't resonate well with her. What could possibly be his interest in her? Was she a challenge to him? Was that the way it was going to be; that men who'd known and not cared for Luke would vie for her affection to prove they were as good as him?

She didn't know and suddenly felt exhausted. She lay her head down on her pillow, with the last thought in her mind being a vision of Luke lying beside her and holding her close. She went to sleep in the comforting circle of his arms.

# Chapter 39

The roar of a Harley-Davidson stopping in front of her apartment the next Sunday afternoon reminded Darlina of her agreement to go riding with Will.

Giving herself a quick glance in the mirror, she was thankful that she'd put on her makeup and gotten dressed today.

Once Will knocked on the door, she hesitated for a brief second before letting him in.

"Hi, Will. Come on in."

"Hi. I was afraid you might've forgotten that I was coming to take you riding today." Will was dressed in faded jeans, motorcycle boots, a black t-shirt and a denim jacket that he'd cut the sleeves out of and sewn Harley emblems on.

Darlina laughed lightly. "To be honest, it had slipped my mind until I heard your Harley. But, I'm still up for it."

Will glanced around the sparsely furnished apartment. "This is a nice place."

"Thanks. I like it. Sit down and make yourself comfortable. I'll just braid my hair right quick and be ready to go."

"That's a good idea. Otherwise your long hair will be a tangled mess." Will sat down on the sofa to wait. "I don't wear a helmet. Hope that's okay with you."

Darlina answered from the other room. "Fine with me. I trust you're a safe rider."

"Always. It's something I totally enjoy doing."

Darlina walked back into the room, as she put a rubber band around her long braid. "I'm ready. Anything else I need?"

"If you have boots, I'd recommend that you wear them."

"I do. I'll grab them."

Once Darlina had her boots on, as an afterthought, she decided to tie a bandana around her head to keep any stray hairs from blowing in her face.

"Now you look ready," Will said. "Let's ride."

Darlina had never been on the back of a motorcycle although she'd avidly read everything she could get her hands on regarding them. She briefly remembered the huge fit her mother had thrown when she found a library book that Darlina had checked out about the Hell's Angels.

She followed Will out to the motorcycle. Her heart pounded with excitement as she looked at the long handlebars, extended chrome front and fancy paint job. "Wow, this is really pretty," she exclaimed.

"Thanks. It's a 1964 Shovelhead. I had the chop work and paint job done on it after I bought it. She's my pride and joy. Have you ever ridden?" Will asked.

"No, but I've always wanted to."

"Well, let me show you a couple of things." Will helped her onto the back of the motorcycle, then threw his leg over and lifted the motorcycle off the kickstand. "First of all, when we turn corners, I want you to lean with me. Not too far, but just lean like I do. Wrap your arms around my waist and hold on. Keep your feet off the tail pipe 'cause it gets hot. Ready?"

"Yes." Darlina said excitedly, as she put on her sunshades.

Will jumped up and down on the kick-starter twice before the motorcycle roared into action. He pulled out on the street and took off toward Treadaway.

Darlina's heart raced and she held on to Will with a death grip. She began to notice people staring as they whizzed by and felt a smile form on her lips. This was exhilarating.

Once they were out of town, Will kicked it into high gear and they went flying down the road. Darlina loosened her grip and began to relax, finally letting her hands rest on top of her legs.

They'd ridden for over an hour when Will stopped under a shade tree and killed the motor. He got off the bike and then helped Darlina off.

Her legs wobbled and her ears rang. "That is really fun Will. I can see why you love it so much."

"Glad you're enjoying yourself." He reached in his pocket and pulled out a small tin case. "Wanna share a joint with me?"

"I don't know. I've never smoked pot."

"Let's sit on that rock over there behind the tree and I'll show you how. It makes the ride even better."

"Are you sure it won't mess me up?"

Will laughed. "Well, I guess it depends on your definition of messed up. It will make you relax, colors will be brighter and birds will sing louder. It might make you hungry and thirsty too, but that's it. I promise."

"Okay. I'll try it." She thought about Luke and could almost visualize him frowning at her. She shook her head as if to clear the image. Luke wasn't here. Luke wasn't going to be here. It was up to her to live her life however she chose and right now, she was choosing to try pot with Will.

He lit the joint, took a long drag off it and held his breath. When he finally let it out, he coughed. "That's how you do it. Pull it into your lungs and hold your breath until you can't hold it anymore. Here try it." He passed the joint to Darlina.

She held it gingerly between her thumb and finger and took a small puff. She immediately choked and her eyes watered. "I don't know if I can do this."

"Try it again. Only this time, breathe in real slow and easy."

Darlina tried it again, following Will's instructions. She managed not to cough and held her breath as long as she could. When she released it, she felt a little lightheaded. She gave it back to Will. "That was better. How long have you been smoking pot?"

"Since high school. I can't believe you've never tried it." Will took another long drag and handed it to Darlina.

"I was pretty sheltered." She took a puff, pulling it deeper into her lungs this time, and passed it back to Will. "I've only been in Abilene a little over a year."

"I've lived here pretty much all my life. It's not a bad town."

"How long have you had your bike?" Darlina asked, accepting the joint from Will.

"About a year. It was a full dress police motorcycle when I bought it. I'll show you pictures sometime. My folks think I've lost my mind, but I love it."

"I certainly understand about your folks thinkin' you've lost your mind. My mom and dad won't even speak to me right now."

Darlina and Will sat on the rock for close to half an hour; talking and passing the joint back and forth while getting to know each other. Much to her surprise, she conversed and laughed easily with Will.

She could tell she was high, but it was different from anything she'd ever experienced. Everything began to feel easy, as her stress and worries drifted away. This was a nice change.

After a while, Will stood. "Guess I better be gettin' you back to town. Do you want to grab a bite to eat before I take you home?"

Darlina giggled. "You were right about pot making you hungry and thirsty. Yes, I'd love to eat, but I'd give my eye teeth for a drink of water right now."

Will laughed along with her. "I'll go fast and we'll be back in Abilene before you know it."

He helped Darlina back on the motorcycle, jumped to start it and was soon roaring back down the road they'd just come.

Darlina was in awe of how beautiful the scenery they were passing had become and she felt completely relaxed. She enjoyed the exhilaration of the ride. She wondered what Luke would think and for the first time in a very long time, she didn't care.

Once they were back in town, Will pulled into the first Whataburger he came to.

This time, Darlina easily swung her leg over and off of the motorcycle without any assistance from Will. She walked beside him as they went inside, noticing that they were drawing stares from the people around.

After a hamburger and Coke, they were back on the motorcycle and Will weaved in and out of traffic while shifting gears. When they reached the underpass on Mockingbird, he wracked the pipes making a deafening roar. Darlina covered her ears and people in the cars nearby, shot them angry looks. One more time, oddly enough, she found herself smiling.

She began to feel a rebellious spirit rise up in her, as she thought about how Luke had been unjustly convicted of a crime he had not committed and how society looked down on people who rode Harleys.

She sat tall and proud on the back of the 1964 Shovelhead and imagined that she was riding in protest to what had been done to Luke. She'd show society just how messed up it was. She looked at Will's long blonde hair blowing back and thought that he must also be somewhat rebellious, with his fancy chopper and long hair. Perhaps they had more in common than she first thought.

Back at her apartment, Will turned off the motor and leaned the motorcycle over on the kickstand. Darlina again easily got herself off without his help.

"That was really a lot of fun Will. Thank you for taking me riding and for showing me how to smoke pot."

"I enjoyed it too. I hope you'll go with me again sometime soon."

"I would love to. Drop by anytime you are out and want a rider. I still don't have a phone yet, but you can always reach me at the boiler factory."

"Sounds good, I'll see you soon." Will got back on the motorcycle and jumped to start it. He then roared off, waving to Darlina.

She turned and walked into her apartment, taking the bandana off her head as she went through the door. She liked that Will hadn't tried to touch her or kiss her. That was nice and he hadn't pushed her to talk about Luke either. Perhaps she'd just found a friend.

She'd no sooner got inside and unbraided her hair when a knock came on her door. She opened it to find Sherry standing on her doorstep.

"Hi, Sherry. What are you up to? Come on in."

"I need to talk to you, Darlina. Where have you been? I've been by here a couple of times and you weren't home."

"I went motorcycle riding with a guy I met at Norma's house last week. It was the most fun I've had in a long time."

"How did you like Henry?" Sherry made herself comfortable on the sofa.

"He was nice enough, but when he started saying ugly things about Luke I asked him to bring me home." Darlina joined her sitting on the sofa and kicking off her boots.

"You have to realize that there are lots of people in Abilene that have no love for Luke or his brother. They worked hard to earn their badass reputation."

"It doesn't matter. I won't tolerate anyone talking bad about him to me. I really did enjoy The Sensations' music though. I'm sure I'll go see them again."

"That's sorta' what I want to talk to you about. I wanted to talk to you last night, but you were having such a good time and I didn't want to spoil it. I think I might be pregnant."

"Oh shit! Ken's baby?"

"Yes, and he's freaking out because he's got a wife and a couple of kids already. I don't know what I'm going to do. I'll find out for sure tomorrow because I'm going to the clinic for a pregnancy test." Sherry nervously chewed her fingernails.

"Well, try not to worry about it until you know for sure. Aren't you on birth control?"

"I missed a couple of pills a few weeks back and I should have had my period over a week ago. I just know I am and I don't want a baby."

"I don't know what to say. I'll help you in any way I can."

"I can't believe this is happening. The last thing in the world I need or want is a baby, especially with a man who is married and doesn't want it either."

"Let's worry about it tomorrow. Come over when I get off work and I'll fix us supper. Want a glass of iced tea?"

"No, I have to get going. I just had to tell somebody. I'll see you tomorrow and maybe we can figure out what to do." Sherry stood and walked toward the door.

"Don't be too upset until you know for sure." Darlina stood and hugged her friend. "See you tomorrow."

"Okay. Thanks, Darlina. You're a good friend."

Once Sherry was gone, Darlina turned the radio on and hummed along with Aretha Franklin singing Respect. She brushed out her hair and chose clothes she'd wear for her first day back to work at the boiler factory.

She thought about the exhilaration she'd felt riding on the motorcycle and how she'd begun to feel like she was doing it in protest to the injustice that Luke was suffering.

She liked the way smoking pot had affected her. She decided it wasn't a bad drug at all, but instead, rather a pleasant one. She wished she could tell Luke about everything that had happened or at least Leann. Her sister hadn't gotten a phone in Hobbs yet so she hadn't been able to call her like she'd hoped to.

She decided she would get a telephone for her apartment with her first paycheck from the boiler factory. With that thought, she climbed into bed and, for the first time in months, fell asleep the instant her head hit the pillow. It had been a good day for Darlina Flowers.

# Chapter 40

"Welcome back, Darlina" was a phrase that was echoed many times that morning at ABCO boiler factory. She couldn't help feeling apprehensive and afraid that people would ask her a lot of questions. But, to her surprise, no one asked a single thing.

Everyone seemed genuinely glad to see her and she was thrilled not to be winding watches on this hot August morning.

"Well, little sister, looks like everyone's glad to have you back here." Norma approached her desk with a cup of coffee.

"I can't tell you how happy I am to be back. Thanks for the coffee." She accepted the cup Norma handed to her.

"It sure helps me out that I don't have to train someone new." Norma pointed to an overflowing bin sitting next to the typewriter. "Here is the stack of contracts that need to be re-typed. The corrections and changes are highlighted. Let me know if you have any questions."

Darlina took the stack of papers from the bin and turned to the IBM typewriter. In no time, the clicking of the keys was the only sound in the same office where Darlina had received her first gift from Luke Stone. She touched the gold heart necklace nestled around her neck and for a brief moment remembered how excited she'd been when he'd given it to her. It seemed like a lifetime ago.

Dragging her attention back to the contracts, she pushed the memory out of her mind. That was then and this is now.

Periodically, the phone rang and she answered it quickly and efficiently.

David, the owner of the company, stopped at her receptionist window when he came through the door. "Darlina; I'm so glad to see you back in this office. We missed you. Looks like you're catching us up on those contracts."

"Thank you, sir. It's really good to be back. I'll have them ready for your signature before the end of the day."

"Keep up the good work." He walked on to his office and closed the door.

It felt good to be appreciated and she would work hard to make sure no one was disappointed in her.

At eleven o'clock, Norma came to check on her. "Honey, there are a couple of salesmen in today and they want to take me to lunch. Do you want to go? Is everything going okay in here?"

"Sure. Why not? Just let me know when you're ready to leave. Everything's going great."

"Okay. I'll come and get you a little before twelve."

Norma and Darlina entered the restaurant where the two men were already there waiting. Darlina found herself sizing them up. They both wore nice business suits, ties and their shoes were shined to a high gloss. She couldn't help comparing every man she met to Luke. These two men together wouldn't make one of Luke, but they were nice enough and lunch was free.

She watched as they flirted with Norma. Her older sister was a very attractive lady, with a perfect figure and she knew how to play the game. She had them eating out of her hand and Darlina knew before lunch was over that Norma would be joining them for drinks after work.

She smiled inwardly. She loved her sister and learned from her, although she knew she'd never be as good at the game as Norma was. She truly had no desire to play the game. What she wanted and loved more than life itself had disappeared and nothing or no one would ever fill the void Luke had left in her.

As they were finished with lunch and getting ready to leave, the invitation came. "Would you girls like to have drinks with us tonight? We're staying at the Lamplighter." The older of the two men picked up the check.

"I'd love to. How about you, Darlina?" Norma asked.

"I'm sure it would be fun, but I already have plans. Thank you for lunch and the invitation, though."

"Maybe next time," the younger of the two salesmen said.

"Yes, maybe next time." Darlina and Norma walked to the door then turned to wave.

"See you guys later," Norma smiled at the men.

In the car, Norma turned to Darlina. "Do you really have plans or do you just not want to go?"

"No, I really do have plans. Sherry's coming over for supper."

"Oh, that's good; as long as you aren't trying to go back into hibernation."

"I'm not. We're going to hear The Sensations again this weekend."

Norma refreshed her lipstick in the rearview mirror. "I'm proud of you Darlina. At least you're trying to put your life back together."

"I don't see that I have much of a choice. The bottom line is that Luke is gone and he's not coming back."

"Hey, I was thinking. How about me and you go to Hobbs to see Leann for your birthday?"

"Oh I would love that. I really do miss her. I'll be glad when she gets a telephone so we can talk. I'm going to have one put in my apartment next week. Letters aren't quite the same as talkin'."

"Then we'll take a trip to Hobbs and see her."

"That sounds wonderful," Darlina replied excitedly. "That's only three weeks away."

"It will be my birthday present to you. Happy Birthday."

"Oh, thank you Norma. You're the best."

The girls returned to work and Darlina tackled the stack of contracts with a concentrated energy. How exciting it was to go see Leann. She should be looking very pregnant by now. They'd exchanged letters, but she really missed talking to her sister.

The day flew by and five o'clock came quickly. Darlina thought about Sherry's situation as she drove home. She hoped her friend could find a solution to her predicament.

She'd barely gotten home and changed out of her work clothes when Sherry knocked on the door. She hurried to let her in.

"Hi, honey. Come in. I just got home from work." Darlina closed the door behind her and headed into the kitchen.

"How did it go?" Sherry followed her.

"It was absolutely wonderful. Everyone seemed very happy that I was back and not a single person questioned me about where I'd been. What can I get you to drink?"

"Do you have any liquor?"

Darlina laughed. "No I don't. How about a Dr. Pepper?"

Sherry sighed. "Alright. Can I do anything to help you with supper?"

"Nope. I've got it all under control. Just sit and talk to me." Darlina switched on the radio and Henry's smooth baritone voice announced the next song.

"Henry's working tonight. If you had a phone, we could call him up and request something. When are you going to get one?"

"Actually, with my first check next week." Darlina peeled a small stack of potatoes. "Okay. I want to hear what you found out today."

"I'm pregnant. I spent most of the day with Ken. He told me that he will leave his wife and take care of me."

"How do you feel about that?"

"I don't know, Darlina. I like him okay, but I don't know if I want that."

"Well, honey, I think it's something that you will have to decide."

"I don't know what I want to do." Sherry took a sip of her Dr. Pepper.

"I'm sure you don't."

"If I had to say what I really feel and want to do, I don't want to have this baby. I wish Luke was here. He'd know where I could go for an abortion."

"I wish Luke was here too, but for different reasons." Darlina turned to hide the tears that sprang up so quickly.

"Guess I'll just see what happens. If Ken leaves his wife I'll consider keeping it, but if not, I'll find a way to end it."

"It's something you'll have to figure out, but you can't wait too long or it will be too late for an abortion. You know I'll help you however I can."

"I know and I really appreciate it."

The two girls ate their dinner with the music of radio station KNIT playing in the background.

"I want to go see Marketa sometime soon," Darlina said breaking the silence.

"She'll be very happy to see you. Every time I go to The Faded Rose she asks about you. Why don't you go back to work there?"

"I don't want to dance there again. I just want to go visit her. I think I'll go Thursday."

"I'm working Thursday night or I'd go with you."

"It's alright. I can go by myself. I am a big girl, you know."

Sherry laughed. "That you are and I'm very proud of the way you are picking yourself back up. I know it's not easy."

"It's the hardest thing I've ever done in my life, but what choice do I have? If I could magically make things the way I want them, I would be with Luke for the rest of my life, but I can't because he's gone."

"Would you go on a date with Henry if he asks you?"

"Probably, but he hasn't asked. I really enjoyed spending time with Will yesterday. Riding the motorcycle was the most fun I've had in a long time. He was easy to talk to and best of all, he didn't try to kiss me or even touch me."

"That's kinda' strange. Are you sure he's a man?"

Darlina laughed. "Yeah, I'm pretty sure he's a man. I told him I'd go riding with him again. Oh yeah I almost forgot to tell you that I smoked pot with him."

"Oh you did, did you? Some friend you are. You won't smoke pot with me, your best friend, but you'll try it with a stranger." Sherry joked.

"It was all so easy with him. I loved it and the ride back to town was even better than it was going out." Darlina began to clear the dishes from the table.

Sherry joined in helping her and once the dishes were all washed, dried and put away, she said her goodbyes, leaving Darlina by herself in her apartment, with Henry on the radio.

Darlina sat on the sofa, kicked her shoes off and let her thoughts drift where they may.

As always, they immediately turned to Luke. She closed her eyes and remembered the many hours they'd spent making love and how he taught her to be bold in telling him what she wanted. She sighed heavily. She would never know another touch like Luke's and she longed for him with all of her being.

She opened her eyes, a tear escaping and trickling down her cheek. No need to keep thinking about something that couldn't be, but she'd always cherish her memories of Luke.

She didn't know what life ahead of her would be like, but she did know what it wouldn't be. It wouldn't be with Luke. He faced a lifetime behind bars and her sentence was a lifetime of missing him and never forgetting the love they shared.

How was she supposed to smile and pretend her heart wasn't shattered into a million pieces? She didn't know but no matter what came or went, she'd never forget her blue-eyed rebel whose voice and music could charm the angels.

# Chapter 41

The four hours it took to drive from Abilene, Texas to Hobbs, New Mexico seemed like forever to Darlina. She couldn't contain her excitement and anxiousness to see Leann again. Leann and Wayne had been living in Hobbs for over two months and her letters seemed to indicate that things were going good for them. Darlina wanted to see for herself.

When Norma pulled the car to a stop in front of the old home place on Avenue A, Darlina leaped out of the car and ran to the front door like an overanxious puppy.

Leann had the door open before she got there. "Darlina! I'm so glad to see you."

The two sisters hugged each other tightly.

"I'm glad to see you too, but it's weird to be coming back to this house."

"Yeah, I know. Try living in it."

"Look at you. You have a belly." Darlina held her sister at arm's length.

"That I do." Leann laughed. "Norma, I'm glad to see you too."

"I thought we needed to come celebrate Darlina's twentieth birthday with you." Norma hugged Leann.

"I'm so glad you did. I've missed both of you." Leann held the door open while her two sisters went in the house ahead of her.

Darlina stood looking around at the familiar walls of the house she'd grown up in. "It looks pretty much the same, except for the TV and stereo."

"That's true. We certainly never had those when we lived here with mama and daddy." Leann agreed. "I've got a pitcher of iced tea in the kitchen. I'm sure you both must be thirsty."

The girls walked through the hallway and into the big kitchen their mother had cooked many meals in. Leann opened the refrigerator and retrieved a frosty pitcher of tea. Then she got glasses from the cabinet and sat down at the table.

Norma and Darlina joined her.

"I have a surprise for you," Leann said, as she poured the glasses full.

"Oh yeah? What's that?" Darlina asked.

"Mama and daddy are going to be here his afternoon. They want to see both of you."

Darlina felt immediate apprehension. "Are you sure they want to see me?"

"Yeah, and me too?" Norma added

"They said they did. Since it is Darlina's birthday, they wanted to be here."

"I do want to see them," Darlina said, taking a sip of her tea. "It's been almost two years. I just hope mama won't be so upset and angry."

"She'll be fine," Leann assured. "You just have to take her with the grain of salt."

"I'm going to leave you two to visit for a little while. I want to go see my friend, Alice, while I'm in town. I'll be back in a few hours." Norma stood and picked up her purse. "What time will mama and daddy be here?"

"They said they'd be getting into town around three or so. They're driving from up north."

"That will work out good. See you then." With that, Norma left and the two sisters who had grown up in this house, sat at the table together.

"I have so much to tell you Leann. I don't know where to start."

"Let's go into the living room, by the air conditioner, so I can put my swollen feet up and you can tell me everything."

Darlina shared every detail of her life since Leann had moved from Abilene, not leaving out anything. Leann sat listening, occasionally asking a question, but mostly letting her sister talk.

After a while, she said, "Wow, little sister, you've certainly had lots of changes. I'm proud of you for trying new things and looking for ways to keep living without Luke. Want to come help me make some sandwiches? Wayne will be home for lunch in a few minutes."

"How is he doing? How's the drinking since you moved here?"

"At first it was better, but now he's drinking with our brother and uncle, so I really don't know if we accomplished anything by moving here."

Darlina laughed. "If he's hanging around with Uncle Ellison, then he's sure in good drinking company. Remember how he used to come to the house so drunk he didn't know which way was up? And the time he came to the door with his artificial leg turned around backwards? I still laugh when I think about that."

"I remember and also how mama would yell at him and get on him all the time. Not that it ever helped any."

"He was always my favorite uncle, in spite of his crazy drinking."

"Mine too, although I'm not too fond of him right now. I don't think it matters where we live, Wayne is going to find someone to drink with."

"I'm so sorry. I thought with you being pregnant, he'd do better."

"He did for a little while, but now he's right back to drinking every day. I think we'll wind up moving back to Abilene at some point."

Darlina didn't try to hide her excitement. "Oh, that would be wonderful and tomorrow wouldn't be too soon for me."

Darlina hugged Wayne when he came in the door. "Hi, brother-in-law. How are you doing?"

He gave her a quick hug and then washed his hands. "I'm doing alright. I'm learning how to butcher cows."

Darlina laughed. "Our brother certainly knows how to do that."

"Happy Birthday," he said, as he sat down at the table.

"Thank you. Getting to come and see Leann is the best birthday present ever. So, what do you think about Hobbs?"

"Guess it's alright, but I'm about ready to go back to Abilene."

"That's what I hear and like I told Leann, tomorrow wouldn't be too soon to suit me."

The three of them sat at the table in the kitchen, ate sandwiches and chatted. Once Wayne had gone back to work, Leann got a big roast out of the refrigerator, along with a bag of carrots, potatoes and an onion.

"Here, let me do that sister. I can get everything ready and in the oven for you. You need to get off your feet."

Leann reluctantly agreed. "I hate to turn the oven on in this God awful heat, but a roast was all I could think of to fix that would feed everyone."

"Soon as I get it all in the oven, we'll go back in the living room by the air conditioner," Darlina said, as she began to scrape carrots.

Looking through the kitchen window, Darlina asked Leann, "Remember how we used to stand here at the sink and watch the Mexican boys on the next street over?"

Leann laughed. "Boy, were we stupid. We didn't know shit from Shinola, but we thought we were pretty cool."

"We've come a long way, huh sister?"

"Yeah, a long way...I can't believe I'm fixing to become a mother. I hope I can be a good one. Everybody tells me this is a boy because of the way I'm carrying it. It doesn't matter to me as long as he or she is healthy."

"I agree. Either one will be just fine. Do you think you'll stay here in Hobbs until the baby comes?"

"I don't know. Guess only time will answer that one."

The two girls continued sharing everything they could think of, making up for lost time. Before they knew it, they heard a car pulling up in the driveway.

Leann looked out the window. "Mama and daddy are here."

Darlina's breath caught in her throat. She hoped everything would go alright. She and Leann stood at the same time and went out onto the porch.

Their father was the first one out of the car and when he reached the porch, he hugged both girls. Their mother followed him. She still wore her hair in a tight bun at the nape of her neck. Her greeting was cool, but her hugs were genuine.

Darlina noticed her father's thinning hair that was turning white and the lines around her mother's mouth and eyes that weren't there the last time she'd seen them.

"It sure is hot down here," their father said. "When we left Trinidad this morning, we had jackets on. I forgot how hot it gets down here."

"You sure are right about the heat, daddy. Ya'll come on in by the air conditioner." Leann held the door open for their parents to enter the house.

Their mother looked around. "Looks the same as it did when we left it."

"It's home, mama." Darlina nervously twisted a strand of her hair.

"Humph. Wasn't much home to you and Leann or you wouldn't have left like you did." A flash of anger shot from her eyes.

"Mama, we just wanted to get out and start our lives." Leann took up for herself and her sister.

"Some lives. You're married to a drunk and Darlina, you did even worse. I don't know what to think about you girls. I certainly raised you better."

"Now, honey," their father interrupted, "let's just visit and have a good time. Let bygones be bygones."

Their mother looked away and squared her shoulders. Both girls knew she wasn't done, no matter what their daddy had said. "I have the right to speak my piece."

"Yes, you do mama." Darlina said. "And no matter what we have or haven't done, we still love you and daddy. Thank you both so much for coming down. It's the best birthday present I could ever have."

Darlina's daddy put his arm around her shoulders. "I can't believe our baby girl is twenty years old today. Me and your mama are getting old."

"Oh daddy...ya'll aren't old. You're free for the first time since you've been married to go and have adventures."

Norma's return interrupted the conversation. Once they had greeted her, everyone sat down and conversation began flowing between the family members.

The girls' mother and father had stories to tell them about Northern New Mexico and the disasters they'd had with all the snow. Leann talked about the baby that was on the way and Darlina talked about working at the boiler factory. There really wasn't much else about her life that she could share with her parents and Norma was pretty much in the same boat.

She certainly couldn't tell them that she was riding a Harley with Will every chance she got, or that she was smoking pot with him. She also didn't want to talk about Luke or any of the circumstances surrounding him.

Darlina was relieved when Wayne returned from work, along with their brother, Raymond and his wife. There were so many different conversations going on that it was easy not to focus on any one thing.

Soon, they could smell the aroma of the roast coming from the kitchen and Darlina escaped the chaos to go check on it. Her mother followed her into the kitchen.

"I cooked many a meal in this kitchen for you girls."

"Yes, you did mama. And they were all delicious. You are the best cook I know. I'm sure my roast won't compare to yours."

"Darlina, what are you doing with your life? The last I heard, you had moved in with Luke Stone and were going to live happily ever after."

Darlina felt tears gather in her eyes as she turned to face her mother. "Mama, something real bad happened to Luke. He's being sent to prison for something he didn't do and no matter what, I still love him with all my heart."

"Well, I'm sorry the man is going to prison, but I'm not sorry he's out of your life. I hope you learned your lesson."

Her tears began to fall in, spite of her strongest resolve. "Please don't say anything ugly about Luke. I still love him, mama."

Darlina's mother began to cry with her. "I just want the best for you and taking up with a married man, that has a house full of kids, isn't what's best for you. That's all I'll say."

Darlina wrapped her arms around her mother. Then, wiping their eyes, they took the roast out of the oven.

"It looks ready to me. I'll cut the roast if you'll get all the others in here," her mother said.

Making sure all traces of her tears were wiped away, Darlina walked down the hallway to where the rest of her family sat visiting. "Supper's ready everyone. Mama's cutting the roast. She said to come on."

Soon, everyone gathered in the kitchen with plates of food. The conversation and laughter continued amongst Darlina and her siblings. She began to feel a comforting warmth creep in. She'd missed her family and in spite of all their differences, her family still cared about each other.

She was glad they'd come and happy that their mama and daddy had joined them. As she looked around the room, she remembered a similar dinner when Luke had come to Norma's house to move her in with him. Everything had seemed so magical and wonderful that day.

How quickly life had changed, and what seemed as though it would last forever, had become nothing but a memory. She vowed to hold every precious second she'd spent with Luke close to her heart.

That was one thing that could and would last forever, along with her love for him.

# Chapter 42

Luke Stone flinched inwardly when the aging judge slammed the gavel down on the wooden block, signaling court was adjourned. He quietly placed his hands behind his back, as the bailiff clicked the handcuffs onto his wrists and led him from the courtroom.

In his cell, he sat wearily on the side of the bunk. The chill of an early December seeped through the walls of the jail and deep into his soul. Another twenty-five years to go with the fifty year sentence he already had. For seventy-five years, he would be locked behind bars. The future looked very grim and hopeless indeed. His lawyer would file another appeal, but since the first one had already been overturned, so he didn't hold out any hope that the second one would fare any better. It appeared that he'd never see life again outside of prison walls.

"Luke Stone," a gruff voice called out.

Luke looked up to see the jailer standing in front of his cell. "Yeah, what do you want?"

"The sheriff told me to come tell you that you'll be transferred to Leavenworth Penitentiary in two weeks."

"And I s'pose that bit of news was meant to cheer me up."

"I'm just delivering the message. You and Johnson will be transferred together."

"Whatever man..." Luke turned away from the jailer. He lay back on his bunk covering his face with his arm.

This certainly wasn't the way he'd planned for his life to turn out. He'd wished it a thousand times, but couldn't help wishing once more that he could go back and do it all over again.

He jumped at the sound of the cell door opening and saw Red being escorted back in.

"Hoss, this sure looks bad," Luke said as Red sat dejectedly on his own bunk.

"Sure as hell does. Looks like we may both die old men in prison."

"Shit man, Butch and Joe didn't even make it that far. You'll never make me believe that Butch hung himself and Joe accidently caught his death of pneumonia."

"I know. Especially after what Pat told us he overheard between that Texas Ranger and the sheriff."

"Yeah. This is a bunch of dirty rotten shit for sure. What will happen to my kids is my biggest worry."

"I know. At least I ain't got a family to leave in a bind like you do."

"Hell man, Joyce can't hold it together. It'll be up to mom and dad to look after them and that ain't fair." Luke ran his fingers through his hair.

"That's for sure. Her trying to commit suicide twice since you've been in here is some kind of shit. Your mom and dad will do their best to look after them though."

"I know they will, but it sure as hell don't make me feel any better about the situation."

"There ain't nothin' about any of this shit that could make a man feel better. Hell Luke, we've already been locked up for eight months and it seems like eight years. I don't know if I can do this kind of time."

"We ain't got no choice, Red."

Red chuckled under his breath. "There's always choices, hoss. The way I see it, we've got three. We can try to escape, kill ourselves, or we can try to do the time and figure it out as we go."

"From where I stand, I see only one choice. We'll do the time and figure it out as we go." Luke stated emphatically. "There's only one thing I do feel good about from this whole damned mess."

"What's that?" Red lit a Camel cigarette, passed it to Luke and then lit another for himself.

"At least Darlina didn't get drug off into all this shit with me." He took a long drag off the cigarette.

"That's true."

"I can't help but think about her and wonder how she's doing."

"I'm sure she's doing just fine. She's young and she'll be alright."

"Sure as hell hope so." Luke's voice trailed off. Both men smoked the rest of their cigarettes in silence.

Luke's thoughts swirled around his head like a dust devil in the hot West Texas sand. So many things were left undone and none of it that he could do a damned thing about. He thought about his brother, Bobby, and was glad he'd decided to take his family and move to Alaska. Maybe he could get straightened out up there.

Mostly, he thought about his kids and his parents. He hated leaving all of them behind. His thoughts returned to the man who'd been sent by the Irish Republican Army, with the offer to bust him and Red out of the Eastland County jail and take them to Ireland. If he'd known then what he knew now, the lies that were going to be told and the false statements signed, he'd have taken him up on that offer in a heartbeat.

As it stood, he was now thirty-six years old with a seventy-five year prison sentence ahead of him. He'd told the truth, as much as he could without being a rat, and look what it got him. Bitterness, much like bile, rose up inside him and threatened to choke him. His eyes narrowed to a squint. How he'd give anything to get even with the ones who had lied to save their own hides.

Never before in his entire life, had Luke Stone felt so helpless and hopeless. He and Red would be arriving in Leavenworth Penitentiary just two weeks before Christmas.

As always, his thoughts returned to Darlina. He closed his eyes and breathed in the imagined scent of her hair and felt her silky skin under his fingertips. This was what he was left with. A vivid imagination fueled by memories and a bleak future ahead.

Miles away from the Tom Green County Jail, Darlina had settled into somewhat of a routine in her life without Luke. She still thought about him with each day that passed, but especially each night when she lay down to sleep.

She had found a determination to make a life for herself and have some fun as she went along.

Will had become a regular fixture in her life and she loved it every single time he took her riding on the back of his Harley, which had become quite often.

She didn't feel any romantic attraction to him, but instead, a comfortable and easy friendship, for which she was very thankful. She was also happy that Will didn't seem to feel the need to push anything romantic on her. Her tender heart wasn't ready for that yet.

She'd gone on a couple of dates with Henry, but decided she didn't like his attitude. He was somewhat full of himself and seemed to think he was a little bit better than everyone else.

Sherry had tried to abort the baby she was carrying after Ken made it clear that he wasn't going to leave his wife. She spent two days and two nights at Darlina's apartment, drinking castor oil, hoping that would cause the baby to abort. Finally, she had decided to move back to Colorado where her brother lived and have the baby. She still didn't want to keep it and most likely would put it up for adoption. Darlina missed her friend.

Leann had delivered a baby boy in Hobbs, and they had plans to move back to Abilene before Christmas.

And so it was going on December 2, 1971, when Darlina heard the news report on the radio in the car. Luke Stone and Thomas "Red" Johnson had been found guilty of robbing the Bangs bank and given an additional twenty five-year prison sentence on top of the fifty years they had previously received in Eastland.

Her heart sank to her toes. Seventy-five years was a very long time. She could not begin to imagine how he was feeling and how sad his parents must be but most especially his children.

How awful, that his children would grow up without a father. Her heart broke for them.

She arrived at her apartment just as the teardrops started to fall. Who would have thought that in America, the land of the free and the home of the brave, a man could be convicted twice of crimes he did not commit and be sent to prison? Yet, it had happened.

The phone rang just as she walked in the door. When she answered, she heard Will's voice on the other end. "Hi Darlina. I know it's chilly outside and a Thursday night, but I really want to go riding. Do you want to go?"

"Will, I can't think of anything I'd like better. I'll dress warm and be waiting for you."

"I'll be there in thirty minutes."

She hung up the phone and sat on the sofa with tears streaming down her face. Maybe it was time that she talked to Will about Luke. Maybe it would help to talk to a friend. She dried her eyes, got on her warmest jeans, sweatshirt and had her coat waiting by the door when Will arrived.

"You're anxious to ride tonight," Will said, when he saw her dressed and ready to go.

"You have no idea. Let's go."

Soon, they were whizzing down side streets and heading to Lake Fort Phantom on a country road. Darlina didn't try to hold the tears back. She let the wind whisk them from her eyes.

Justice didn't exist. She'd become a rebel like Luke, and in her own way, defy society with all of its screwed up rules and laws.

She doubted that one person could make a difference, but was determined to try. At least she wouldn't buy into the bullshit rules society had created for everyone to live by in hypocrisy.

When they reached the lake, Will stopped and turned off the motor. The full moon reflected off the still water with an eerie glow. Its luminous brightness made it seem more like day instead of night.

Will spotted a half burned fire pit and after adding another large stick of wood, lit it. They stood by the fire, warming their hands.

Staring into the fire, Darlina spoke. "There's something I'd really like to talk to you about."

"I knew something was on your mind." He took a small tin case out of his pocket and lit a joint.

"You know I was just coming out of a very intense relationship when I met you at Norma's house, don't you?"

"I remember." He passed the joint to Darlina.

"I had been living with Luke Stone. Not long before I met you he'd brought me back to Norma's and left me there. I was devastated because I had no idea why."

"I've heard about Luke Stone. Never met him, but heard lots of things about him. He got arrested, didn't he?"

"Yes, and today he was convicted of a second bank robbery. He now has a seventy-five year prison sentence."

"Shit! That's rough."

"I loved him with all my heart and still do. If there is such a thing as soul-mates, then that's what Luke and I are." Darlina took an experienced drag off of the joint Will passed to her.

"Things change. Time doesn't stand still. It marches on and drags you right along with it. What seems like a permanent thing one day can suddenly vanish the next. When you're given no choice about something, what can you do but try to adapt?"

"I know. I'm so angry that the justice system is all screwed up and the way society dictates how we are supposed to look and act."

"Why the hell do you think I have this motorcycle? I've been fed up with it for a long time. This is my little way of rebelling."

"It's a good way. I love riding behind you. I see the looks people give us and it makes me smile every time. They're looking down their righteous noses at us. They think we are trash, but in truth, they are the trash. People are so falsely judgmental."

"Not everyone Darlina. I agree that lots are, but when you say people, that includes every person and that's not true. Don't let yourself get bitter." Will picked up a stick and stirred the fire.

"You are a good friend, Will. I feel like I can talk to you about anything and you don't think I'm stupid or silly."

Will laughed. "Why would I think that? I think you're a beautiful, sweet girl and I love being around you."

"How come you've never tried to kiss me?"

"I don't know. I figured you didn't want me to."

"What if I do now?"

Will turned to face her, looking deep into her eyes. He put both arms around Darlina and pulled her against him. She laid her head on his shoulder and closed her eyes.

"I'll kiss you when you're ready for me to and right now you aren't. There's no rush. We've got plenty of time. Let's just see where it all goes."

Darlina lifted her head. "Thank you, Will."

"Let's ride." Will picked up a few hands full of sand and doused the fire. Darlina kneeled down to help.

Once the fire was out, they both got back on the motorcycle and roared off down the moonlit road.

When Will had put his arms around her and she had closed her eyes, Darlina had imagined it was Luke holding her. Maybe that was how she could open herself up to someone new, by always pretending it was Luke.

She put her arms around Will's waist and let the wild rough wind rip away every thought she had in her head. Soon it was as crystal clear as the bright moonlight above her.

Once she was back in her apartment and nestled in her warm bed, she picked up a pillow and wrapped both her arms around it tightly. Closing her eyes, she whispered sweet loving words to her imaginary Luke.

Just before she drifted off to sleep, she decided this was how she would be able to go on living. She'd keep her imaginary Luke with her at all times and whisper to him when she needed to talk.

If and when she ever made love to another man, in her mind, it would be Luke and no one else.

Luke Stone might be locked away in a prison, but in her heart, he was free and alive.

At exactly three a.m., Luke Stone opened his eyes, fully aware that he was lying on the hard narrow bunk in a jail cell. His heart raced and his breath came in short gasps. He'd been given a vision of the future that would sustain him through many difficult years ahead. He had seen himself walking with Darlina down the aisle in a small church to say their wedding vows. Her radiant face, angelic smile and long flowing gown had taken his breath away. Could a man possibly be so foolish to dream of a bright happy future against all the odds?

Darlina sat upright in her bed, clutching the pillow, with tears streaming down her face. The ticking clock told her it was three in the morning. What had just happened? Had she been given a glimpse into the future? In her dream, she and Luke were walking down the aisle in a small church, with all of their families gathered to witness. Luke appeared older and much thinner, but his blue eyes and crooked smile were the same. Her heart pounded in her chest. Could it be that they would survive prison and eventually be together?

Every once in a great while, in life, there is a love so strong between two human beings that neither time nor space can erase nor destroy it.

This is precisely the kind of love that Luke Stone and Darlina Flowers shared. It would live on through eternity in both of their hearts and neither of them would give up hope of being reunited again.

Perhaps if two people believe something strongly enough, they can move heaven and earth, even open prison doors, to make it happen.

## THE END

# About the Author

Jan Sikes is a new author, although not new to writing. She has written songs, poetry, screenplays and short stories. Growing up in a small dusty town on the Texas-New Mexico border, she and her sister found adventures untold through avidly reading books (many times late into the night, under the covers, with a flashlight). Little did she know, all of that reading was early training to become an author.

Her years of being married to Rick Sikes proved to be the launching pad for her writing career. After his death in 2009, she got serious about it and the result is the book that you now hold in your hands.

She resides in North Texas and when she isn't writing, you will find her volunteering at the various music festivals across Texas or playing with her three grandchildren.

To learn more about Jan, please visit her website at:
www.jansikes.com

Made in the USA
San Bernardino, CA
12 July 2016